The Logic and Rhetoric

of Exposition

The Logic

Harold C. Martin HARVARD UNIVERSITY

New York

& Rhetoric

of Exposition

Rinehart & Company, Inc.

Second Printing, July 1958

© *1957, 1958 by Harold C. Martin*
Printed in the United States of America
All Rights Reserved
Library of Congress Catalog Card Number: 58–5758

☞ *Preface*

COURSES IN EXPOSITORY WRITING differ so greatly from teacher to teacher, from institution to institution, and from year to year that the making of textbooks for them is really never ended. Although each new one necessarily duplicates characteristics of its predecessors, each is in some measure an effort to find a new and efficient means of helping students to write well. Most try to provide as generally useful an approach as can be achieved; a smaller number, of which this book is one, focus more narrowly on students or programs of a particular kind. Without pretending to hold a brief for the superiority of the "method" of this book, I offer it as a helpful way of bringing average and better-than-average students to a recognition of their responsibilities as speculative and critical writers.

The first part of the book adapts a few important matters in logic to the immediate purposes of the writer of expository prose. The subjects chosen for treatment—definition, assertion, proof, and persuasion—are those which seem to uncover and help to remove the principal difficulties of the young writer trying to find solid ground in the mist and muck of new intellectual experience. The second part of the book presents the familiar matters of rhetoric in a manner intended to lead the student to something better than desultory acceptance of imposed dicta about form. The concluding section, that concerned with mechanics, footnotes, and bibliography, is abbreviated to the matters that most frequently need correction in students' essays.

This book grew out of a writing course closely associated with courses in the humanities, the social sciences, and the natural sciences. That association accounts for the range of allusions and the variety in examples and illustrative matter. The more connectedness there is between a writing course and the writer's whole intellectual life, the better; it justifies, I think, an emphasis on the serious side of higher education—leaving the lighter side largely to extracurricular activities.

Although I assume full responsibility for the faults of this book, minor or grave as they may be, I am happy to acknowledge my indebtedness to colleagues for many, if not all, of whatever virtues it possesses. Members of the staff of General Education A, past and present, have been inestimably helpful in their suggestions; from that goodly crew I wish to single out Richard Ohmann, Dudley Shapere, Clifton Orlebeke, and Max Bluestone for especial thanks. Professor Martin Steinmann, Jr., of the University of Minnesota, gave me good advice and sound criticism when I needed it most. To a late request for a "fresh" reading Professor S. O. A. Ullmann, of Union College, responded with characteristic readiness and competence. The staff of the college department of Rinehart and Company has been consistently patient and helpful in its editorial activity. Miss Dorothy Buck transformed disordered manuscript into clean and accurate copy. To all I am grateful.

Finally, I wish to thank the authors of volumes perused in the process of working out the shape and character of this book. They are too numerous to acknowledge one by one, but many readers will recognize their influence even as I am happy to own it.

H. C. M.

Cambridge, Massachusetts
January, 1958

Contents

Part Two

The Logic and Rhetoric

of Exposition

☙ *Introduction: Experience*

and Language

WHEN WE WRITE, we translate experience into arbitrary symbols which we call words. To write at all, we must have had experiences and we must be able to use one or more sets of symbols. To write well, we must understand the experiences we have had and we must be able to manipulate words so that they give the reader a clear sense of the experiences which they translate. For that reason, a book which proposes to help people to write well must concern itself with ways of knowing experience as well as with ways of expressing it. Such a book must face, like the head of Janus, in two directions at once: toward the old, the experiences we have had or are having, and toward the new, the fresh communication of the experiences themselves.

There is a paradox in this matter of knowing and telling, however, which is of first importance. For a reason hard to understand, we do not seem to have a full grasp on experience itself until we have symbolized it in some fashion; we do not *know* until we have *told*. The telling may be done, of course, by many kinds of symbols—words spoken or written, musical notes, paints brushed on canvas, and so on. But whatever the kind of symbol, it appears to be true that we do not really know our experiences until we have expressed them. Yet it is also certainly true that when we express, we express *something;* that is to say, we do not use words at random when we begin to write about an experience but instead seem to be directed by our *un*expressed consciousness of the experience to choose certain words and ignore others.

One attempt to resolve this paradox appears in the common remark, "I know what I mean, but I can't find the words to express it." There is something attractive about this simple account of a baffling matter, but the account is probably a misstatement or at least an overstatement. It would be more accurate to say, "I know very vaguely what I mean, but so vaguely that I can't find any words inclusive enough to represent the notion I have of what I think I know." Put in those terms, the resolution of the paradox is closer: if we begin to describe an experience by

1

testing one series of words after another, rejecting or altering as we do so, gradually the vagueness of our understanding diminishes as "wrong" words are eliminated and as "right" or "nearly right" words are accepted as proper symbols of the experience. We are directed by a vague understanding of the experience to words roughly suitable for its expression; by testing a variety of words which are roughly suitable we refine our understanding of the experience. Thus we come to know the shape of experience through the process of using words to describe it. There is, then, a serious observation behind the superficially laughable question: "How can I know what I mean until I hear myself say it?" As we say or write words, as we set notes on a scale, as we blend pigments on canvas, we discover the complete nature of our experiences. We have had the experience before we begin to express it; we *know* or understand it only when we find means to transform it into some symbolic pattern.

A reader may be inclined to ask at this point if it is always true that telling and knowing are inseparable and interdependent. It is hard to give an answer to such a question because so little is known about the way of knowing anything. Still, it is clear that some experiences are either so violent or so simple that their expression requires no reflection at all. If we bark our shins against a table in the dark, we say, "Ow!" almost as quickly as we pull back our leg from the offending piece of furniture. If, like Archimedes, we suddenly discover what we have long been trying to find, we give a shout of delight. Both ejaculations may be called "noises," and they are certainly expressive noises. Yet neither is informative enough by itself to communicate more than a very vague notion of the experience from which the ejaculations spring. An enraged child expresses his rage *un*symbolically by crying; an enraged man may do the same, but because he is an adult and therefore richer in experience he is more likely to seek fuller means of expression. He knows that his rage has causes and probable effects and he uses language to convey his awareness of those causes and effects to the world around him. In giving expression to complexities of which the child is not aware, he necessarily and instinctively tries to understand the complexities himself in order that the symbols he uses may properly represent the subtlety of his feelings. Here he encounters the two obstacles mentioned above: the difficulty of knowing himself and the difficulty of choosing symbols which will adequately and accurately represent what he comes to know. It is awareness of these obstacles that may lie behind the proverbial maxim to count ten before you speak; if, instead of blurting "noises," you take the time necessary to analyze an irritating experience, you are more likely to understand the experience and therefore to comment or to act on it intelligently and informatively. In one sense, then, words not only discover and express experience but put some restraint on it as well;

they fit one experience into the whole range of experience of which we are aware and prevent it from exercising an unmanageable control over us.

There are some people for whom the thought of restraint is infuriating or even profane. They feel that only the rush of words that seems to be stimulated by an experience is to be respected and that interference and analysis destroy the vitality and "truth" of the experience itself. Now there is certainly some truth in the contention that analysis may affect the flow of inspiration; if there were not, philosophers since the time of the Greeks would not have speculated about such matters as inspiration and intuition. If truth lay entirely in the uninhibited flow of "inspired" utterance, however, the same men would not have given their attention to analysis. It is clear that one of the problems of this book, and one of the principal problems of a writer, is to consider the relationship between spontaneous expression and controlled expression and to use the resources of both wisely.

Besides those who believe that only spontaneous expression properly represents experience and those who believe that experience is not even fully known until it has been analytically expressed, there are some who claim that expression is either impossible or, if not impossible, is detrimental to experience. In Ernest Hemingway's *The Sun Also Rises*, the leading character advises another who wants to explain her delight in a particular experience, "You'll lose it if you tell it." Followed to its logical conclusion, that advice implies the death of all communication, of all art, perhaps even of all but ecstatic self-knowing. It is probably true that some experiences are incommunicable because symbolic structures (of words, notes, pigments) are man's creations and our experiences undoubtedly do often exceed in their variety and intensity any instruments we are capable of devising for their expression. Yet symbols are always helpful in reducing the amount of the uncommunicable in experience by fixing some portion of it, so to speak, in a frozen state, thus permitting us to turn our attention to the portions that remain still fluid and uncontrolled. In physics, the "law of the variable function" depends on a procedure by which all but one of the parts of a process are controlled so that the one left free may be observed without interference. Such a degree of regulation is possible only for simple experiences, but it is certainly one of the functions of symbols to control some parts of an experience while we attempt to observe other parts with undivided attention. Thus, confronted by an unusual experience to which we have reacted in ways we do not ourselves fully understand, we begin to work out of our confusion by labeling parts of our reaction: "Well, at first I was shocked. No, not exactly shocked, but surprised, I think. And the surprise was partly fear, or perhaps I should say 'dread.' Then. . . ." In such fashion as this, we blunder about with words, trying one after the other in the hope of reaching terms capable of translating a private affair into a public form.

The words we use in this effort to translate our private experience of the world into terms that others can understand, unlike the symbols used in mathematical computations, for instance, are themselves variable and indefinite. Words change meaning over the years and, even at a given moment, do not mean precisely the same to all who use them. In writing, then, there cannot be absolute control either of experience or of expression. Moreover, because the use of words and the knowledge of experience interact, there cannot be perfect communication. If we could say, "First we experience, then we know, then we express" and could take "then" to mean "consequently," we might hope for a formula or a foolproof procedure like that which Jonathan Swift satirized in his account of the writing-machine in the laboratory at Laputa; and modern electronic "brains" often seem, to the layman, to have solved the problem entirely. But Swift's writing-machine and the electronic calculator have this limitation in common: both require that the raw material of experience be translated into some kind of symbolic form before they can begin to work on it at all. The human being, on the other hand, can do his own translating; in fact, he gains command of experience only when he *does* do his own translating. Although his "translating" is never perfect, it is one of the principal glories of the human being that he has found so many means of sharing with others such a large measure of the necessarily private response each man has to all that touches him.

It is wise to begin the discussion about writing by openly facing these difficulties because writing is a serious matter for all who seek a liberal education. It is no less than the principal means by which the educated man tries to discover and transmit the truth about himself and about the world as he understands it. If we cannot fully resolve the paradox with which we began—experience as necessary to symbols and symbols as necessary to a knowledge of experience—we can at least say that, in practice, we do find it possible to communicate. This we find it possible to do because we have the conviction that we know and because we instinctively distinguish between knowing and having an experience, which is to say that we do recognize something external to our own mental processes. If this separation is an illusion, as some claim, it is a necessary illusion, natural to our existence and apparently important to our lives. We must assume the separability of events from knowledge of events in order to write at all; we must recognize the interdependence in order to write well.

This book is built on the premise that writing is a way of coming to know as well as a way of communicating what is known. It recognizes that perfection in both processes is beyond human attainment, but it assumes that the proper role of writing in a liberal education is that of moving toward perfection in each. Moreover, it takes as axiomatic the proposition that the two processes, though in fact indivisible, can be separately analyzed, as well as the further proposition that attention in practice to one will result in improvement not only of the one practiced but of the other as well. To the process of coming to know, it gives the title "Inquiry"; to the process of communicating what is known, the title "Expression." For the purposes of teaching, it goes beyond simple division of the processes to suggest that students who are intent on improving their writing will generally achieve success most rapidly if they begin with some analysis of the process of coming to know and then move on to study and practice of the means by which we express what we know. This order is the reverse of the one often practiced, but it is adopted here in the belief that analysis, far from deadening the nerve ends, makes them increasingly sensitive and increasingly reliable in what they report. The words we use when we write are not simply blown through us by the winds of the Muses; they come out of the turbulence of our minds. And the reins that analysis puts on the wild chargers of the imagination alone make it possible for the chariot to move swiftly and well. Stephen Spender has observed that the poet's use of rhyme does not so much stifle as stimulate thought and feed inspiration. Analysis does much the same service for prose. Even so, it is only half of the process by which we transform thought and feeling into language. In practice, analysis works in tandem with experimentation in forms of expression; neither does well without the other. Both, then, are proper subjects of study for the person who is concerned about the improvement of his own writing and about a deeper appreciation of the writing of others.

Part One

⏏ Defining and Describing

> . . . things have got so twisted round and wrapped up i' un-
> reasonable words, as aren't a bit like 'em, as I'm clean at fault,
> often an' often. Everything winds about so—the more straight-
> forward you are, the more you're puzzled.
>
> MR. TOLLIVER, in *The Mill on the Floss*

ONE OF THE PARADOXES of learning is that a beginner must accept much that he cannot prove before he can understand anything. Each of us works with certain "givens," as they are called in geometry, and builds his structures of knowledge and belief in the confidence that those "givens" are more or less unassailable. Gradually he becomes aware that those postulates may themselves be subject to question or in need of re-interpretation; and finally he learns that the simple propositions from which he started are the ones that continue to challenge the intelligence of wise and thoughtful men. A perceptive study by Jean Piaget of the child's use of language (*The Language and Thought of the Child*) shows that a large part of early speech is monologue in which the child works out, in more or less dramatic fashion, his role in the world and the significance of the objects and persons with which he comes into contact. For no reason apparent to an observer, he repeats words and phrases over and over, as though to fix identities firmly in his own mind and to guarantee their authority in his own little world. In various circuitous fashions, much of his verbal activity is what he will later come to call "defining"—attaching a set of characteristics to a word in order to relate it to and distinguish it from other words and the object to which it refers from other objects. Moreover, in this perhaps only half-conscious activity, he deals quite *unconsciously* with one of the most perplexing and important problems in the great number of problems associated with explaining the nature of language.

Anyone who thinks at all about the world he lives in and attempts to communicate his thoughts about it must inevitably, from time to time, have an almost overwhelming sense of confusion and frustration. In its simpler form, his trouble may resolve itself into uncertainty about the meaning to be ascribed to some word or expression; in more com-

9

plex form, it is likely to concern the nature of the *thing* talked about.
It is at this stage of complexity that a thinking man may begin to wonder whether the definitions with which he tries to dispel his troubles are
related only to the words he uses or whether they deal with the reality,
the things and events, to which the words make reference. In the terminology of the logician, he wonders whether definitions are *nominal* only,
or whether they may also be *real*. The arguments for each side of what
remains a major philosophical controversy have difficulties beyond delineation here, but the importance of the issue is too great to be
ignored. If definitions are concerned only with words (that is, if they are
nominal only), then the definer must always hold in mind the possibility
that what he is defining perhaps does not, did not, and never will exist,
and that his definition is only a part of the complicated calculus of language, essentially an artificial structure of linguistic conventions. If his
definition has to do not only with words but with the things that words
refer to (if it is, in short, a *real* definition), then its claims and responsibilities may be much more extensive. A *real* definition of "table," for
example, purports to talk about something which all tables have in
common, a set of characteristics which all tables possess; a *nominal*
definition assumes that it deals only with the word "table" and recognizes, as a condition of the definition, that the word changes meaning
from situation to situation and from one time to another. Obviously,
this book cannot resolve the argument; it does suggest, however, that
for most human purposes it is necessary to believe either that some
definitions are real or that, in order to act at all, we must assume them
to be so. Justice Holmes spoke of certain undemonstrable postulates of
law as "can't helps," and real definitions seem to make somewhat the
same claim to inclusion in our habits of thinking and writing.

CONVENTIONAL DEFINING

In its largest sense, defining is taken here to comprise all those activities *immediately* connected with apprehending the full significance
of a word. It is what I. A. Richards has divided into the three activities:
indicating, characterizing, and realizing. For the writer's purposes, to the
word "defining" may be added the word "describing," words used because they are commonplaces of ordinary discourse, words readily understood as satisfying the demands raised by the defining question "What
is *x*?" As soon as describing is joined to defining, however, it is apparent
that the answer to the defining question may require more than an equation, more than a sentence or a paragraph, more even than an entire
volume. Even in the face of such elaborateness, it is still certain that
much can be done to make defining comprehensible and efficient. If it
could not, men would move blindly in the welter of experience and,

moreover, would find themselves frequently unable to transmit to others or receive from them any account of experience at all.

As it rises in daily life, defining has come to be a procedure with clearly discernible patterns. Most commonly it appears as the expression of an equation, an equivalence between an unknown and something known, between an x and a y where y is something which is already familiar. This is the pattern most often found in desk dictionaries—an assertion of the sameness in meaning conveyed by two or more words:

> **institution,** *n.* **1.** an organization or establishment for the promotion of a particular object, usually one for some public, educational, charitable, or similar purpose. **2.** the building devoted to such work. **3.** a concern engaged in some activity, as a retail store, broker, or insurance company. **4.** *Sociol.* an organized pattern of group behavior, well-established and accepted as a fundamental part of a culture, such as slavery. **5.** any established law, custom, etc. **6.** *Colloq.* any familiar practice or object. **7.** act of instituting or setting up; establishment: *the institution of laws.* **8.** *Eccles.* **a.** the origination of the Eucharist, and enactment of its observance, by Christ. **b.** the investment of a clergyman with a spiritual charge.
>
> *American College Dictionary*

Definition, as the example shows, is a highly refined procedure; and, as our experience with the use of dictionaries, even of the best dictionaries, makes clear, it is not always a satisfactory one. To begin with, a good dictionary presents many y's for the x whose meaning its user wishes to know, and he is sometimes perplexed as to which he is to choose; more than that, the y's themselves may often be as unfamiliar to him as the x from which he begins. If, for example, he finds that an equivalent for "profuse" is "prodigal," he may plunge further into darkness; conversely, if he finds "instable" equated with "not stable," he gets almost nowhere at all since he is merely told that x is not *not-x*. Reliable dictionaries, of course, have many ways of obviating the awkwardness illustrated by the equivalents, or synonyms, for "profuse" and "instable." Yet their best devices will often not be helpful enough unless the user understands the nature of the process of defining, the first step in which is understanding that the process is far from simple.

The procedures of formal logic provide a starting point. A definition, according to those procedures, has two initial components: the term-to-be-defined (*definiendum*) and the defining term (*definiens*). In the example given above, "institution" is the *definiendum,* the term-to-be-defined, and each part of the lengthy series of words and phrases following it is a *definiens,* a defining term. It is immediately apparent that the term-to-be-defined is limited to a single grammatical unit, generally to a single word. To ask, "What is an ecclesiastical institution?" is to imply that one already knows what "institution" means and wants only to know what it means when it is modified by the word "ecclesiastical," or it is to ask for two definitions, one for each word in the term-to-be-defined. The simplicity required in the term-to-be-defined, however, is neither expected nor desired in the defining term. In it one may properly anticipate more than one word, more than one grammatical unit, more than one logical division.

Consider this simple definition: "A gig is a two-wheeled, horse-drawn passenger vehicle." The defining term is composed of four informative expressions: "two-wheeled," "horse-drawn," "passenger," and "vehicle." Of the four, one is a noun, and refers to a *class* of objects meant to include the referent of the term-to-be-defined. If it alone is used ("A gig is a vehicle"), there is indeed a definition, and for some purposes that definition may be adequate. That it may not be, this colloquy makes apparent:

X: What is a gig?
Y: A gig is a vehicle.
X: Oh, I understand. A gig and a wagon are the same thing.
Y: Not at all. A gig is designed to carry passengers.
X: Well, a wagon may carry passengers.
Y: Yes, but a gig is designed especially to carry passengers, and a wagon is designed to carry freight rather than, or in addition to, passengers.
X: Well, then, a gig is a special kind of wagon.
Y: No, it's really not a wagon at all. Its particular function is different. A wagon carries passengers only incidentally. That is not what it is designed to do.
X: I think I understand you now. A gig is a carriage.
Y: That's more like it, but there is another difference I forgot to mention. Most carriages have four wheels and a gig has only two.
X: Is a gig, then, like a bicycle?
Y: Not at all. For one thing, the two wheels on a gig are joined by an axle and operate in parallel; the two wheels of a bicycle are placed one behind the other and are connected not by an axle but by a rigid frame which permits one to follow the other or, as a matter of fact, one to precede the other. Besides that, I said passengers, not passenger.
X: My brother and I often ride together on a bicycle.
Y: True, but a gig is *designed* to carry more than one passenger, and a bicycle is not.
X: *Must* there be more than one passenger in a gig?
Y: No, there need not be, but a gig is designed to accommodate more than one, though generally not more than two or three without crowding. It has only one seat, and a carriage has one or more.
X: Now I know what you mean. When I was in Japan I rode in gigs, but the name used for them there is "rickshaws."
Y: A rickshaw is a different thing because it is pulled along by a human being.
X: Could an ox draw it—or a dog?

Y: Neither one, I think. An ox requires a yoke, and a gig has shafts; and
the shafts are too far apart and too far raised from the ground to be
attached by harness to a dog. At any rate, a gig is designed to be
drawn by a horse.

X: I conclude, then, that a gig is a vehicle for one or more passengers,
operating on two wheels joined by an axle, and drawn by a horse.
Why didn't you say so in the first place?

The example is not so preposterous as it may seem in the form
of a dialogue. The backing and filling illustrate quite accurately the
mental process of framing a definition, and it is to avoid such round-
aboutness in exposition that a pattern of formal definition is useful.
Compressed, the defining term turns out to have two parts: first, a term
to indicate a *class* of objects (vehicle) to which the referent of the
term-to-be-defined properly belongs; and, second, one or more terms
to distinguish it from other objects (wagon, carriage, bicycle, rickshaw) in the same class. The defining term, then, is a composite. It
names (a) what the referent of the defined term has in common with
other objects (class terms) and (b) what distinguishes it from other
objects in the same class (differentiating terms).

If Y had first answered X's question by saying, "A gig is a thing,"
the process would, of course, have been even longer. From this one
may deduce that the class to be used in the defining term should be as
limited as it can be without excluding "gig," the term-to-be-defined. The
limitation can be stated in this way: the class word of the defining term
should be of the order of generality *next above* the term-to-be-defined.
To find that class word may in itself be no easy matter, but unless it,
or one near it, is found, the definer makes for himself exactly the kind
of difficulty Y would have had with X had he started with "thing" instead of with "vehicle."

Selection of the distinguishing characteristics presents similar difficulties. Y might have described the vehicle as "made of wood and
metal," for instance, but had he done so he would have added little
that is helpful, since wood and metal are markedly less specific properties of the object he has in mind than are its two-wheeledness or its
limited carrying capacity or its mode of locomotion. The general rule for
choice of differentiating terms is that they should be the ones that most
strikingly distinguish the object referred to by the term-to-be-defined from
other objects in the same class.

One more part of the definition requires attention. What of the
equation sign between the term-to-be-defined and the defining term, of
the word "is" in the original definition of "gig" and in the definition
finally arrived at? Considering the false leads and the tediousness of
that definition, one might say that it more nearly represents an intention than a certainty. The definer intends, when he is done defining, that

the expressions on each side of the copula ("is") will balance perfectly, like the two pans of a scale in which one might measure out a quantity of potash by putting a metal weight of known quantity in one pan and sifting potash into the other until the indicator of the scale rested at dead center. Since measuring an amount of potash is very much simpler than measuring words, it is natural to regard with suspicion this indication of equivalence between the two sides of a definition. Indeed, it is not uncommon to hear people say that there are no such things as synonyms or synonymous expressions in language and that precise definition is, therefore, impossible. For the practicing writer such an assertion is academic, to say the least; he is much less concerned to know whether or not a precise definition is possible than to know what degree of precision is necessary for the answer demanded by the question "What is x?" Potash, too, can be more or less accurately measured in truckloads on a feed-store weighing scale or in delicate balances in the laboratory.

If uneasiness about the copula persists, one may be tempted to look on it less as a statement of equivalence than as a command, as though the definer were saying not "x is y" or "x means y" but "Use x to mean y." This restricted kind of definition—stipulative definition, as it is usually called—is very useful and must eventually be examined with care. For the present, however, it is best to confine attention to those definitions that assert, rather than command one to accept, an equivalence between terms and, by inference, between the objects to which they refer.

LEXICAL OR HISTORICAL DEFINING

The largest class of definitions is that known as *lexical* or *historical*. The definitions in dictionaries, for instance, are lexical: they present the meanings of a word which have had or still have currency, those which various men at various times and for various purposes have made use of. An abridged dictionary records as many meanings as suit its purposes and size; an unabridged dictionary purports to record all the meanings that have sound claim to attention, all that have had enough currency at any time to be successful vehicles of communication.

One of the editorial consultants of the *American College Dictionary* (abridged) reports that he and his colleagues tabulated 832 meanings of the word "run," but that they included only 104 of those meanings in the "desk" dictionary which they helped to compile. The reason for their making so drastic a reduction is obvious enough, but the grounds on which they chose one meaning rather than another for inclusion may be less evident. They might, of course, have excluded all meanings no longer current, but to do so would have been to reduce the useful-

ness of the dictionary for anyone dealing with the writing of past centuries. They might have limited their choice to meanings common in
the general use of language, barring all technical usages. Or they might
have made more or less arbitrary choices, setting down the meanings
they approved or those which the etymology of the word seemed to
justify. The inadequacy of any of those criteria is readily apparent.
What lexicographers actually do in such a case is attempt to determine
which words are most frequently "looked up" by readers and which of
their meanings are most frequently used in general discourse, and then
to make special provision for technical, rare, purely colloquial, and
dialectical meanings. If they have done their work well, the meanings
they record are all proper, the equivalences true equivalences, and the
definitions "good" ones.

Unabridged dictionaries are of two kinds: (1) those which record
the full range of meanings detected by lexicographers, arranging them
in groups to indicate context and listing them, perhaps, in order of
frequency of use; (2) those which attempt to locate the earliest appearance of a particular meaning and to record the persistence of that
meaning at subsequent periods. Both kinds may, and generally do, document the meanings they provide by brief quotations. The foremost
American dictionary of this kind is *Webster's New International,* a one-
volume work of great size which not only contains a much greater
number of meanings for each word than an abridged dictionary but
also defines a much greater number of words. Even more extensive and
elaborate is the *Oxford English Dictionary,* the great historical dictionary of the English language. Its thirteen folio-size volumes make it
possible to scan in one place the entire history of a word, and it is for
that reason an invaluable resource for students and scholars alike. Some
idea of its approach to the problem of defining can be gathered from a
greatly abbreviated account of its treatment of the highly ambiguous
word "nice," a word so variously used today that one would be hard
put to answer quickly a demand for its definition. Since the *OED* is
a dictionary built on historical principles, it is appropriate to rephrase
the defining question to read not "What does 'nice' mean?" or "What is
'nice'?" but "What did, and does, 'nice' mean?" or "What was, and is,
'nice'?" A few (perhaps one one-hundredth) of the answers to that defining question are set down here so that the peculiar virtue of this
kind of dictionary can be made apparent.

Foolish, stupid, senseless. *Obs.* (Common in 14th and 15th c.) **a.** Of persons.

> **1387** TREVISA *Higden* (Rolls) VI. 23 He made the lady so mad and
> so nice that she worshipped him as the greatest prophet of God
> Almighty.

Wanton, loose-mannered; lascivious. *Obs.* **c.** Of dress: Extravagant, flaunt-
ing. *Obs.*

> **1563** *Homilies* ii. *Idolatry* iii. (1640) 72 An Image with a nice and
> wanton apparell and countenance.

Slothful, lazy, indolent. *Obs. rare.* **b.** Effeminate, unmanly. *Obs. rare.*

> **1598** Florio, *Paranimpha* . . , an effeminate, nice, milkesop, puling
> fellow.

Fastidious, dainty, difficult to please, esp. in respect of food or cleanliness;
also in good sense, refined, having refined tastes.

> **1782** Cowper *Mut. Forbearance* 20 Some people are more nice than
> wise.

d. Precise or strict in matters of reputation or conduct; punctilious, scru-
pulous, sensitive.

> **1887** Baring-Gould *Red Spider* xvii, I should get it back again . . ,
> and not be too nice about the means.

Not obvious or readily apprehended; difficult to decide or settle; demand-
ing close consideration or thought; intricate. **b.** Minute, subtle; also of
differences, slight, small.

> **1870** Howson *Metaph. St. Paul* ii. 41 When we desire to appreciate
> the nicer shades of meaning.

Agreeable; that one derives pleasure or satisfaction from; delightful.

> **1837** Maj. Richardson *Brit. Legion* ix. (ed. 2) 220 The Comman-
> dant, whom I subsequently found to be a very nice fellow.

The soundness of such definitions as are recorded above is beyond
dispute simply because the cited text is evidence that the word once
had the meaning attributed to it by the lexicographer. The importance
of appreciating the historical "truth" of a definition is more apparent
for reading, of course, than it is for writing. A man writes, for the most
part, with his own age in mind, and he defines words with the assumption that his readers will know that he means their definition to
be taken as referring to his and his readers' present existence. If for
any reason he prefers to use a word in a manner no longer common, he
prefixes to his use of it a reminder: "When I call Miss Grundy a spin-
ster, I use the word *in its now almost forgotten sense,* not of an unmarried woman past her prime, but of one who makes her living at
the spinning wheel." But the reading of books from other periods is
not made easy in this way. In dealing with them, the reader must always be aware that meanings do change and that his understanding of a
passage depends on his knowing the words in it as their author knew
them. To read "humorous" in these lines from Kyd's *Spanish Tragedy*
as though it means "amusing" is to miss the point altogether:

> My Lord, be not dismay'd for what is pass'd;
> You know that women oft are humorous.

Kyd's use of "humorous" is conventional for his time, and a check on
the meaning of that word in the sixteenth century will provide the in-

formation needed to make the passage intelligible. Meaning in this instance, however difficult it may be to come at, is literal. When it is more than literal, when, for instance, a pun is involved, the reader may have to resort to historical knowledge of other kinds, to etymology, for example, as in these lines from Milton's *Paradise Lost:*

> As we erewhile, astounded and amaz'd
> No wonder, fall'n such a pernicious highth.
>   (1, 281-2)

Both "pernicious" and "astounded" are serious puns; both mean what they still mean today in common usage, but both have additional meanings drawn from their Latin ancestry. "Astounded" comes from *extonare* and thus refers to being struck by, or hurled out by, thunder, a reference to the battle in which Satan was cast out of heaven by God. "Pernicious" comes from *per-nex* and means "through death" or "death-giving," a description of the "highth" much more impressive than one is likely to understand if the word is taken only to mean "bad" or "undesirable."

Now if historical definitions have a truth-value, are either true or false, it might seem that they should provide no particular complexities. Faced with the problem of knowing what is meant by a word historically used, one might think it necessary only to determine the range of meanings possible for the word, as of the time in which it was used and of the context in which it appears, and then make a choice among those meanings. Yet it does not take much reflection to discover that the procedure is not so simple as it sounds. Even if the choice among many meanings could be made without difficulty, another characteristic of words would give reason to doubt that defining is a process to be casually passed over. That characteristic is commonly referred to as their "connotation."

DENOTATION AND CONNOTATION

It is necessary at this point to make a distinction between the way the two words "denotation" and "connotation" are used in formal logic and in ordinary discourse. In logic, "denotation" is synonymous with "extension," and it refers to a class of objects; "connotation" is synonymous with "intension," and it refers to a set of attributes or characteristics which determine the objects. Thus, the denotation (or extension) of "general" is "Eisenhower," "Washington," "Juin," and its connotation (or intension) is "leader," "strategist," "bold," "forceful," and so on. This two-part classification of the meanings of a term, first carefully distinguished by John Stuart Mill and adopted by most logicians since his time, is particularly useful for dealing with one problem of meaning, and its persistence is no doubt largely due to that particular usefulness. If it is argued, for instance, that, since the statement "A unicorn is a quadruped with a single, spiral horn protruding from its forehead" is meaningful, there must in fact be such a thing as a unicorn, the logician can point out that the word "unicorn" does indeed have connotative meanings but does not have any denotative meanings. In other words, there are attributes, or characteristics which can properly be ascribed to "unicorn" but there are no unicorns, no objects in the class called "unicorn."

The distinction which Mill developed has turned out to be less useful for the purposes of general discourse than for those of logic, unfortunately, and the result is that the two words are now commonly used with somewhat altered meanings. In general language, "denotation" has come to mean something very close to "definition," and "connotation," something rather like "suggestion." *Webster's New Collegiate Dictionary* makes the distinction in these words: ". . . **denote** implies all that strictly belongs to the definition of the word, **connote** all of the ideas that are suggested by the term; thus, 'home' *denotes* the place where one lives with one's family, but it usually *connotes* comfort, intimacy, and privacy. The same implications distinguish **denotation** and **connotation**." One reason for this shift may be an inadequacy in the second of Mill's divisions: our everyday habit is to think that certain attributes are necessarily a part of the meaning of a word and that others are less necessarily so. We like, therefore, to separate the essential from the unessential ones, and we do so by making the essential ones a part of what we call "denotation" and reserving the word "connotation" for those which we regard as associated with the term but not essential to it.

Obviously, the name we give to these divisions is not so important as the divisions themselves, but it is important to see that ordinary language blurs rather than sharpens the distinction. One way out is suggested by Morris R. Cohen and Ernest Nagel (in *An Introduction to Logic and Scientific Method*). They follow the divisions traditional to logic but note that the term "intension" (or "connotation") is commonly used to mean three things: (1) the sum total of attributes which are present to the mind of any person employing the term (*subjective intension*); (2) the set of attributes that are essential to it (*conventional intension*); (3) *all* the attributes which the objects in the denotation of a term have in common, whether these attributes are known or not (*objective intension*). And, consistently with logical practice, they add that it is the second meaning that is important.

Without pressing any further into this matter, we can take from it at least this much for our present purposes: our casual use of the word "connotation" seems to cover less ground than the logician's use of that word but at the same time to be less clear since it includes both those characteristics, or attributes, which might come to almost everyone's mind when the word is mentioned as well as those which might occur only to a few, or even to a single person. What, in fact, most of us seem to mean when we say "connotation" is what Cohen and Nagel call "subjective intension" as well as what they call "objective intension." In general language, then, "denotation" has come to mean "the meaning of a word," and "connotation," to mean "what a word suggests." Since what a word suggests to me may be different from what it suggests to you, this extralogical meaning of the word "connotation" is a dangerous one. But, dangerous or not, it is too well entrenched to be ignored, and the remainder of this account will deal with it as it is and not as, perhaps, it should be.

The distinction between denotation and connotation, in this extralogical sense, becomes clear if we consider such a definition as this one:

"Mother" means "female animal parent."

In this example, "female animal parent" is what we loosely call the "denotative meaning" of the word "mother." How far from being complete it is, one has no trouble in discovering. In the 1930's, for instance, Gertrude Stein and Virgil Thomson wrote an opera about the great suffragette, Susan B. Anthony, and to it they gave the title, *The Mother of Us All.* Now it does not even occur to us to take only the denotative meaning of "mother" in this instance; we recognize readily enough that the word "mother" in the title is used figuratively, that it is meant to imply that, in one or more ways, Susan B. Anthony stands in relationship to those who have followed her as a female animal parent stands in relationship to her offspring. What we do is desert, or minimize, the denotative meaning and jump directly to one or more of the connotations of "mother." And, although those connotations are many, we are not very likely to go wrong in making the jump. We may have to see, or read, the opera to know which ones of the many connotations Miss Stein had in mind, but, for this word, at least, the range of possibilities has more similarity than dissimilarity: protector, inspirer, lover, encourager—such are the connotations that immediately come to mind. Perhaps Miss Stein had no more than a slight extension of the denotative meaning in mind, a "parent" not of children but of ideas or conceptions of freedom and human independence. In that case, it is "parent" that is used connotatively: the jump, at any rate, is the same. When, conscious of his immigrant forebears, a man speaks of the "mother country" or of the "fatherland," he recognizes in the same way that the words we use have connotative as well as denotative character; when adolescents say that they no longer want to be "mothered," they are protesting not against parenthood but against activities which they associate with it. In ordinary discourse, then, connotative meanings are projections beyond denotative meanings, neither better nor worse but different.

Some words, of course, lend themselves more readily than others to the development of connotative meanings. Why that is so, it is not easy to say. Familiarity undoubtedly plays an important role in the process, but that role is not definitive: "house" is a familiar enough word, but it has few connotations; "home," on the other hand, though denotatively similar to "house," has many powerful ones. Nor is the historical development of a word necessarily the determinant of its connotative activity: "egregiously" derives from the Latin *e* plus *grex*, *gregis*, meaning "out of the herd" or "outstanding." Through the seventeenth century it was used primarily as an adverb of admiration and praise; gradually, perhaps through irony at first, the word began to mean "outstandingly" in a pejorative, or unflattering, sense. Today it is exclusively used to mean "monstrously" or "flagrantly" or "outrageously."

The example just cited suggests that connotations may have an effect on denotations, that what is more or less vaguely suggested by a word may in time affect the "meaning" of the word itself. For the writer, this fact is of less importance than the fact that connotations do cling to nearly every word he uses. He must therefore recognize that, even in the act of defining, he deals with the volatility of language, with its power to suggest more than it states. Defining is, in part, a procedure for reducing vagueness in statement; it calls for precise selection of defining terms, and there is no possibility of precision without respect for the connotative, as well as the denotative, activity of words.

STIPULATIVE DEFINING

The statement that defining is a procedure for reducing vagueness is itself a definition, but it is an imperfect one. A definition may do more than reduce vagueness; it may also resolve, or remove, ambiguity. The definition of "institution" at the beginning of this chapter offers many meanings for the word, some of them quite different from others. Since all of the meanings are proper ones, it is clear that the use of the word "institution" in a sentence might very well produce confusion for the reader or hearer. For that reason there must be devices for indicating a choice among the many meanings—devices, in short, for eliminating ambiguity. Two of those devices deserve special attention.

The first has already been mentioned in connection with the copula or sign of equivalence in a definition. In its usual form, a definition is a statement and has, therefore, a truth-value. It is either true or false that "gig" means "a two-wheeled, horse-drawn passenger vehicle." But it is also either true or false that "gig" means "a narrow, light ship's boat for oars or sail," "a wooden box used to draw miners up and down a pit or shaft," "an instrument used for spearing fish," "a textile machine which raises nap on cloth," and "a top." Actually, "gig" means all of those things; each of the definitions is a good definition, each of the defining statements a true statement. Yet it is obvious that, in a given sentence, "gig" is not likely to mean more than one of the things named above. To make clear which of the meanings is meant, a writer must sometimes resort to *stipulative definition*. And to indicate the kind of defining he is about to do, he may find it necessary to make an explicit announcement: "By 'gig' let us mean 'instrument for spearing fish,'" or "Understand 'gig' to mean 'top.'"

The need for stipulative definition may occur wherever a word has several distinct meanings, and it is particularly valuable wherever a writer needs to distinguish between conventional and technical meanings of a word in common use. Such is the case with the words "denotation" and "connotation" as they were treated above. After a distinction had been made between the meanings given to those words in logic and those given to them in general language, it was stipulated that both words would be used with their extralogical meanings in the discussion that followed.

Because stipulative definitions provide a convenient way for keeping discussion on a single track, they often tempt expositors more than they should. It is sometimes possible, for instance, to win an argument by insisting on a stipulative definition of a key term at one stage of the argument and then using different, and perhaps more inclusive, definitions at another stage. And it is also possible to confuse an opponent by stipulating so unusual a meaning for a key term that he cannot accustom himself to it in time to assemble his forces for reply. That is approximately what happens in a famous colloquy between Humpty Dumpty and Alice:

"I don't know what you mean by 'glory,'" Alice said.

Humpty Dumpty smiled contemptuously. "Of course you don't—till I tell you. I meant 'there's a nice knock-down argument for you!'"

"But 'glory' doesn't mean 'a nice knock-down argument,'" Alice objected.

"When I use a word," Humpty Dumpty said in rather a scornful tone, "it means just what I choose it to mean—neither more nor less."

"The question is," said Alice, "whether you *can* make words mean so many different things."

"The question is," said Humpty Dumpty, "which is to be master—that's all."

Alice was too much puzzled to say anything, so after a minute Humpty Dumpty began again. "They've a temper, some of them—particularly verbs, they're the proudest—adjectives you can do anything with, but not verbs. However, I can manage the whole lot of them! Impenetrability! That's what I say!"

"Would you tell me, please," said Alice, "what that means?"

"Now you talk like a reasonable child," said Humpty Dumpty, looking very much pleased. "I meant by 'impenetrability' that we've had enough of that subject, and it would be just as well if you'd mention what you mean to do next, as I suppose you don't mean to stop here all the rest of your life."

"That's a great deal to make one word mean," Alice said, in a thoughtful tone.

"When I make a word do a lot of work like that," said Humpty Dumpty, "I always pay it extra."

"Oh!" said Alice. She was too much puzzled to make any other remark.   LEWIS CARROLL, *Through the Looking Glass*

Humpty has solved the whole problem of defining with admirable facility and forthrightness, but perhaps he ought to pay extra not only to the words he finds so manipulable but also to Alice, who is in the uncomfortable position of having to make sense out of his conversation. The trouble with Humpty's stipulative definitions, if they can be dignified by such a name, is that they are entirely capricious and absurd. They will probably not be the same tomorrow, or an hour from now, as they are at this moment; and, no matter what they are now or later, they have meaning and usefulness only for Humpty. Genuine stipulative definitions are neither less permanent nor less public than lexical definitions; they are simply definitions chosen from the range of lexical definitions, and so chosen in order to exclude meanings inappropriate to the immediate purpose.

Ordinarily, the resort to stipulative definition takes place only where words in common use must be restricted to a limited meaning for a special purpose. In all technical writing, therefore, the amount of stipulative defining is likely to be large. And even in general discourse the amount is large enough to justify listing the obligations relevant to it: first, the definer has an obligation to make sure that his reader knows that he is defining stipulatively; secondly, he has an obligation to be consistent in his stipulation; and thirdly, he has an obligation to guard against stipulative defining which contradicts the whole weight of established usage. To go back to Alice and her patronizing companion: try as she will, Alice is going to have a hard time remembering that when she talks to Humpty Dumpty she must always take "glory" to mean "a nice knock-down argument" but that, when she talks to the White Rabbit or to her mother, "glory" is going to mean just what it did before she had the misfortune to encounter Humpty. And even if she keeps her wits about her at all times she is going to have trouble *feeling* that "glory" means "a nice knock-down argument" when all her life she has used it to mean "fame" or something of the sort.

Stipulative defining is a direct and explicit device for removing ambiguity; a second device, less direct and sometimes entirely implicit, is the use of *context.* A technical writer, whether he be a literary critic or a nuclear engineer, may feel free to use ambiguous terms without taking the precaution of providing stipulative definitions simply because he knows that the audience for which he writes will understand the specialized meanings which he intends. In a broad sense of the word "context," he can be said to rely on context to supply the stipulation he has not provided. If Alice had known Humpty Dumpty over a period of years, and if Humpty had been consistent in his use of words, however unusually he defined them, communication between the two would eventually have become possible. Just so, one artist can speak to another about "mass" in a painting without detailing the special way in which he uses that word.

In a narrower sense of the word "context"—the passage of writing in which a word occurs, for instance—the writer may effectively avoid ambiguity in any of several ways. Fortunately, most of the time the situation in which a word occurs makes clear the restriction to be put on its meaning. Where the situation does not clearly do so, an announcement to make the context explicit is useful. Such an announcement may be very simple: *"According to this law,* 'residence' does not necessarily mean 'the place in which one actually lives' but may also mean 'the place in which one owns taxable property.'"* Or it may be as elaborate as this passage from a textbook in sociology:

> This process of rationalization is punctured, however, by certain discontinuities of history. Hardened institutional fabrics may thus disintegrate and routine forms of life prove insufficient for mastering a growing state of tension, stress, or suffering. It is in such crises that Weber introduces a balancing conception for bureaucracy: the concept of "charisma."
>
> Weber borrowed this concept from Rudolf Sohm, the Strassburg church historian and jurist. Charisma, meaning literally "gift of grace," is used by Weber to characterize self-appointed leaders who are followed by those who are in distress and who need to follow the leader because they believe him to be extraordinarily qualified. The founders of world religions and the prophets as well as military and political heroes are the archetypes of the charismatic leader. Miracles and revelations, heroic feats of valor and baffling success are characteristic marks of their stature. Failure is their ruin.
>
> H. H. GERTH and C. WRIGHT MILLS, introduction to *From Max Weber: Essays in Sociology* (New York: Oxford University Press, 1946).

The phrase "is used by Weber" signals a stipulative definition which is to be attached to the word "charisma" wherever it is found in the writing of that author.

Since this book is concerned with writing in all its stages, from the puzzling over of a problem to its final delineation in clear and forceful prose, an additional word about the usefulness of stipulative definition is pertinent. Even when a person is only communicating with himself—or "inquiring," as this book names the process—stipulative definitions are often valuable. Thinking about a knotty problem, one in which all the terms seem to have more meanings than he can conveniently cope with at once, may force a writer to limit one or more of the terms to a single meaning, arbitrarily chosen, in order to make any headway at all in the solution of the problem itself. If, for example, he is trying to decide whether or not *Pride and Prejudice* is a "sociological" novel, he may temporarily stipulate that "sociological" means "concerned with the solution of social problems." Having made a decision on the basis of that definition, he may stipulate that "sociological" means "concerned with depicting as exactly as possible a social problem" and then proceed to another decision. Next he may decide that "sociological" means "concerned with presenting a picture of society, or of a part of it, in a given time and place," and go on to a third decision. What he would *not* do, of course, and what Humpty Dumpty did do with his words, is stipulate that "sociological" means "divided into three parts" or "enjoying custard pie more than ice cream."

DEFINING IN THE NATURAL SCIENCES

More than once in the preceding pages, some mention has been made of the particular needs of "technical" writers. While those needs are, in the main, fairly obvious, it is worth while to speculate briefly about the different demands on words, and therefore on the definition of words, that are made in the various intellectual disciplines. For the sake of convenience, the discussion makes use of a three-part division of those disciplines which has wide general acceptance: the natural (or physical) sciences, the social sciences, the humanities.

The natural sciences are concerned to deal, in so far as such dealing is possible, with the world apart from man's experience of it. That is, they try to find out what is constant in the world, and to do so they try to separate matter from the sensations it produces in sentient beings. In order to make their measurements as precise as possible, they regularly attempt to reduce the world to quantities of this or that. In the little essay which follows, an English scientist discusses the way in which the common word "hard" is made useful for scientific measurement by strict exclusion of connotative meaning and careful transformation of denotative meaning into quantitative form.

WHAT "HARD" MEANS

In the last article I wrote about the way in which ordinary words change their meaning as they are used in science and technology, taking as an example the word "hot." All adjectives start as descriptions of qualities. They end up as descriptions of quantities, if they are taken over by science. A word like "big" or "long" is entirely relative. A mile is a long swim but a short walk, because an ordinary man often walks a mile, but seldom swims a mile. A man is large compared to a cat, and small compared to an elephant, and so on. This sort of contradiction does not trouble anyone but philosophers, because we are accustomed to measure lengths, and we all know what a foot or a mile means.

But we are in much greater difficulties with some other common adjectives such as "hard." Of course we use the word metaphorically, as when we talk of a hard question, meaning one which is difficult to answer, or hard X-rays, meaning rays which penetrate easily through matter. But I want to deal with the word in its ordinary sense, as when we say that iron is harder than butter. Everyone will agree that this is true. But it is not so easy to decide which of two pieces of iron is harder, and as a matter of fact there may be no definite answer to the question. When we come to accurate measurement, we find that the word "hard" has dozens of slightly different meanings.

The most usual test of hardness in steels is that of Brinell. A very hard steel ball of 10 millimetres diameter is pressed onto a steel plate for 30 seconds with a load of 3 tons. The hardness number decreases with the depth of the indentation.

Another test of hardness which generally agrees pretty well with the Brinell test is the weight which must be put on a diamond point in order that it should just produce a visible scratch when pulled sideways. But as soon as we use moving bodies to measure hardness things become very complicated. For example at a relative speed of 30 feet per second a disc of "soft" iron was cut by a steel tool; at 100 feet per second the disc cut the tool itself, and at 300 feet per second the disc cut quartz. In the same way hardness varies with temperature.

If we compare an ordinary hardened carbon tool steel and a high-speed tool steel at ordinary temperatures, the former is probably a little harder by the Brinell test. But at a dull red heat the high-speed steel is still hard, while the ordinary tool steel is about as soft as is copper at room temperature. . . .

Hardness is also used as a measure of the amount of wear which a material will stand. But here again the details are very important. We may want to test how a metal stands up to rolling friction without lubricant. This is essential in tests of rails, and wheels of railway vehicles. Or we may want to know how a metal stands up to sliding abrasion, either with or without a film of oil. One steel may stand up better to rolling friction, and another to sliding friction. Here their differences in hardness probably depend on the fact that metals sliding over one another actually melt at the point of contact, so their properties at high temperatures become important.

Within a century or less we shall probably be able to calculate the various kinds of hardness with great exactitude from a knowledge of the forces between atoms. At present we can only do so very roughly. Probably the physicists of the future will be able to specify the different kinds of hardness very completely in terms of a few numbers.

It would be possible to deal in the same way with the meanings of various words such as toughness, elasticity, and brittleness, which are applied to solids. None of these can be expressed by a single number.

The properties of liquids are a good deal simpler than those of solids, and the properties of gases are simpler still, though anyone concerned with the design of aeroplanes finds even gases quite complicated enough. And when we come to such a property of material systems as life, the complications are of course vastly greater. Scientists are reproached because they cannot say in simple terms what life is. It is easy enough to point out differences between a dog or a cabbage and a stone or a machine. It is much harder to draw the line when we get down to the agents of smallpox and other diseases, which behave in some ways as if alive and in others as if dead. But if anyone reproaches science because it cannot yet give a complete account of life, it is a fair reply to ask him what he means by hardness, and how he would tell if one thing is harder than another.   J. B. S. HALDANE, *A Banned Broadcast and Other Essays* (London: Chatto & Windus, 1946).

Another definition, this time of the equally common word "work," makes the point even clearer by showing how the definition that is useful to the natural sciences may actually contradict ordinary usage.

WORK

We feel we have been doing more "work" when we have lifted 20 lb from the floor to a bench 1 ft high, than if we had lifted only 10 lb; and we feel it takes more work to lift 10 lb from the floor to a table 2 ft high, than to a bench 1 ft high. Such qualitative judgments may have been the starting point for the following quantitative definition:

The *work* done by a force F lb, constant in magnitude and direction, when it has moved its point of application a distance D ft along its own direction, is the product $F \times D$:

$$\text{Work} = \text{force} \times \text{distance.}$$

The unit of work is the foot-pound (ft-lb), a derived unit:

$$W \text{ (ft-lb)} = F \text{ (lb)} \times D \text{ (ft).}$$

Note that this is a definition, not a physical law. Note also that it contradicts some of our experiences. If we lift 20 lb through 3 ft twenty times in succession, the definition says we are doing the same "work" each time, namely, 60 ft-lb, whereas we know our work gets harder as the task progresses. The same would be true if we tried to climb the stairs in the Hancock Building. The fact is that physics uses some of the words of the English language, "work" for instance, in a new and specialized sense entirely its own. Also we must not make physics say more than it does: "physics" is concerned with measurements of length, time, force, and derived quantities; it says nothing about sensations. Scientists know very little as yet about "biophysics" in general, and physiological fatigue in particular. (They are working at it, just as Leonardo da Vinci and Simon Steven and Galileo were working at understanding mechanics.)

PROFESSOR PHILIPPE LECORBEILLIER, Natural
Sciences I Syllabus (Harvard University, 1951).

DEFINING IN THE SOCIAL SCIENCES

Not even in all of the natural sciences, however, is such precision as these definitions of "hard" and "work" propose possible; psychology, for instance, has not yet found ways, nor is it likely that it ever will, to make its definitions mathematically manipulable. Yet all critical writing, within or outside the natural sciences, aspires to precision in its definitions, and it would be foolish indeed to conclude that precision is unachievable except by the means congenial to science. There are other means of reaching toward exactness in definition, and it is with such other means that the social sciences and the humanities must do most of their work. The passage quoted earlier from the introduction to Max Weber's work provides a good illustration. The writers define the word "charisma," as Weber used it, by several means: they indicate its provenience from the work of a church historian and jurist, they refer to its etymology ("meaning literally 'gift of grace'"), they explain in what situation Weber uses the word ("to characterize self-appointed leaders who . . ."), they add examples of people who possess the quality represented by the word they are defining ("founders of world religions and . . . prophets as well as military and political heroes") and, finally, they list achievements of those who possess it ("Miracles and revelations, heroic feats of valor and baffling success . . .").

The main reason that defining in the social sciences is very different from that in the natural sciences is quite obvious: the complexity of relationships which the social scientist sets out to describe is much greater and is not so readily reducible to simplicity. If the chemist needs to define "catalyst," he can do so in symbols and, even if he decides to use words, entirely in terms which have concrete and particular reference. But the social scientist who must define "prejudice" or "motivation" or "progress" is faced at once with the connotative activity of words and with a phenomenon so intricate that it almost defies analysis.

Therefore he must refine as much as words will allow him to do and then resort to supplementary devices of example, comparison, and so on to finish the job.

DEFINING IN THE HUMANITIES

What is true of the social sciences is true of the humanities so long as one is thinking of critical efforts to determine the meaning of a term; both areas of knowledge are most commonly expressed in words rather than in mathematical symbols or in operational demonstrations (like the Brinell test cited by Haldane), and both must therefore rely on controlling rather than on ignoring the connotative activity of language.

In some ways, the problem in the humanities is even more difficult than it is in the social sciences because so large a part of the critical vocabulary used in discussing works of art is metaphorical. For each of the arts there is a vocabulary that is particularly appropriate ("mass" in sculpture, for instance, and "euphony" in poetry), but the specific vocabulary has never been adequate to meet critical needs. The tendency to borrow the words appropriate to one art for the description of another is therefore almost irresistible, and such borrowing immediately raises problems of definition. The word "texture" used to describe a piece of cloth is immediately comprehensible; used to describe one aspect of a painting, it calls up much the same response; but used to describe a passage of poetry, it obviously requires an imaginative translation from imagery of feeling to imagery of hearing. In the same way a translation from the imagery of hearing to the imagery of seeing is necessary when the word "tone" is used to describe painting. If these "translations" are left entirely to the whim of the reader, confusion is bound to occur, and it does indeed occur in some criticism. The careful critic may be unwilling, nonetheless, to abandon the suggestiveness of such words and will find himself constrained, therefore, to make stipulative definitions for them. These stipulative definitions he will reinforce as the social scientist reinforces his definitions—by example, allusion, comparison.

The principal difference between the means used to define "hard" and "work" and that used to define "charisma" is quickly apparent. The first means is single; the second, multiple. The first sacrifices some of the complexity of the term-to-be-defined in order to achieve abstractness and manipulability. The second sacrifices neatness of formula in order to preserve complexity. If the final test of a definition is that, at its conclusion, both the definer and the person for whom the word is being defined are in agreement about its meaning, then both of these definitions may be successful, though for different reasons.

PATTERNS OF DEFINITION

Such examples make it possible to move away from the some-what confining formula of logical definition and look at the process of defining in the fullness that is valuable in writing. This is not to suggest that the logical formulation with which this discussion began is useless; in one way or another, a definer is constantly pressed back to it, not only to make clear to others what he means but to make meaning clear to himself. It is only to say that exposition is not logic, though it cannot ignore logic. It serves a different purpose and must sometimes use different means to do so.

Most of the means of definition appropriate to expository writing have already been illustrated, and a brief discussion of them, in orderly fashion, is now in order. The simplest in form is also the one most common to an abridged dictionary: *definition by synonym*. Putting aside the claim that no two words mean the same, one can recognize in synonyms a very helpful device for conveying meaning. To say that "heroism" means "bravery" does not indeed exhaust the possibilities of meaning for the word "heroism," but it directs the mind effectively toward one small range of possible meanings. How much the word "bravery" excludes can be gathered from Mark Twain's story of the collie who made her reputation in dogdom by the extensiveness of her vocabulary and who defined "heroism" as "agriculture" and "agriculture" as "intramural incandescence." Synonyms are useful in defining, and the search for semantic perfection should not make the perfectionist lose sight of that fact.

Where synonyms do not satisfy because the defining term is as little agreed upon or as hard to pin down as the term-to-be-defined, *definition by analysis* will help. This is the kind of definition used in the discussion of "gig" above, one in which the defining term includes mention of the class of objects to which the term-to-be-defined belongs and of the characteristics which distinguish it from other members of that class. Like definition by synonym, it, too, is commonly found in abridged dictionaries, though much less elaborated than a writer may wish to make it in his own work. In definition by analysis, the definer comes closer than in any other means to the search for full meaning that is the primary end of the use of language as an instrument of inquiry. The resources of the analytic definition are exhausted only when there remain no more questions to ask, no more distinctions to make. It may do its job adequately in one sentence or may fail to come to the end of it in a volume. Whether a sentence or a volume is needed depends on the purpose the definition is meant to serve and on the perceptiveness of the definer.

Another means, very close to that of analytic definition, is that in

which the defining term contains a class word and distinguishing characteristics but in which the distinguishing characteristics depend on relationship with other members of the class. To define "lion" as "the
king of the beasts" is to define *synthetically;* so, also, is to define "atom"
as "the smallest known particle of matter." Synthetic definitions are
useful, but their reliability is limited. A hundred years ago, for instance,
the definition of "atom" as "the smallest known particle of matter"
might have gone unchallenged; today it would not. Despite its unreliabil-
ity, *definition by synthesis* has one particular virtue: it singles out a
characteristic of the term-to-be-defined and directs attention to that characteristic. The kingliness of the lion and the smallness of an atom are,
by this means, firmly fixed in the mind. The synthetic definition is incomplete, but it is emphatic.

The three kinds of definition reviewed so far—definition by synonym, by analysis, and by synthesis—all use the method of equivalence
$(x = y)$. For writers, though perhaps not for logicians, there is one other
kind of definition belonging to this group, one which may be called
definition by connotation. One of Robert Frost's most impressive son-
nets begins with the line

She is as in a field a silken tent

and goes on to mention the characteristics of "a silken tent" which can
be taken, figuratively, to suggest equivalents in the nature of the
"She" from whom the poem begins. The equivalents it suggests, however, are not the ones stated but those which the image, fully per-
ceived, brings to mind: fragility, resilience, strength, sensitivity, serene
aloofness, surprising stability. These are the connotations of the image of the "silken tent," as it is described in the poem, and it is in these
connotations that we discover the definition of "She." The same kind
of definition occurs in the simplest metaphorical statement: "The earth
is a ball." Analysis of this kind of definition shows that it has two striking characteristics: (1) it compares objects which have (or seem to
have) few, rather than many, properties in common; (2) it relies for
equivalence on those more distantly associated properties rather than
on the ones which we commonly associate with the object to be defined. Because extended discussion of connotation occurs in the chapter
entitled "Persuading," no more need be said here than that this kind of
definition is one of the most useful the writer has at his command.
What it fails to provide in precision it makes up for in suggestiveness
and power.

Defining by connotation is on the border line between those processes which use equivalence and those which do not. Of the latter,
three demand attention. The first, and least important, is the *ostensive
definition,* or definition by showing. This means is more common in

speech than in writing, but it is useful in both. In conversation with children particularly, one is often forced, by the limitations of a common vocabulary, to point to objects as a way of defining them. Ordinarily some sort of demonstrative phrase accompanies the gesture: "That is a daffodil," or "This is what I mean by 'skipping.'" A writer may use diagrams or pictures to perform the function of ostensive definition, just as dictionaries regularly print line drawings of animals and of mechanical objects alongside their verbal definitions. Although the means is clearly not a primary one for the writer, as a supplement it can be of considerable use to him—witness the fables and seriocomic essays of James Thurber.

The second kind of definition which makes no effort to produce a logical equivalent for the term-to-be-defined is *definition by example.* If a friend says that he is interested in Lepidoptera, we may be forced to ask him what he means by "Lepidoptera." If he answers, "You know, moths and butterflies," he is defining by example. (In the language of logic, "moths" and "butterflies" would be called *denotations* of the word "Lepidoptera.") The distinctive characteristic of this kind of definition is that the referent of the defining term falls within the class of referents of the term-to-be-defined, and the significance of that characteristic is in what it assumes. In the definition by analysis ("A gig is a vehicle for one or more passengers . . ."), the definer generally assumes that his reader or hearer does not know the object (gig) which he is defining. In the definition by example, the definer assumes that the reader *does* know the object but that he is simply not familiar with the term which has been used to name it ("Lepidoptera"). Definition by example is useful, therefore, only where the definer can make that assumption. A further limitation on its usefulness comes from the fact that the examples cited in the defining term may have several characteristics in common; if that is so, the reader may be uncertain about which one, or ones, he is to select as a guide to understanding the term-to-be-defined. Will he be surprised to find larvae in his friend's collection, or not to find mosquitoes? In short, is the class of objects suggested by the examples clearly enough defined by the examples alone? In most cases, the definition by example, like the ostensive definition, is a valuable supplement to other forms of definition but is not by itself adequate.

The third kind of definition-without-equivalence is *definition by function,* a kind so common that it needs only summary illustration. "A thermometer tells temperature" is a definition by function. It may be objected that the definition is really elliptic, that it omits words which would make it also a definition using equivalence ("A thermometer is an instrument for taking temperature"), and that may be so. Since it commonly occurs in the abbreviated form, however, it may reasonably be distinguished from other definitions-by-equivalence. Its strength is that it draws directly on a person's experience with an object rather than on his power to abstract its properties; its weakness is that it may be very ambiguous, as the sentence "A gig is designed to carry passengers" proved to be in the dialogue presented earlier in this chapter.

Although they do not fully cover the range of the possible ways of defining, the seven means just discussed and illustrated are those most commonly encountered and most useful to the writer. If a writer knows all of them and appreciates their particular limitations and virtues, he is reasonably well prepared to deal with the often difficult problem of explaining to a reader or of determining for himself the complete significance of the terms he uses in discourse. Once the means are at his command, he can deal readily enough with the form in which he casts definition and with a series of checks against the success of his efforts to define.

FORM IN DEFINITION

In one way this chapter has stayed quite close to the manner of defining common to the study of logic, that of stating the term-to-be-defined, using a sign of equivalence, and then stating the defining term (x is y). The neatness and efficiency of that form recommend it particularly for analytic work. Where it is used, the writer must make sure that the term-to-be-defined and the defining term are similar grammatical elements: a noun on one side of the equation demands a noun on the other, an adjective demands an adjective, and so on. The following definitions, though adequate as far as meaning is concerned, are both breaches of form:

> Rent is paying money to an owner for the use of his property.

> Cramming is when you study very hard immediately before an examination.

A simple correction in each preserves the proprieties of expression:

> Rent is money paid to an owner for the use of his property.

> Cramming is studying very hard immediately before an examination.

Despite its neatness, the invariability of the formula $x = y$ may make it disagreeable to the writer. To avoid the mechanical balancing of term-to-be-defined against defining term, he may resort to several other patterns. He may, for instance, compress a definition in this fashion: "A square joins four equal straight lines at right angles so as to form a complete enclosure." This is the same as the analytic definition, "A square is a geometrical figure in which four equal straight lines meet at right angles so as to form an enclosure," but substituting an active verb for the copula and class term of the analytic definition considerably reduces formality. Another way of reducing formality and providing variety is to use the grammatical structure known as "apposition." This also has the advantage of reducing emphasis on the definition so that the forward movement of the discourse is not interrupted:

> Paul used the Greek term *agape,* a word meaning "brotherly love," to distinguish a kind of Christian love which he believed to be entirely different from love as the unrelieved search for fulfillment discussed in Plato's *Symposium* and deeply rooted in subsequent Greek thought.

In "*agape,* a word meaning 'brotherly love.'" there is a definition (by translation) which is presented as an appositive. The reader gets the explanation of *agape* which the definition supplies without having his attention drawn away from the principal focus of the sentence (a contrast between two concepts of love). If the writer had wished to provide the Greek equivalent for "love as the unrelieved search . . ." as he did for "brotherly love," he could have used the same device as for *agape,* or he could have set the word *eros* in parentheses after "fulfillment." If his intent had been to follow this paragraph with a discussion of the Platonic concept, he might have wished to emphasize the term for it, preparatory to beginning a discussion. To do so, he could have separated the definition from the preceding sentence in this way:

> . . . entirely different from the Platonic concept of love. That concept, given the name *eros,* was the embodiment of the human faculty of desire, of yearning, of lust to possess. It included every manifestation of powerful longing from the most sensual to the completely sublimated.

In this example of a definition to which importance has been lent by its presentation in an independent sentence, one can see also the most common device writers have for making definitions fully effective— that of adding definition to definition until a complex series of equations is established for the term-to-be-defined.

CHECKS ON DEFINITION

The various ways in which a definition can be presented give the writer no excuse for failing to clarify as he goes along, unless, of course, his purpose at a given point in the discourse is to mystify or to create suspense by withholding information. He may use one means of definition only, or many; he may set down his definition with all the starkness of a mathematical equation or with the unobtrusiveness of an aside. Which means and which manner he uses will depend on his intent and on his assessment of his readers' needs.

Once the writer understands the nature of the defining process and knows how to handle definitions deftly in the regular flow of discourse, he may still need to check himself occasionally to make sure that his definitions will hold up under careful scrutiny. The process of writing is such that a writer is often carried along by his own words, the words seeming at times to come almost of themselves. So great is their impetus at such times that the writer may neither wish, nor be able, to check the rush of words. He will be convinced that the words say what he means to say and will not dare to test them at the time of the writing for fear of shutting off the flow itself. When he comes back to his work and looks at it soberly and critically, however, he may find inadequacies and contradictions where he would earlier have sworn that completeness and harmony reigned. At such times—and they are common—the writer finds system to be the best buckler against despair. If he can ask a series of questions about his terminology, if he can systematically test his definitions, he may swiftly discover the weaknesses and discrepancies and remedy them; if he cannot, he must write and rewrite until the sentences satisfy his inner ear. Both methods work, and most writers make use of one or the other as occasion demands.

A system of checks on what one has written is essentially negative. Like a mechanic checking an automobile engine to discover the cause of sluggish operation, the writer eliminates one by one the possible causes of disorder until he has found and corrected the faulty mechanism. This hunt for the causes of trouble is seldom as orderly an affair as a book will make it out to be, but that is true of the entire process of writing and will not here impede the setting down, in formal fashion, of the most common faults made in defining.

Overinclusion. Complete confidence about the meaning of some words and equal confidence that others are sure to understand them as the user does often make him rather summary and careless in definition. For example, to define "patriotism" as "the feeling a man has for his country" is less than enough simply because men have many feelings about their country which do not at all belong in the sense of the word "patriotism." This is the fault of overinclusion, of failing to qualify the class word in the defining term as much as it needs to be qualified. In the example given here the addition of qualifying phrases to "feeling" will correct the deficiency: "Patriotism is the feeling of respect, love, and pride which a man has for his country."

Overrestriction. At the other extreme, a definition may suffer from overrestriction, from being so closely confined by the class word or the qualifiers in the defining term that not all of the things to which the term-to-be-defined may properly refer are covered by it. "Kings are rulers by hereditary right" is an overrestrictive definition of the word "king" since it makes no provision for rulers who have taken thrones by force or who have been elevated to them without any hereditary claim at all. Both overinclusiveness and overrestriction can be detected by sampling, that is, by asking if all the examples one can call to mind have the attributes named or implied in the defining term.

Duplication. It is sometimes convenient and useful, though often dangerous, to define a term simply by using a second term which has a different linguistic history but the same meaning. The definition, " 'Liberty' means 'freedom,' " uses a word of Latin origin on one side of the verb and a word of Germanic origin on the other. Where definition is needed because the term-to-be-defined is simply unfamiliar to the reader, this kind of definition may be valuable: " 'Prophylaxis' means 'cleaning' " is an example. Where definition is needed because the term-to-be-defined stands for something which the reader actually does not know, a definition of this kind is of little help. In general it is best avoided except in the act of translation ("Rot" in German means "red" in English) because it may appear to give information without actually doing so.

Circularity. A definition which uses the term-to-be-defined in the defining term is said to be circular. Most instances of circularity occur not in single sentences ("Freedom is the state of being free") but in a series of sentences long enough so that the repetition of the term-to-be-defined is not immediately noticeable:

> *Freedom* is not easily defined except by reference to what it is not. The closest one can come, in positive terms, may be to call it "independence of action." Independent action is that which is free from coercion or control by any external agent whatsoever.

Ambiguity. In any writing, the danger of ambiguity is always great because words shift and multiply meanings so rapidly and because there is sometimes actually an accidental identity between the appearance or sound of words having very different meanings and origins (between "herd" and "heard," or "foul" and "fowl" in sound, for instance, or between the two meanings of the word "mean," one from Medieval French, the other from Old English, in this sentence: "The average man is the mean man of the population"). Definition is often thought of as the means of eradicating ambiguity, and it is true that stipulative definition, at least, does have that as its main purpose. Lexical, or historical, definition, however, does not so much eradicate as describe the essential ambiguity of words because it indicates all or a large number of the meanings which a word may have. Yet, despite the fact that definitions can seldom divorce themselves from ambiguity, there is a sense in which they must attempt to avoid it. The examples given above deal with *semantic* ambiguity, that deriving directly from the meanings of words themselves. Another kind of ambiguity, that known as syntactical, is more likely to plague the definer because it results from the careless handling of punctuation or of the order of words. To define a "willful abstainer" as "one who does not do something because he does not wish to" is to produce such ambiguity: in this instance, a simple cure is effected by placing a comma after "something." The definition "In gin rummy, a discard is a card placed by a player of no value to him in the center of the table face up in return for a card previously drawn from a face-down stack also in the center of the table" has all the words needed to make an accurate definition but arranges them so badly that their meaning is ambiguous.

Obscurity. The person who defines stipulatively usually does so in order to clarify meaning; by selecting one of several possible definitions of a word and limiting himself to that one, he hopes to avert misunderstanding. It is only a short step from stipulative defining of the right kind to another kind that is less defensible, the stipulation of newly invented meanings for words in common use. The writer who insists on the privilege of making up his own definitions for words which, in ordinary discourse, have different meanings from the ones he attributes to them runs several risks. If the word for which he makes a private definition has strong connotations, nothing he can do will relieve it of them, no matter how he defines it. Moreover, because the writer, like his readers, is accustomed to using words with their conventional meanings, he is very likely to be caught off guard in any extended passage of writing and to find, too late, that he has used an important word both in a private sense and in the sense common to everyone. Should he be skilled enough to escape both dangers, he faces a third, that of developing a vocabulary so special and private that a reader needs a special lexicon to make use of his works. It is safe to say that a writer must have rare talents to find and keep readers willing to make such an effort for him. In most cases, such private defining is less the product of special insight than of laziness or pretentiousness; when either is the cause, the reader is fully warranted in leaving the writer to contemplate his glory alone.

These formal checks on one's defining are mechanical aids only. Good definitions can come only from some understanding of what is involved in the defining process. Enough has been said here to suggest the ramifications of that process and to indicate the respect it deserves from a serious writer.

EXERCISES

1. Improve these definitions:

    a. When a group can maintain conformity, it is called equilibrium.

    b. Network: anything reticulated and decussated at equal intervals, with interstices between the intersections. (From Dr. Samuel Johnson's *Dictionary of the English Language.*)

c. Verse is prose cut into lines of equal length.

d. Osmosis is where one thing filters into another.

e. The policy of containment can best be described as one in which the idea is to contain the spread of control.

f. In underworld parlance, a rod is a gat.

g. What Weber means by "charisma" is leadership. (Refer to page 23.)

h. Sculpture is the representation of human or animal figures in marble.

2. Common words often lose precision through overuse. When that happens, the only recourse for the careful writer is to indicate by direct definition the meaning he wishes to convey. Remembering the summary of cautions to be observed in defining, prepare a careful definition of each of these words:

a. democracy (politics)

b. communism (economics)

c. friction (physics)

d. motivation (psychology)

e. fever (medicine)

f. radical (linguistics)

g. stanza (poetry)

h. interval (music)

i. hue (painting)

j. plot (fiction)

3. Often a definition can be *reinforced* by distinguishing the object referred to from others with which it might be confused. Define the first word in each of the groups below, making proper distinctions between it and the others in the group:

a. planet, star, sun, asteroid

b. sonnet, ode, quatrain, rondeau

c. capitalism, socialism, communism

d. rectangle, parallelogram

e. deviation, difference, variation

4. The more difficult something is to define and describe, the more likely are the terms of definition and description to become metaphorical. Discuss the metaphorical adequacy of these common terms about wine:

balanced	hard
coarse	rough
dry	soft
fat	bouquet
flowery	breed

5. Invent a word ("igran," "porin," or the like) to serve as a noun or adjective expressing some substance or quality for which there is not at present a proper word in English. (It has been noted, for example, that there is no dignified but unpretentious word in English meaning "the regular male companion of a young, unmarried female"—what is rather embarrassingly called a "boy friend.") Without defining the word you invent, use it in a paragraph until its meaning becomes clear.

6. Some new words become public property very quickly by virtue of their sudden usefulness; some are unheard of on Monday, on everyone's tongue on Tuesday, and all but forgotten on Wednesday; some give no clue to their meaning and others depend largely on the clues within the word to supply, or suggest, their meaning. Analyze each of these words on the basis of your own experience with it:

simulcast	longhair
tranquilizer	motel
brinkmanship	private eye
fall-out	kickback

7. One of Santayana's essays begins with this sentence: "Patriotism is a form of piety." What kind of definition is this? What obligation does it lay on the definer? How would you meet the obligation?

8. Throughout the chapter on definition the process of defining is treated with an eye to ordinary discourse, that is, to a freer relationship between defining and describing than formal logic permits. Following the principles of that treatment, develop an extended definition of an abstract word: honor, virtue, pleasure, wealth, vanity.

9. To what degree is the following informal definition analytic, to what degree persuasive? Is it possible to deduce a formal definition from it? What is gained and lost by the attempt?

July 3, 1943

We received a letter from the Writers' War Board the other day asking for a statement on "The Meaning of Democracy." It presumably is our duty to comply with such a request, and it is certainly our pleasure.

Surely the Board knows what democracy is. It is the line that forms on the right. It is the don't in Don't Shove. It is the hole in the stuffed shirt through which the sawdust slowly trickles; it is the dent in the high hat. Democracy is the recurrent suspicion that more than half of the people are right more than half of the time. It is the feeling of privacy in the voting booths, the feeling of communion in the libraries, the feeling of vitality everywhere. Democracy is the score at the beginning of the ninth. It is an idea which hasn't been disproved yet, a song the words of which have not gone bad. It's the mustard on the hot dog and the cream in the rationed coffee. Democracy is a request from a War Board, in the middle of a morning in the middle of a war, wanting to know what democracy is.   E. B. WHITE, *The Wild Flag*

10. In the *Nature of Prejudice* Gordon Allport develops a definition for the word "prejudice" as he intends to use it in his book. He begins with a "dictionary" definition (a. below); from analysis of it he discovers the need to develop another (b. below); and finally he alters the second definition to make it serve his particular purposes (c. below). Examine the three definitions and then explain each change in terms of the account given above.

   a. thinking ill of others without sufficient warrant
   b. a feeling, favorable or unfavorable, toward a person or thing, prior to, or not based on, actual experience
   c. an avertive or hostile attitude toward a person who belongs to a group, simply because he belongs to that group, and is therefore presumed to have the objectionable qualities ascribed to the group.

⊂⊐ *Asserting*

. . . *opinion in good men is but knowledge in the making.*

JOHN MILTON

SOME OF THE MOST INTERESTING FACTS about language are such commonplaces that their provocative character is easily overlooked. It may appear completely platitudinous, for instance, to say that people make assertions more frequently than they ask questions, give commands, express wishes or resolutions, and emit ejaculations. And it is only when one asks *why* assertions predominate that the differences between sentences that are assertions and sentences that are not begin to seem important.

ASSERTIONS AND NONASSERTIVE UTTERANCES

One way to get at those differences is to consider the responses which assertions and the various kinds of sentences that are not assertions provoke in listeners or readers. First, note that an assertion comprises two elements: an identification of the matter spoken of or written about (*subject*), and an observation about that matter (*predication*):

The hero (subject) won the battle (predication).

Essentially, an assertion claims that something (the predication) is true about something else (the subject). The response to it, therefore, is an affirmation or denial of the claim. The hearer or reader agrees or denies that the assertion is true.

The response to a question is very different because a question calls upon the hearer or reader to supply information, not to deny or assent to an observation. It would make no sense to reply to the question "Who won the battle?" by saying, "That is false" or "That is true." Not even when the question *suggests* the information which is to be supplied ("Did the hero win the battle?") is it possible for the respondent to declare that the *question* is true or false, though he may by his answer indicate that the suggested assertion (that the hero won the battle) is, or is not, true: "The hero did win the battle."

In one sense, a wish may be said to be an assertion. It is either true or false that I wish that the hero would win the battle. Such is the case if the wish is said to be the same as the sentence that contains it. The actual wish itself, however, is something separate from the expression that announces it ("I wish") and from the sentence in which it occurs, and if it is so considered it, too, does not warrant the reply "That is true." The most that a respondent can do is to indicate that he approves or disapproves the wish; his response is not a judgment of the truth or falsity of the wish but of its meritoriousness.

Both resolutions ("Let us win the battle") and commands ("Be a hero!") call for a still different kind of response, one that involves not a judgment or an indication of approval but an action or a refusal to act. And ejaculations (Oh!), in some ways the most interesting of all these nonassertive sentences, seem to be capable of soliciting several kinds of response, though never the one response that is consistently provoked by an assertion.

Having made this preliminary examination, we can set down a simple definition:

An assertion is a sentence that is either true or false.

To seize the implications of this simple definition, we shall have to back off from the definition for a moment and examine the way we are accustomed to treat assertions in ordinary discourse. When we do so, we discover almost at once that they are treated somewhat differently in the general use of language than they are in logic and, further, that the difference in treatment is both a gain and a loss.

In the chapter on defining, it was necessary to make clear that the words "denotation" and "connotation" are differently used in ordinary discourse than in logic; after both uses had been explained, the chapter adopted the general usage as preferable for its purposes, noting as it did so that a certain blurring of categories would be the result. In the treatment of assertions, too, popular terminology blurs categories, but here the blurring has even more serious consequences. For that reason, although it begins with the distinctions common in everyday language, this discussion will go on to examine the distinctions made in logic and to propose that *they* be the ones adopted for use in expository writing.

RHETORICAL CATEGORIES: FACT, OPINION, PREFERENCE

A simple assertion and two responses to it will provide a starting point:

Melville is a greater novelist than Hawthorne.
1. That's a fact.
2. Well, now, that's a matter of opinion.

In the two responses, the statement is classified as fact and as opinion. Now it is clear that, in this instance, the classification does not depend on the statement (since there is only one statement) but on something in the attitude of the respondent. The two responses might be altered to read (1) "I agree" and (2) "I'm not sure whether I agree or not." Or those responses may be a way of saying (1) that the statement is one that can be proved true and (2) that it is one that can probably not be proved either true or false. Since these reponses contradict each other, one of them must logically be wrong. Yet no one reading the two responses is at all likely to be misled about them; nor is he likely to think one a wrong, another a right, response. Instead, he will recognize that they represent different aspects of a complex act of judgment and are therefore perhaps as much descriptions of the respondents as of the assertion.

Where simpler acts of judgment are called for, the inadequacy of this kind of classification is not so obvious, and a sort of rough justice may be achieved with it, as discussion of several assertions will show.

Horses have manes.

Peter wears glasses.

These two are the most intelligent students in the class.

Lemon pie tastes better than apple.

Each of these statements poses a different problem of verification, but all are alike in requiring that we turn to experience for the tests of truth or falsity.

Although it is true that all of the statements just cited are alike in requiring verification by reference to experience, it is also true that they are unlike in several ways. Some concern a whole class of objects; some are confined to particular members of a class. Some would appear to require very little in the way of verification; some, to require a great deal. Some seem susceptible of almost certain proof; others, impossible to prove at all. And, finally, some appear to invite tests of validity; others, to warn that such tests are irrelevant. Because these assertions are different in so many ways, a writer commonly uses signals to warn his reader about the differences, signals ranging from parenthetical remarks ("so far as I can tell," "in my judgment," "from one point of view," "considered superficially," and so on) to the development of an informative tone of voice in the paragraph (that, for instance, of reassurance, of decisiveness, of hesitancy, of cautious speculation, of skepticism). In general, these signals are intended to make the distinctions which we commonly indicate by the loose, and more or less rhetorical, categories *statements of fact, statements of opinion,* and *statements of preference or taste.*

If we attempt to locate each of the sentences above in one or another of these three rhetorical categories, we can get some idea of the strengths and weaknesses of the categories for analytic purposes. For each, we must first speculate about the kind and amount of "evidence" we are likely to be able to accumulate, and on that basis proceed to assign it to a category.

The statement "Horses have manes" would require for verification the examination of, or a reliable report on, all horses now living and all that have ever lived or will do so; most of us would settle for less, it is true, just as testers of all kinds now draw conclusions from "sample populations." Whether or not we require reference to all horses, we are satisfied that it takes only the simple tests of direct observation to determine the truth or falsity of the statement. And it is that feeling of the simplicity or relative certainty of proof that leads us to treat such a statement without qualification and to refer to it as though it represented something about whose truth or falsity we could eventually reach an unassailable decision. Statements of this kind we conventionally call "statements of fact," meaning not that they are beyond doubt true but that we are sure that their truth or falsity *can be readily and finally determined by reference to experience.*

(In ordinary language, we occasionally distinguish between "factual statements" and "statements of fact," meaning, by the former, statements whose truth *or* falsity can readily be determined and, by the latter, those whose *truth* is readily demonstrable. In this discussion, the two terms are not distinguished: a "statement of fact" may be either true or false, and it is different from other statements primarily because of its high degree of susceptibility to tests of validity.)

If we treat "Horses have manes" as a statement of fact because we know that the proofs for establishing its truth or falsity are within our power to produce, we shall not hesitate to classify "Peter wears glasses" in the same group. Provided that we understand "wears" to mean "sometimes wears" or even "usually wears," we know that there are easy ways of finding out whether or not the statement is true. The statement "These two are the most intelligent students in the class" presents somewhat greater, but certainly no insuperable, difficulties. As soon as we get agreement on a means of measuring intelligence, we can proceed to test the truth of the statement. If the means agreed upon is a pencil-and-paper test, verification will be easy; if the means is a record of responses to crises in actual experience, verification will be extremely difficult. In the former case, we are likely to think of the statement as one of "fact"; in the latter, as one of "opinion." The difference is in part the result of our lack of confidence in tests necessary to establish validity; and in part the result of the nature of the word "intelligent."

Obviously, "intelligent" is an ambiguous word; that is, it means different things to various people. What one will find adequate as the meaning of "intelligent," another will find inadequate or completely irrelevant. The more ambiguous the predication of a statement, the more difficult it will be to find generally acceptable tests of validity; the more difficult it is to find such tests, the more uncertain we are that any statement requiring them is sure to be found true or false by everyone. It is the increase of uncertainty that leads us to think of such statements as "statements of opinion" rather than as "statements of fact." To repeat, there is no strictly logical difference between them: both kinds require reference to experience for verification. The difference lies either in the ambiguity of a term or in the difficulty of determining truth or falsity, or in both.

Another source of uncertainty in the classification of such statements is the connotative effect of words. For various reasons we respond favorably or unfavorably to certain words. Most words, indeed, besides directing us to consider something, influence us to take an attitude toward it as well. Suppose that a man regularly puts away all the money he earns except what he must spend on the necessities of life. Then consider these two statements about him:

He saves his money.

He hoards his money.

Whether we think of one as a statement of fact and of the other as a statement of opinion will depend partly on the denotation of the words "saves" and "hoards" but even more on their connotation, on the associations they raise in our minds. "Hoards" carries the sense of secret and greedy accumulation; testing the truth of the assertion which contains it would be difficult. If "saves" means only "puts away," testing the truth of the statement would be theoretically not hard at all; if it means more than that—if, for instance, it suggests prudence and self-control—then the statement in which it appears is, like the other, hard to verify. The connotative power of the key words might therefore lead us to classify both statements as statements of opinion.

Within this class of assertions whose truth or falsity is determined by reference to experience, two extralogical subdivisions of some importance to the writer have so far been distinguished. The first, that of statements of fact, represents the writer's feeling of assurance that the test of truth or falsity can be readily determined and that there is already general agreement about the truth of the statement itself. The second, that of statements of opinion, reflects the writer's uncertainty about the possibility of producing satisfactory proofs of the validity of the statement and his recognition that disagreement about its validity is more likely than not. This uncertainty sometimes is the result of the difficulty of the procedures necessary for testing, sometimes of the ambiguity of terms in the statement, sometimes of the connotative effect of terms in the statement. The progression, then, has been from relative certainty to considerable uncertainty.

To continue that progress is to move into another category common to everyday discourse about statements, that of statements of preference or of taste. In some ways, these are the most interesting statements of all to writer and reader. The medieval proverb, *De gustibus non est disputandum* ("There is no disputing about tastes"), reflects the popular view that the grounds of choice, being subjective, are neither logically defensible nor attackable, and probably not even analyzable. Yet, for the very reason that they are subjective, that is, that they refer not simply to the data presented to our senses but to our experience of it, we are likely to hold to statements of preference or taste with singular tenacity. At the same time, we recognize that there is no convenient means of testing the truth or falsity of such a statement as "Lemon pie tastes better than apple," and we do not try to do so. But if this statement is changed into "I like lemon pie better than apple pie," it then becomes an autobiographical statement, and not very different, as far as proof is concerned, from "These two are the most intelligent students in the class." The tests which someone else would apply to determine the truth or falsity of our stated preference for lemon pie (seeing which kind we eat when we are given a choice, for example) are not different in kind from those he would apply to detect the intelligence of students in the class.

In its original form, however ("Lemon pie tastes better than apple"), the statement of preference means something more than "I like lemon pie better than apple." It either assumes agreement among people of "right" perception or it indicates that no agreement is expected and that the statement is really one about the condition of the stater rather than about lemon and apple pie. A proper feeling for the meanings of a statement of preference will often lead a writer to qualify it ("Connoisseurs agree that . . .") or to overstate deliberately in order to emphasize the limitedness of intention ("Every man who has ever put fork to piecrust knows that lemon pie tastes better than apple").

To this point, no attempt has been made to classify into the categories of fact, opinion, and preference those assertions whose verification seems to lie not in the "facts" of experience but in some general idea of the order of the universe. To do so now is to emphasize the ultimate inadequacy of the "rhetorical categories" of ordinary discourse. Yet assertions of that kind occur too frequently to be entirely ignored, and some attention must be given to them here. How *do* we classify such statements as the ones that follow?

Man is inherently noble.

God is good.

Clearly enough, these are assertions; that is, they are either true or false. But, just as clearly, they involve much more than reference to experience. In practice, we are likely to say that they are *statements of belief*, statements held to be true (or false) despite inadequate information or even in the face of contradictory evidence, statements which we accept (or reject) as starting points for our thinking. In short, to deal with them at all satisfactorily, we have to make a fourth category, that of statements of belief, and as soon as we do that we find ourselves crossing lines with all three of the other categories.

LOGICAL CATEGORIES: DEDUCTIVE AND INDUCTIVE ASSERTIONS, STATEMENTS OF OBLIGATION

After this rather abortive attempt to classify assertions in the loose categories of everyday language, it is refreshing to turn to the tighter categories worked out by logicians. The refreshment comes, moreover, not simply from the firmness of the logical divisions but from the fact that those divisions provide insight into the responsibilities which various kinds of assertion entail for those who make them.

Starting from the definition of "statement" as "a sentence that is either true or false," modern logicians proceed to make a distinction between (1) those statements whose truth or falsity is determined by their relationship to other statements and (2) those whose truth or falsity is determined by reference to the facts of experience. (Whether or not a given statement is of the first or second kind depends, in most cases, on its context or on the conditions of proof which its context indicates to be relevant.) To use terms which will be more fully developed in the next chapter, the distinction is one between statements whose truth is arrived at *deductively* and those whose truth is arrived at *inductively*. Statements arrived at deductively are judged to be true if they are valid consequences of postulated statements, false if they are incompatible with such statements. Their truth or falsity, therefore, is dependent on the verbal structure of which they are a part. So, in this sentence, the truth of the main statement is deduced from the other two statements; if they are true and if they imply the main statement, the main statement is true:

> If mercifulness is a characteristic of human greatness and if it is true that Hitler condemned five million Jews to death between 1935 and the end of World War II, then Hitler was certainly not a great man.

The main statement we judge to be "true" if the series of statements is logically related. It does not matter for the truth of this statement whether or not mercifulness is a characteristic of greatness, whether or not Hitler actually did condemn five million Jews to death, or whether or not he was "really" great. Provided only that we accept the conventional definition of "mercifulness," we can describe the assertion as a true one.

A simpler example illustrates the nature of these assertions in a different way. If a child were to say, "Aunt Mary is a bachelor," we would correct his error by referring not to the facts of experience but to definition. The falsity of the statement would be apparent to us simply because it contravenes the conventional meaning of a word, a meaning upon which it must depend to make sense.

We might even say that truth or falsity is, for such statements, a verbal matter, not a substantive one; that is, it is a matter only of the relationship between groups of words, not of the actual state of things as we apprehend them to be by our senses.

About the second group of statements, those whose truth is arrived at inductively, there cannot be the same degree of certainty. If we say, "Freshmen spend more time studying than sophomores do," we make a statement which is reached from observation of freshmen and sophomores. For logicians, the important thing about such a statement is that its truth or falsity requires reference to experience, to the knowledge brought to us by our senses. The possibility of determining the truth or falsity of such statements varies widely, but logicians are satisfied, for purposes of classification, to put all assertions of this kind into one group.

Besides those assertions whose truth or falsity is determined by reference to the assertions from which they are deduced and those whose probable truth or falsity is determined by reference to the facts of experience, there are some which many logicians choose to classify separately. These assertions, which they denominate *statements of obligation* or *ethical statements,* are like one of the two which were lumped together earlier as statements of belief.

Everyone should love his country.

Men ought to help each other.

For such assertions, which cannot be arrived at deductively except from other assertions of the same kind, the inductive tests by reference to experience are useless because such tests are not applicable to "should" or "ought." The test of truth or falsity for these statements lies not in the terms of the predications themselves but in some standard external to them. If we challenge the first statement with "Why should everyone love his country?" the answer must be of this order: "Because loving one's country makes one willing to work for its betterment." The answer provokes another question: "Why should one work for the betterment of one's country?" And the answer to that question will provoke another until, eventually, the terms by which we account for "should" in the original statement come to the further, and independent, statement that some kinds of action (feeling, thought) are good. Every statement of obligation, then, assumes or proposes another statement about what is good or right. Not even in those sentences which indicate the consequence of prescribed action ("People of sedentary habit should exercise regularly *in order to keep their bodies healthy*") can the verb of obligation be meaningful without there having been some assumption about what is "good" or "right"—in this example, an assumption about the desirability of keeping bodies healthy.

When the assumption is overtly stated, it becomes the premise from which the statement of obligation is deduced. And the truth or falsity of the statement, as in all deductive structures, will then depend on the truth or falsity of the assumption (premise) and on the logical correctness of the relationship between assumption and statement of, obligation. The statement may, of course, contain in its predication an element to be dealt with in another fashion. "You should drink forty quarts of milk a day" is a statement of obligation; besides the unstated assumption related to "should," however, there is included in the predication the assumption that "you" *can* drink forty quarts of milk a day. The second assumption is subject to the usual tests of verifiability; the first is not. This statement of obligation, therefore, is a compound of the testable and the nontestable, and most statements of obligation are of that kind. They are truly statements, or assertions—that is, they are true or false— but some part of them resists empirical verification and refers one to basic assumptions which cannot be "tested" at all.

ASSUMPTIONS

The role that assumptions play in writing and reading extends far beyond statements of obligation. One way to describe assumptions would be to call them "what we take for granted" or "what we do not feel obliged to prove," or "what else must be true in order for this statement to be true." Certainly we "take for granted" fully as much as we make explicit in our writing. Most of the time we do not even give a thought to the assumptions from which we begin; we simply *assume* that others make the same assumptions as we do. When we do have any cause to doubt agreement, we may make the assumption explicit (*"Assuming that it is better to go now than to stay and fail,* you still have to decide whether or not there is any likelihood of your passing if you do stay"). But very often we assume agreement when there may not be any; in fact, we may make statements whose assumptions we neither have investigated nor would accept if we were to do so. To write in ignorance of one's own assumptions is to write irresponsibly; it is, in fact, to make writing a matter of limited "communication" and of no "inquiry" at all.

The need to reckon with unstated assumption does not usually arise in simple assertions of the kind presented above. When assertions are combined causally, however, the unstated assertion may be fully as important as any assertion explicitly stated. Consider this sentence:

Jefferson was an extensive landowner and was therefore interested in securing the independence of the American colonies from England.

Underneath this sentence there is an unstated assumption to the effect that all landowners at that time and in that place were interested in securing the independence of the colonies. And behind that assumption there may well be another, more general, one to the effect that all landowners everywhere and at all times are interested in securing the independence from foreign control of the political territory in which they hold land. The criteria for testing these assumptions are historical; if we apply such criteria, we shall have no difficulty in finding that the assumptions are false; we might say of the original sentence about Jefferson, then, that it is based on an *unwarranted assumption*.

In passing, however, it must be noted that an assertion may be true in spite of the fact that what it assumes is unwarranted. The statement "Because Poe was a writer, he never became wealthy" contains the assumption that no writers become wealthy; the assumption is certainly unwarranted, but both of the explicit assertions in the sentence are true. In such instances as this one, it is clear that the connection between the two assertions ("because") is what damages the sentence. To substitute "even though" for "because" would be equally misleading (some writers *have not* become wealthy). The solution for this particular sentence lies in separating the assertions entirely; in others, a change in the connective might suffice. *The point of the illustration is that a sentence may be composed of true statements and still be untrue because the relationship stated or implied by the connective is false.*

IMPLICATIONS

To talk about assumptions is to talk about the logical precedents of an assertion, about what must be true in order for that assertion to be true. Because it is a looking backward, a search for antecedent condition, the search for assumptions is not always easy: a particular statement may rest on many assumptions, each of which must be acknowledged if the writer is to feel secure about his statement. To appreciate the logical consequences, or *implications,* of an assertion is to ask, "If this assertion is true, then what other assertions are necessarily true?" If, for instance, someone says that maple trees always shed their leaves in winter and if he is able to demonstrate that the statement is true, then it is perfectly obvious that a particular maple tree in your front yard will

shed its leaves when winter comes. The truth of the first assertion necessarily implies the truth of the second. This form of implication is the
simplest of all since the fact that a particular maple is part of the category of all maple trees makes the implication unmistakably clear.

In the ordinary course of reading and writing, however, implications do not appear in this openly deductive fashion. Instead, they operate subtly, often by omission rather than by announcement; frequently
they arise from a sudden or peculiar emphasis; sometimes juxtaposition
produces them. In a recent political convention, one speaker praised by
name all of the President's principal advisers except one, thereby implying by omission his disapproval or dislike of that one. Had he gone
through the list and then made a pointedly offhand addition of that one
name to his list, he would have achieved the same implication by emphasis. Or had he dealt with each name in ascending order according to
the value he placed on the services of each, and coupled the one name
with others early in his list, in defiance of the man's actual status, he
would have implied, by juxtaposition, what he actually did imply by omission. The use of implication is not confined, of course, to getting revenge
on one's enemies; it is also a primary instrument of humor and of satire
("all the necessities of life—food, shelter, clothing, and a TV set"), and
an important means of enlarging the significance of a statement without
making it seem unnecessarily explicit.

"Enlarging the significance of a statement" points to an ampler meaning often given to the word "implication" in ordinary discourse, a meaning
roughly synonymous with "suggestion." When Laborite Aneurin Bevan
called an opponent "that Parliamentary doodlebug," he probably implied
—in this loose sense of the word—that the opponent was unfit to hold
office or, at least, a fellow incapable of constructive action. Implication,
in this sense, may reach to the furthest limits of association; in the
stricter sense described above it includes only those additional statements
logically entailed by the statement made.

Implications and assumptions really represent the gap between all
that a man means and the language he uses to express it. Without them
we should all be required to lengthen our assertions almost endlessly, and
we should be deprived, as well, of many of the artful devices by which
we convey subtleties of understanding and feeling which lose some of
their character when they are put into words. A considerable amount
of the effectiveness, and therefore of the informativeness, of our language
derives from the fact that we do not need to express explicitly everything we would have our readers or listeners understand. Were it not for
assumptions and implications, a simple command like "Shut the door"
would have to be elaborated in this fashion: "There is a door here, and it
is now open, and you are able to shut it, and I want it shut; therefore,
I order you to shut it." And an exclamation like "Fire!" would require

expansion to "There is a fire here; it is a dangerous fire; I advise everyone to get away from it as quickly as possible." There is no doubt, then, about the usefulness of this mode of saying less than we mean to have our listeners understand; it is only the matter of determining precisely what is meant in addition to what is explicitly asserted that makes a problem.

Every extended piece of serious discourse is made up of a series of assertions, however disguised. If a writer had to deal with each as elaborately as this book suggests, he would never get done; yet, if he is reponsible about his work, he cannot ignore the one consideration about asserting which underlies all that has been said here: that *a writer must know the nature of the assertions he makes in order to understand what meanings they can convey and what responsibilities for proof they impose upon him*. If that consideration becomes important to him, he has the kind of command over language that prepares him to represent honestly the world as he understands it.

THE USE OF ANALYSIS OF STATEMENT IN WRITING

To conclude this chapter on asserting, it may be useful to point out two ways in which the skillful construction of assertions may be of practical help to the student in developing both the early and the final drafts of an expository paper.

As practical instruments of speculation, assertions are of great value primarily because they bring thought into focus. It is sometimes said that the greatest educational achievement is learning what questions to ask; the statement is true enough, but only because questions, as noted above, themselves often suggest assertions. A question such as "Did Napoleon's ambition really have anything to do with his smallness of stature?" implies a tentative assertion which might not have occurred to the listener at all if the question had simply been "What were the causes of Napoleon's ambition?" The point of the illustration is that it is really tentative assertions, and not questions, that mark the inquiring mind, though the assertions may be cloaked in interrogative form.

The usefulness of assertions and assertion-containing questions in the process of writing is easy to demonstrate. Every writer, professional or amateur, begins, of course, from experience. The more fully digested the experience is, the easier will be the preliminary stages of writing. But no matter how completely the writer has assimilated the material he wishes to write about, and no matter how great his experience, he is bound to find that writing itself opens new possibilities of interpretation to him. When it does, he must explore those possibilities; that is, he must engage in the process which this book calls "inquiry" just as though he were entering new country. The adult amateur may have thought and felt as deeply as the professional, but he lacks the training in the solution of problems of expression that keeps the professional going when writing becomes difficult; the student writer lacks that training, too, and lacks also the kind and quality of experience that helps to provide quick and sound perceptions. For that reason, the student writer, and in some measure the adult amateur, can make asserting a practical instrument for dealing with difficulties at the beginning of, or anywhere in the course of, a piece of writing.

Assume that a student is preparing a paper on the federal Soil Bank Bill of 1956, a bill paying farmers a yearly fee for each acre, up to a specified number, taken out of production if that land was previously used for the growing of any one of several "surplus" crops (corn, wheat, and so on). The writer has read widely in preparation for his paper and has found sharply conflicting claims about the bill, not only from the politicians who framed it but from organizations of farmers, from economists, and even from sociologists. He is, in fact, almost submerged by what he has read, and his writing must be, first of all, an attempt to bring some order into the mental and written notes he has accumulated. It is precisely at this point that a conscious use of assertions is of most value to him.

Setting up general "topics" and "subtopics" (Causes, Purposes, Means) does little more than fence the field into sections, as does asking general questions: "What are the causes of the demand for a soil bank?" "What are its purposes?" "How does it operate?" Such topics and such questions provide only the subjects to be discussed; the predication, that is, the heart of the discussion, they scarcely hint at. For that reason it is not until the writer is ready to frame tentative assertions that he can even come close to grappling with his subject matter. It does not matter particularly that the first assertions are very general or even that they are wrong. They provide the focus for fruitful activity. The assertion "The Soil Bank Bill was designed primarily to silence Democratic charges that the Republican administration was indifferent to the plight of the farmer" offers a limited and specific matter for consideration; as the writer marshals his knowledge and information around this assertion, he may come to the conclusion that what evidence he has does not warrant the expression "primarily," and change it to suit the data he has at hand. Having tested the value of this assertion, he proposes another, and so on until an order (in this instance, an order of purposes) begins to make itself apparent. In such a process, assertions become first the temporary scaffolding and eventually the permanent framework for the structure of the essay.

Moreover, when the writer alters a temporary assertion until it satisfies his evidence and his understanding, not only has he taken a major step in getting his paper under way, but he has also laid out for himself the responsibilities he must meet. Each final assertion is at the same time a demand. It demands that each of its parts be developed: the "subject" ("The Soil Bank Bill") must be *explained,* and the "predication" ("was designed primarily to give farmers immediate, though temporary, financial assistance in areas where surplus crops had seriously depressed prices") must be *defended.* The steps by which the writer thinks his way from other assertions to this one in the preliminary stage of his work become the steps by which he defends the predication at which he finally arrives.

Even if he works cautiously and slowly on the first draft of his paper, the student is likely to find, when he reads over what he has written, that for all his caution the first draft is as circuitous as a bird dog hunting pheasants in tall grass. It is at this point that skill in the framing of assertions can perform a second service for him.

What a first draft, even a very disorderly one, comprises is a series of coagulations of thought. By translating each of these coagulations into a single, clear assertion, the student can distill the draft into a few statements—any number from a half dozen to a score. Thus distilled, the several steps of the paper become evident, and the relationships between them reasonably easy to detect. Reduction of the sheer mass of the paper to a few statements also makes it possible for the student to see clearly what his obligations for explanation and defense are in each. In effect, he does nothing here that he was not doing earlier, as he wrote the first draft, but now he has the advantage of hindsight. He does not have to think about where the paper is going but may judge, more or less dispassionately, where it went. Through the medium of the abstracted assertions, he looks at it, so to speak, from outside, which is to say that he looks at it, in some measure, as his reader will do. As with the other matters which are discussed in this book, there is nothing automatic about the transfer of skill in analysis of assertions to skill in composition. Yet, if the development of skill in the making and understanding of assertions does no more than provide this partial perspective on what one has written, it is worth a great deal of study and effort indeed.

EXERCISES

1. Break each of the following assertions into components which can be separately analyzed for propositional content.

   a. One of the persistent delusions of mankind is that some sections of the human race are morally better or worse than others.
   b. The musical mind is concerned predominantly with the mechanism of tonal memory.
   c. No man who is as well abreast of modern science as the Founding

Fathers were of eighteenth-century science believes any longer in unchanging human nature.

d. Under a government which imprisons any unjustly, the true place for a just man is also a prison.
e. Birds seem as subject as men to the emotion of jealousy.
f. No man should spend his small store of energy in the wasteful habit of hoping for better times.
g. Of all earth's beauties, mountains and chasms are the most appealing to the noble mind.

2. Analyze the components of the preceding assertions according to the "rhetorical categories" discussed in this chapter. Analyze them next according to the "logical categories." For which are the rhetorical categories insufficient?

3. By analysis point out the assertions *contained in* the following non-assertive sentences.

a. Let him who is a patriot speak now or forever keep silence.
b. Oh, for the free and easy life of the schoolboy!
c. Have you stopped wasting your time and become useful?

4. What assumptions underlie these statements?

a. The students who cut classes, scamp their reading, and turn in essays in their first draft do irreparable damage to their ability to make a good income after they leave school.
b. I know he was enjoying the party because I saw him smiling.
c. When this man, or *any* demagogue, challenges us, we have a sacred duty to accept the challenge.
d. When he was asked whom he considered the greatest of French poets, André Gide is reported to have answered, "Victor Hugo, alas!"
e. Officials admitted that radioactive particles transmitted by high winds from Nevada may have been responsible for the blurring of photographic plates as far away as New York.
f. Because Kant was by nature an orderly sort of person, he was deeply distressed by Hume's restless and skeptical turn of mind.
g. The quartet played the third movement of the sonata too slowly for it to be at all enjoyable.

5. Epigrammatic language is powerful partly because its implications are so extensive. What are the implications of these epigrams?

a. Lie is the contrary to Passion.
b. Imitation is criticism.
c. If Morality was Christianity, Socrates was the Saviour.
d. A fat paunch never breeds fine thoughts.
e. The world cannot live at the level of its great men.

⊂₴ *Proving*

Logic is the ethics of thinking in the sense in which ethics is the bringing to bear of self-control for the purpose of realizing our desires. CHARLES SANDERS PEIRCE

. . . the last proceeding of reason is to recognize that there is an infinity of things which are beyond it. BLAISE PASCAL

IN THE PRECEDING CHAPTER assertions were classified primarily in terms of their verifiability, that is, as to whether or not they could be proved true. And three rhetorical subclassifications (statements of fact, opinion, and preference) were examined because they attempt to provide for important distinctions in the attitude we take toward, and the expectation we have about, certain assertions. Still other classifications and subclassifications are conceivable, but the ones used are more valuable for the writer's purposes because they lead directly to one of his most important responsibilities, that of testing and demonstrating the truth of his statements. Throughout this chapter that responsibility is called "proving," a term used here to mean both the writer's private testing of a tentative statement and his public and formal demonstration of its validity, if he finds such demonstration necessary or desirable.

In many instances, perhaps in most, a writer's explicit "proof" for a statement will be the same as that by which he originally came to make the statement in the first place. For rhetorical purposes, he may rearrange the steps of the process, but essentially it will remain the same. Yet we all know that the two procedures sometimes vary in more than form: some of the things we say, even some of those we feel most certain about, come from no careful analytic procedure of testing but from an impulse or an intuitive perception, and it is only after the statement is uttered that we "find reasons" to explain or support our remark.

The impulsive remark and the intuitive assertion are baffling to deal with, both for the asserter and for the hearer or reader. Aldous Huxley remarks that D. H. Lawrence rejected the theory of evolution because he "did not feel it *here*," meaning "here in the solar plexus." Although Mr. Huxley does not report his reaction to Lawrence's answer, he would have found the "proof" hard to contest or accept: the solar plexus resists argumentation, for the "truth" of Lawrence's statement is beyond analysis by others even if they know what "solar plexus" means in Lawrence's psychophysiology (*Fantasia of the Unconscious*). Proof is not really irrelevant to it, but probably impossible because the assertion arises not from ratiocinative procedures but from a subordination, in this case deliberate, of the mind to feeling. In some measure, everyone relies on such practically unprovable statements for a certain part of his daily life; most of them he holds tentatively and uses for what they are worth, rejecting them if, on being forced to examination, he discovers that they seem to be groundless or less solid than alternative statements. And, of course, some of the principal premises of all our living (that our existence is real and not phantasmagoric, for example) are likewise useful and unprovable.

By and large, however, it is not with entirely unprovable statements that the writer has to deal. Few of his assertions will be easy to prove, but toward nearly all of them he will feel some responsibility to make sure that they are credible to others, and to make sure of that he will have to be sure himself that they are based on a sound line of reasoning. According to the nature and purpose of the assertion and according to the literary form in which it is cast, the writer will require of himself and present to his reader some examinable support for whatever he writes.

This is not by any means to say that man is naturally a logical creature. Logic is his achievement rather than his inheritance. Beneath the subtle structure of logic which he has learned to erect lies a life of perceptions and motivations still largely uncharted. So, to recommend logical procedures is not to ignore other valuable ways of knowing what is true ("The heart has its reasons," said Pascal); it is only to encourage the use of those procedures over which thoughtful men, in the course of two thousand years or more, have learned to exercise control and through which they have learned to reach useful conclusions and make viable judgments.

What psychology has revealed in the past fifty years about man's subconscious and unconscious life, though contestable in detail, is in its broad outlines a genuine addition to man's knowledge of himself and of his fellow man, an addition in some ways at odds with the neat patterns of logic which man has created to explain and deal with the world. The fact that this new knowledge does not always harmonize with the analytic procedures of logic has produced a considerable suspicion of logic in our own day. In so far as the suspicion is founded on understanding, it is a useful check against the abuse of logic; but in so far as it is—as in many instances it seems to be—a revulsion against the rigor, conclusiveness, and universality of logical judgments, it demeans man's dignity and deprives him of the soundest way we know for him to become the best kind of thinker he can be. For that reason the study of formal logic is a proper part of the experience of a liberally educated person and a necessary part of the training of a critical and serious writer.

EXTRALOGICAL "PROOFS": INTUITION, AUTHORITY, PERSISTENCE

Before an attempt is made here to discuss briefly certain procedures of logic, however, certain extralogical "proofs" deserve attention. *Intuition* has already been mentioned. Roughly described, it is the experience of knowing without having analyzed, a sudden and direct revelation of "truth" which may seem to come without warning or search, or which may be the fruit of long and severe self-discipline. The discipline and experience of intuition is a study by itself; without meaning to disparage it at all, discussion here is limited to a warning. The most particular characteristic of intuitive experience is its privateness, and rendering what is essentially private into public language, that is, into communicable form, is not an easy matter. For that reason, if for no other, intuition is seldom useful as proof for an assertion; a man may "know" beyond the shadow of a doubt and yet be unable to tell another how he knows. Moreover, there is adequate evidence in everyone's experience to show that what is called "intuition" is frequently impulsive and mistaken judgment (How often are your "hunches" correct?) or actually the sudden insight that follows and derives from a long period of rumination or study. When intuition is recognized to be the end of a thinking process, however much that process may have been carried on subconsciously, formal procedures of proof can be used to reconstruct that process. Where it seems to have "come like a flash," its conclusions at least must *still* be subjected to logical examination, for only where they stand up to such examination is the intuition likely to be of any value to a writer or reader as a trustworthy ground for action or for further thought.

Authority is a second extralogical ground of proof, and the one most commonly used of all. The cause of its popularity is obvious enough: we all live in daily contact with complexities we only dimly understand, and in order to feel comfortable at all in our dealing with them we have to rely on the reported judgment of men who are supposed to know about those complexities. This is the age of the expert. To know what will happen to the stock market if the Federal Reserve System raises interest rates, one turns to the economist; to know whether or not there is likelihood of striking oil in a piece of ground, one turns to the geologist. Even the housewife listens to the weather report before starting to do the week's laundry. But experience also tells us that experts disagree and that rain sometimes falls in spite of the meteorologist's assertion that it won't. And if we are sensible we ought to know that a gossip columnist is not, by virtue of his having a daily column in a big newspaper, an expert on international affairs; nor a "man of distinction" necessarily an expert on blends of whiskey. Yet everyone today must rely on authority for some of his judgments; or, more precisely, everyone must rely on authority for some of the evidence which he uses to reach judgments. Where conflict occurs between authorities, he has little choice but to wait and see or, if he must act, to choose between them on the best grounds he can summon. In the end, a certain skepticism about all authoritative judgments is warranted: it took a highly complicated study of radioactivity to prove the recency of the bones of Piltdown man, whose antiquity had been "authenticated" by innumerable reputable scientists, but it took only an ingenious fanatic to fabricate them in the first place.

The third extralogical reason frequently adduced for the truth of an assertion is *persistence*. If enough people believe something long enough, soon everyone will take it for granted, and not until some rebel raises a challenge will anyone else think to question it. The history of knowledge is a drama in which theories harden into "laws" which are exploded by new theories which themselves harden and are exploded. What occurs at the forefront of thought does not filter down into everyone's experience, however, so that all of us carry around a stock of notions derived from the past even though they may be at odds with conclusions we have reached after sober thought. We open (or shut) our windows at night in order to let in (or keep out) cold air because we "know" that the night air is (or is not) good for us; we make a Halloween joke of witches, ghosts, and black magic but avoid giving the number thirteen to any floor of a hotel or of a public building; we think that the average man is a dolt about politics but that all of the average men put together are infallible.

Irrational as such activity seems to be, the persistence of an idea is still some argument for its worth simply because persistent ideas generally arise out of some firsthand experience. But, as transmitted, they may become divorced from that experience and overgeneralized, or they may become corrupted (like the prescription "Feed a cold and starve a fever" which was originally a warning, "Feed a cold and starve of [die of] a fever"); and, of course, they may even have been wrong in the first place. Whatever the case, an assertion is not proved true simply because it has been thought to be true for a long time. The odds may seem to be in its favor, as they were when Columbus challenged the conventional idea that the world was flat, but the odds did not keep Columbus from being right all the same.

The statements which we accept on the grounds of intuitive experience are likely to be so convincing at the time that the requirement for proof does not occur to us; when it does, we must either supply additional means of proof or expect others simply "to take our word for it." If the assertion concerns only ourselves, they may be willing enough; if it concerns a reality outside ourselves ("I don't need any evidence to tell me whether or not it will work; I just *know* it will"), they may justifiably be impatient. And they may be impatient, too, if we buttress our assertions only with the claim that "it has always been so" or that "authorities say so." There is a difference here, however, worth noting. What a person accepts as proved by its persistence or by the voice of authority reaches him through *report,* and report, at least, is open to analysis by others, as intuition is not.

PROVING AND HISTORICAL REPORTS

The "proving" of a report, though not actually one of the formal procedures of logic, has much in common with them. It is systematic and it is rigorous. As developed for application in the scrutiny of historical documents (which are, after all, often no more than written "reports" of past events) this kind of proof is essentially inductive in nature: it tests evidence and chains of evidence and proceeds to conclusions only on the basis of the evidence finally admitted as reliable. The easiest way to describe the procedures developed for analyzing reports of this kind is to set down a series of questions which a scholar might ask of a document before him. Obviously, a scholar would not put all of these questions explicitly because he would know the answers to many of them before he chose the document as one worth his investigation; the questions, and their answers, are nonetheless implicit in his choice and are necessary ones to the neophyte.

SOURCE

What is the nature of the source (oral report, written report, personal observation, a combination)? Is the source of the report one from which other reports have come? If so, what is their known reliability? Is the source of a kind that is likely to provide accurate transmission of data? Is it subject to inadvertent error? to distortion because of prejudice, ignorance, the situation or time in which it occurs, necessity to avoid or provide opposition, intention to conceal or deceive?

AUTHOR OR TRANSMITTER

Is the authorship certainly known? If so, is the author's reliability known from any other documents? What are the author's or transmitter's qualifications as a reporter? Did he have opportunity to observe directly the data he uses? Does he display sound knowledge of his subject and general intelligence on other scores? Is there any ground for thinking him susceptible to bias or to pressures likely to cause him to alter or suppress data?

DATA

Are the data such as can be observed directly? If so, *were* they observed directly? If not, are they such as can be indirectly observed with accuracy? With what degree of accuracy can they be recorded? Are they of a kind to make accurate recording likely? Are they verifiable by others? Have they been so verified? Do they stand in conflict with other data? Are they complete or only "representative"? If "representative," what were the grounds of selection? Are the methods of analysis used appropriate? Do the data actually support the conclusions drawn from them? Would they support alternative conclusions as well, or nearly as well?

Whatever its nature, a report which weathers such a line of questioning has a reasonable claim to reliability. Its proof, even if all the questions are favorably answered, may never be beyond dispute, but it is at least a great deal more likely to be sound than a report whose only proof is unexamined persistence or unquestioned authority.

PROVING AND THE SCIENTIFIC METHOD

The series of questions just listed are part of the respect for "scientific method" which has gradually developed in almost every kind of human activity in the past three centuries. To set the phrase within quotation marks may seem unnecessarily cautious, but it is good to remember that what is called "scientific method" is not all of a piece and that its various manifestations have waxed and waned. Seventy years ago John Stuart Mill thought he had developed three principles of scientific investigation which might be applied with almost certain success to all human reasoning; today none of the principles stands unchallenged. In our own time students of the social sciences have elaborated several methodologies, all more or less in imitation of those used in the natural sciences, and all designed to substitute precise measurement and the handling of masses of data for generalizations arrived at by sheer effort of mind. There have even been serious attempts to analyze the style of pieces of literature by statistical counts of vocabulary and syntax. The results from all of this industrious application of scientific method to nonscientific disciplines have not been uniformly satisfactory, to say the least. Sometimes they seem only to affirm what was obvious to begin with, a result not necessarily worthless, to be sure, since it is as good to be sure of the rightness of what you "know" to be right as to be assured of the rightness or wrongness of something about which you are unsure. At other times, the conclusions drawn from such studies seem to be so constricted by the demands of a methodology that they do not satisfy the purpose which they are intended to serve. All the same, it is impossible to imagine a study in economics today, or one in psychology, that does not use some of the procedures developed in the natural sciences for analyzing data and testing hypotheses. Where those procedures have failed, it has not been so much because of their inadequacy as of their application to material for which they are inappropriate. To suggest, then, by the use of quotation marks, that it is advisable to use the expression "scientific method" with some caution is to do no more than pay proper respect to the method itself.

Actually, the so-called scientific method comprises a variety of procedures which have in common primarily one thing: that the steps of formal proof for an assertion be repeatable and verifiable by others. For the rest, scientific methodology is a compound of practices ranging from knowledgeable guesses to highly refined statistical analyses, and one part of the compound is quite as essential as the other. If the halo is taken away from the popular image of scientific work, it emerges much more like other kinds of work and study than it often appears to be; what is true about proof for assertions in science then becomes proof for the truth about assertions in other disciplines in so far as any particular technique of proof can actually be used with the data available. There is, in short, no *mystique* about it. Habits of thoughtful analysis and of sober judgment are as much a part of the criticism of a poem as of the description of a genetic mutation, and those habits require skill in the handling of the three main formal procedures of proof— analogy, induction, and deduction.

LOGICAL PROOFS: ANALOGY, INDUCTION, DEDUCTION

Analogy is the simplest of the three procedures and partly because of its simplicity perhaps the most deceptive. It consists in arguing from a series of likenesses between two or more things to another likeness or to their identity. Generally speaking, analogy assumes that one of the things being compared is known and the other, or others, only partly known. Thus, a child given his second jigsaw puzzle to work might expect that, like the previous one, when assembled it would show a picture of a locomotive. In assertions, analogy is likely to assume as much as it states. An argument by analogy may therefore appear to leap with considerable suddenness from the particular likeness to the claim of general likeness or identity: a British pathologist recently argued that the similarity between the symptoms which Thucydides describes in victims of the famous plague of Athens (430 B.C.) and those known to characterize typhoid patients today indicates that it was typhoid which caused the Athenian calamity. Here is an argument which, by force of circumstance, must do without the usual kind of proof for the nature of a disease and resorts to symptomatic evidence recorded by a historian

who was also a victim. In one sense, a large amount of even contemporary medical diagnosis (our own as well as our doctors'!) is analogical: it
argues from similarities in symptoms between previous or "typical"
cases and the one at hand. For minor illnesses such a procedure is usually
satisfactory; for more serious ones, doctors today make corroborative
tests of many kinds because they are well aware that *analogy, useful as it
may be, is not adequate for proof.*

The weaknesses of analogical procedure for proof are three. In the
first place, two things may really be alike in nearly every characteristic
except one and, if that one characteristic is important enough, they will
still be very different from each other (helium and oxygen, for example). In the second, everything has so many characteristics that it may
be possible to pick an impressive number of unimportant likenesses between two objects which are different in all important ways (It can be
said of both peaches and hickory nuts that they are round and tough-
skinned, grow on trees, ripen in autumn, and are edible by human beings). Finally, the combinations and interactions of characteristics are
such that even if all *were* the same for two objects, the two objects
might still not be identical. The *finality* of proof by analogy, then, is always in question. It should not, for that reason, be entirely discounted
even in argument, but it is wise to recognize that analogical proofs are
tentative and need supplementation. The best use of analogy, as a matter of fact, is for clarification and description, or for persuasion. Used for
these rhetorical purposes, it often serves better than extended analysis or
argument. Whoever said that one picture is worth a thousand words
might have made almost the same claim for analogy.

Analogy, it was noted above, is essentially an inductive process: it
reaches a probable inference from a sampling of particulars. Its evidence is peculiar in being constantly comparative; in strict inductive
procedure comparison is seldom more than a supplementary device, and
only evidence directly relevant to the subject of the proof is admitted to
examination.

As Francis Bacon elaborated it in the sixteenth century, the new
inductive process was more exciting than it seems to us today simply
because we are now accustomed to it. Bacon demanded that men quit
their habit of starting from traditional assumptions about phenomena
(the "ancients," particularly Aristotle, were the butt of his direct attacks) and use their own senses instead, fortifying them with whatever
instruments might aid their personal observations of the nature of
things. How deeply this challenge stirred men's imaginations and
aroused their curiosity one can gather from early accounts of the pro-
ceedings of the Royal Society and from the fact that, by the beginning
of the eighteenth century, it was fashionable for educated men and
women of the upper classes, particularly in France but to some extent in

other European countries and England as well, to conduct experiments, to write scientific papers, and to sponsor or frequent salons where experimentation was a chief subject of conversation. In our own country, both Benjamin Franklin and Thomas Jefferson showed, in their devotion to scientific studies even in the turbulent years of political struggle, what a great cleft in the clouds of human ignorance about nature was made by the boldness of Bacon's break with the past.

Today there is almost as much danger of popular error from blind adulation of the inductive method as there formerly was from indifference to it. Enthusiasm for "sticking to the facts" is, more often than not, accompanied by general ignorance of what the facts are and of what they can be relied on to provide. There is no need to rehearse the ways in which advertisers, particularly, play up to public gullibility about what they refer to as "the scientific facts in the case." It is more to the point to begin a description of the inductive method of proof with a brief comment on the nature of the evidence from which such a method proceeds.

The English art critic John Ruskin observed that for fifty men who know how to write, there is only one who knows how to think, and for fifty who know how to think, there is only one who knows how to see. What Ruskin's remark implies about intelligent use of sight could as readily be asserted about intelligent use of any of the organs of perceptions. Even so, the remark is fundamentally captious. William Blake's insistence that men learn to see "not with but through the eye" is more apposite. What our organs of perceptions report to the brain is, in part, what the brain has asked for, not what has presented itself to those organs. This is not to say, of course, that we hear, see, smell, taste, and feel *only* by dictation from the brain: more than once you may have mistaken salt for sugar until you actually tasted it. It does mean, however, that our perceptors are exposed to a great many more sensations than they transmit to the brain and that they select among the many partly according to what the brain desires to have transmitted. This is the experience behind the common expression "seeing what you are looking for rather than what's there." Besides being forced to act as selectors (and therefore as ignorers as well), our senses suffer from fatigue and from structural limitations (a tired eye may produce double vision, and a completely healthy one cannot see microbes without a microscope or mesons with one); moreover, they are naturally subject to some kinds of distortion and frequently report what they "remember" rather than what they actually encounter.

If these weaknesses are characteristic of our sensory apparatus, it is clear that the "facts" of direct and personal observation are not incontestably reliable. Even on this fairly simple ground, therefore, the inductive procedure becomes complicated. To go from the recording of sensory data as evidence to any claim about relationship between such data is to complicate the process still further. The easy assumption that, because B consistently follows A, B is caused by A was thoroughly pricked by David Hume in the eighteenth century, but it still survives as the relationship between A and B which most of us would take for granted if we met it in an unfamiliar situation. Some plants always turn light green and then yellow during periods of prolonged rain, yet an observer might be wrong to impute the change in their color to rain rather than to the lack of sunlight. The example is manifestly a simple one, but it illustrates the second complication of the inductive process, even in its most rudimentary form—that of adopting premises about the possibilities and likelihoods of relationship between various bits of evidence. It is no easy matter to decide whether the connection between A and B is that of cause and effect, inclusion or exclusion, derivation, dependency, opposition, or identity; yet until some decision is made the data are as useless to the process of proof as the disassembled pieces of a watch to the process of keeping time.

Even when one grants the acceptability of the evidence and the soundness of the premises upon which it is related, there comes one stage in the march toward proof which no amount of ingenuity can make logically infallible. That is the stage known as the *inductive leap,* the point at which it is necessary to move from the data at hand to the generalization which is meant to satisfy all data of the same kind. In practice, the gap in evidence between the examined data (or "sample," as they are generally called) and the generalization is less likely to be troublesome because of *un*examined data than because of the difficulties that always attend generalization, those of going no further than evidence warrants and of accounting for *all* the relevant data in the generalization.

The fallibility of perception, the complexity of some kinds of data, the difficulty of choosing premises for analysis and of making the leap from particular data to a general conclusion are all obstacles, though not insuperable ones, to the usefulness of induction as a procedure of proof. And to them must be added another, one likely to be overlooked by the inexperienced reporter and hard to manage for even the wary and well trained. Induction almost never begins from a random assemblage of data. Either the investigator has been struck by some odd concatenation and has thus had his attention focused on particular data, or he has been forced to a halt by refractory or contradictory data and is puzzling over what is "wrong"; in either instance, he cannot begin fruitful induction until he has some sort of hypothesis to use as a guide in analyzing the data. It is just here that he runs a risk he can hardly see. The hypothesis will guide his analysis, but it may also damage its accuracy and completeness. Even if he resists the natural tendency to become committed to a hypothesis on which he has spent his time and energy, the investigator may actually become able to view the data only from the point of view implicit in his hypothesis. Not until he can start from an entirely different hypothesis or until he can get another person, uncommitted to any conception about the data, to clarify and freshen his observation, can he be sure that he has not been victimized by the tentative speculation about his material from which he began.

Why, one may ask, is so uncertain and fault-ridden a procedure the one by which the "non-human sciences" (as Arnold Toynbee calls them) regulate their work? The answer is simple enough: it is the one that has, in cooperation with the deductive procedures of mathematics, given them better results than any other. If that is true, then what is the value of any other procedure, in human *or* nonhuman sciences? The second question cannot be so simply answered, but it is important enough to warrant some discussion.

In the two preceding chapters there has been occasional reference to quantification and to the fact that conventional human language resists reduction to entirely controllable form. Haldane's remark (in "What 'Hard' Means") about adjectives of quality becoming terms of quantity in science is pertinent here. In order to prevent data from changing form before their eyes and in order to make them manipulable, scientists attempt to describe them as quantities of matter or energy. And in order to keep the relationship between them equally firm and equally manipulable, they state those relationships in mathematical and other symbols which are largely devoid of connotative meanings. Unfortunately —or fortunately, depending on your point of view—a great many of the data of experience cannot be adequately represented in quantities. Moreover, the relationships implicit in unquantifiable experience are equally recalcitrant: mathematics is all but irrelevant to them, and even language is often inadequate. Such being the case, it is clear that a logical procedure particularly designed to control the capriciousness and volatility of language has still some claim to a modern student's attention, however its eminence may have been overshadowed in recent centuries by the rise of inductive reasoning.

The procedures of *deductive* logic find their classic, though not their only, expression in the syllogism, a succession of assertions so devised and so ordered as to guarantee logical validity, a condition denied to inductive logic by the inevitable "leap" from partial evidence to a generalizing conclusion. Strictly speaking, induction as a system leads to truth, though one can never be sure that the conclusions are beyond doubt truthful ones. Deduction as a system leads to validity, about which one *can* be sure since validity is a matter of observing the regulations of the system. The final purpose of deductive logic, of course, is also to arrive at truth, which it hopes to do by making validity *coincide* with truth. For reasons which will be discussed, however, deduction, too, is a fallible system and quite as likely to fall short of truth as any other. Its single advantage over induction is the one noted above: it is especially equipped to deal with the vagaries of language. Wherever it must refer to the experience which language represents, it becomes susceptible to the same weaknesses as induction and often more liable to them precisely because they are not always anticipated and provided for.

The structure of the syllogism is superficially simple, and its parts are few; but the fact that it is a closed system—that, given the truth of the premises, the consequences are inexorably and infallibly detectable—means that a great deal of care has gone into scrutinizing all the possible combinations of parts to determine which ones lead to a valid conclusion. That care is reflected in the system of scholastic logic developed to a remarkable degree of subtlety during the late Middle Ages and most resolutely illustrated in the great study of Christian theology known as the *Summa Theologica*, the work of Thomas Aquinas.

In the simplest language possible, *a syllogism may be described as the "reckoning together" of three assertions, the first two of which are so related that they imply the third.* The first two assertions are called *premises*, which means only that they are the ground for the third, which is called the *conclusion*.

Every vice is pernicious.	MAJOR PREMISE
Greed is a vice.	MINOR PREMISE
Greed is pernicious.	CONCLUSION

The syllogism above illustrates the form but only hints at its complexities. To begin with, Aristotelian logic notes three kinds of syllogism—the categorical (that in which all terms are unconditional), the hypothetical (or conditional), and the alternative. Further, it distinguishes four kinds of statements—affirmative universal, affirmative particular, negative universal, negative particular—and constructs a series of rules for the use of each in a syllogistic procedure. And, at the very center of the process, it presents a concept of "distribution" designed to prevent error due to misplacement of any of the terms of the syllogism. The subtlety of the system makes necessary initially a considerable amount of memorizing and subsequently a great deal of practice. Indeed, the very ingenuity of the syllogism, and its not uncommon abuse by those skilled in its use, has brought it into some disrepute. A more serious drawback, however, derives from the fact that manipulation of the parts sometimes leads even the manipulator to forget that success in his activity is a verbal, and not necessarily a substantive, achievement. The fact that the premises are stated as assertions and treated as *true* assertions tends to obscure their real character. In short, the classical syllogism suffers from its success as well as from its intricacy.

One mode of simplification for deductive reasoning, originally a supplement to the syllogism, was introduced by John Venn in the nineteenth century. It consists of using circles to show what is included and excluded in each of a series of statements leading to a conclusion. The simple syllogism presented above, for instance, can be translated into Venn diagrams, as follows:

"Every vice is pernicious." (All vices fall within the class of pernicious things.)

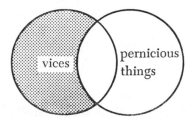

(The blacked-out portion of the circle for "vices" indicates that there are no "vices" other than those that fall within the category of "pernicious things.")

To the circles already linked as a diagram of the major premise, a third circle is added to represent the minor premise: "Greed is a vice."

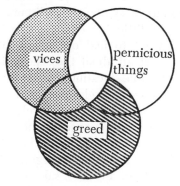

(The blacked-out portion of the circle for "greed" shows that all of "greed" falls within the class of "vices.")

The area in which the three circles overlap, being clear, represents a part of the class of "vices," a part of the class of "pernicious things," and *all* of "greed"; the conclusion of the syllogism ("Greed is pernicious") is thus *shown* to be valid.

The circle diagrams are helpful adjuncts to deductive reasoning, but they, too, must operate without calling attention to the fact that the premises of a deductive argument are not automatically beyond question.

It may have been the desire to insist on the hypothetical condition of premises that led logicians in this century to turn away from the syllogism and seek another means of deductive expression; more likely, it was the handsomeness of mathematical demonstration that attracted them. At any rate, much modern logic is "symbolic" logic, logic carried on by means of symbols which represent the terms and the relationships of deductive reasoning. The fundamental formula is a simple one:

$$P > Q.$$

In this formula, P means "antecedent statement" and Q, "consequent statement"; the symbol $>$ means "implies": "P implies Q" or "If P, then Q."

The purpose of substituting such letters as P and Q for full statements is, of course, to increase manipulability and to reduce what we have called the "connotative" effects of words. As long as P represents an entire statement throughout a series of manipulations, there is no danger that any word in it will be subtly affected by another word or by a change of position. At the conclusion of a computation the symbols may be translated back into the statements in which they originated, and during the process of reaching a conclusion one can work without the encumbrance of those many-word statements.

Now it takes only a beginner's knowledge of algebra to make one conscious of the intricacy of mathematic symbolism. Therefore, to pursue the use of mathematical symbols for discursive thought would involve us in intricacies of little immediate value to this discussion and this book. Those who want to find out all about symbolic logic, like those who want to find out all about the scholastic handling of the syllogism, will have no trouble locating books for their purposes. The proper interest here is in what relevance this new procedure has to expository writing—and, more than what relevance, what usefulness.

The procedure is relevant because deductive reasoning is a large part of any expository discourse. It is useful because it provides a fairly simple formula for checking a deductive argument in one's own writing or in the writing of another. For the sake of making this procedure yield what is useful to present purposes, there must be a brief expansion of the formula given above and a brief explanation of the general rules governing its use.

The syllogism for which Venn diagrams were supplied may be recalled:

> Every vice is pernicious.
> Greed is a vice.
> ∴ Greed is pernicious.

Translated into hypothetical form, it becomes:

If anything is a vice, it is a pernicious thing.
There is at least one thing, greed, such that it is a vice.
∴. Greed is a pernicious thing.

In formula, it looks like this:

$$P > Q$$

$$P$$

$$\therefore \quad Q$$

Now the chief virtue of putting deductive arguments into hypothetical form is that a few rules suffice for handling them, and the chief virtue of using the formula is that the statements themselves need not be repeated again and again. Starting from the first statement of the argument just presented, for example, the various possibilities for a continuation of the argument can be set down in this fashion:

P (statement P of the proposition $P > Q$ is affirmed)
Not P (statement P is denied)
Q (statement Q is affirmed)
Not Q (statement Q is denied).

The conclusion which follows from each of the possibilities is summed up in these axioms:

If P is affirmed, then Q is necessarily affirmed.
If Q is denied, then P is necessarily denied.
If P is denied, then Q is *not* necessarily denied.
If Q is affirmed, then P is *not* necessarily affirmed.

And those axioms may be put into these two generalizations:

If the antecedent is true, the consequent is true.
If the consequent is false, the antecedent is false.

There is always the possibility, of course, that the antecedent (P) or the consequent (Q) will not be simple. Where it is compound, these generalizations govern:

An assertion having two components connected by "and" is affirmed *only* when both components are affirmed.

An assertion having two components connected by "or" is denied *only* when both are denied.

Although the rules given above do make the hypothetical nature of deductive argument apparent, it may be helpful to point out once again that the satisfactoriness of such an argument is a formal matter, not a factual one. For example, the conclusion in the following argument is valid but not factually true:

Monarchs always live well over a hundred years. The king of Persia is a
monarch, so he will live well over a hundred years.

And the conclusion in this argument is valid *and* factually true although one of the premises is false:

All men are Greeks and all Greeks are mortal, so all men must be mortal.

It is even possible that when both of the premises are factually false
the conclusion may still be both valid and factually true:

All normal men are four-legged creatures, and all four-legged creatures
have ten toes. Therefore, all normal men have ten toes.

The point of these three examples is simply to enforce a warning
about the difference between factual truth and validity and to under-
score the statement that deductive reasoning, for all its precision, is not
a meat grinder capable of turning any kind of premises into sausages
of truth.

Despite the initial difficulty of learning to use such a procedure as
that briefly outlined above for verbal proofs, the truth of the matter
is that deductive reasoning, whatever its complication, is really less
difficult than inductive reasoning since it takes only acquaintance with
a few rules and a few formal structures to make one fairly proficient
at reasoning validly from premises but an almost impossible alertness
and perceptiveness to conduct adequate tests of the evidence which is
fundamental to inductive processes.

In the end, any separation of the two processes is artificial anyway.
The premises for a deductive argument are themselves nearly always
the result of some amount of inductive activity, either by the person
using the premises or by someone previous to him. And the process
of moving from data to conclusions about data always involves the acceptance of certain premises about the relationships possible for those
data and a line of deduction from them. Moreover, in ordinary discourse deductive and inductive procedures mix freely, and skill in both
is necessary to the writer who is at all concerned about the validity of
his reasoning and the truth of his conclusions.

PROCEDURES OF PROOF AS AN AID IN ORGANIZATION

Because even a highly abbreviated discussion of the procedures
of proof is bound to be more or less technical, the relevance of those
procedures to the actual process of writing sometimes becomes obscured. As a means of checking on the development of one's exposition,
of ascertaining the cogency of an argument, they show their usefulness
readily enough. But as a means of guiding the exposition itself, they
may seem to be more frustrating than helpful. Yet it is possible to

make use of them as one writes, if only in the more formal kinds of discourse. In them, the procedures of proof provide (a) a constant reminder that truth of assertion and validity of argument or soundness of demonstration are intimately connected and (b) an orderly process for the expansion and proof of a central assertion.

The constant reminder is just that—a reminder only, but a necessary one. To speak figuratively, each assertion lays an obligation on the asserter: for each statement he makes, the asserter must calculate the kind and amount of expansion necessary to make that assertion comprehensible and believable to his reader. To say that he must "calculate" the kind and amount is not to say that all his calculation is conscious. If he has a feeling for style, he will know without reflection how much explanation or proof an assertion requires and whether or not he has provided the right amount. Lacking a "natural" sense of style, the asserter may guard against underdevelopments by remembering the distinctions among assertions and the appropriateness of various procedures of proof to each.

Especially for the writer who has difficulty making his paragraphs cohere, the procedures of proof can be immediately and directly helpful. He can, for instance, build his essay as though it were an inductive exercise even though he knows before he begins what the conclusion will be. His opening paragraph will state the problem and suggest hypothetical solutions, to none of which he gives preference. In subsequent paragraphs examining the evidence he will, step by step, eliminate hypotheses until only one remains. In the concluding part of his essay he will then rehearse briefly the evidence supporting the conclusion he has reached.

If the expositor is developing a proposition for the most part deductively, he can protect his argument against confusion by remembering that deductive conclusions are implied by antecedent assertions and that their validity depends on the soundness of the antecedents. By dealing with the antecedents in order—defining terms, pointing out assumptions—and moving from them to what they necessarily imply, he brings the full force of logic to bear upon his rhetorical presentation. The literal transfer of logical procedures to expository discourse will, to be sure, produce nothing very lively or personal, and it is not recommended here as anything except a way of learning to manage what one has to say in an orderly and lucid manner. If not mistaken for what it is not intended to be, the transfer can be helpful even to those who mistrust any imposed order. As with most things, genuine freedom in writing is greatest when firm boundaries are accepted. The power of invention is increased by the necessity to work within form, and not even the most imaginative writer can afford to feel superior to, or independent of, formal structures, logical and other.

To conclude this chapter, it may be wise to raise again a caution hinted at previously. The formal processes of proof, inductive or deductive, are not for practical purposes the only ways of knowing something to be true or probably true. The ability of a man to arrive at certainty is a complicated psychological matter, and the analytic activities appropriate to proof are not adequate to describe or to document it. Into the judgments of an art critic facing a painting, of a chemist examining the account of an experiment, or of a writer reading the work of another writer there goes such a compound of past experience, intelligent perception, and conviction about premises that no analytic apparatus can dissolve the compound into all of its components. Much of what is referred to as "good taste" is exactly that sort of compound, and it is foolish always to expect neat proof in support of it and equally foolish to think that procedures of analysis or of proof can substitute completely for the experience and training that compose so large a part of the compound. On a particular matter within the general judgment, however, or in any instance where the general judgments of equally competent persons come into conflict, the processes of logic provide the only recourse for the expert and the inexpert alike. There may be arguments beyond the reaches of logical analysis entirely, but it is quite certain that *no* human means will prove one or another conclusion to the general satisfaction of all for whom such arguments are important. Yet, for all that, those arguments are not necessarily futile since the consequences of the different conclusions may be of such importance that it is vital to keep the arguments alive whether or not proof is achievable. Rational proof, in sum, is important as a buttress to responsible thought, even though it may not be the only way of arriving at truth of statement. It is simply the surest way man has thus far been able to develop with the means at his disposal.

EXERCISES

1. Each of the following passages contains egregious errors in deductive reasoning. How many can you detect and identify?

   a. The most honest and convincing of the three authors are the editors of the newspaper because of the pretext at objectivity and fairness. They are thus able to trap the reader with emotive words successfully.

   b. Since the opinion of the North that the South hates the Negro is a misconception, the South doesn't hate the Negro.

   c. Evolution isn't compatible with revealed religion and was not accepted by the great biologist Agassiz. And no scientific theory can be proven anyway. Therefore the theory of evolution is not true.

   d. Generally speaking it is as logical to expect a lawyer to prepare a case without the help of his brief books as it is to expect a student to write an exam entirely from memory. Who ever heard of a doctor performing a major operation without the aid of an X ray?

e. His testimony is trustworthy because trustworthy testimony can only be given by persons who have access to the facts, and he has access to the facts.

f. The gift of reasoning to men is crowning proof of God's providential care. He who cannot see God's providential care in this lacks the gift himself.

g. Economists know that the more a man makes, the more he spends. And the more he spends, the more goods are needed to supply his demands. As demand rises, production goes up; and as production goes up, profits increase. So money flows in all directions, and the products of good living flow in the wake of the money. High wages, then, are good for everyone.

2. This selection is from a speech by a leading English philosopher of the nineteenth century to an American audience. A comparison has already been made between the "spasmodic" energy of the savage and the "persistent industry" of the American.

> What I have seen and heard during my stay among you has forced on me the belief that this slow change from habitual inertness to persistent activity has reached an extreme from which there must begin a counter-change—a reaction. Everywhere I have been struck with the number of faces which told in strong lines of the burdens that had to be borne. I have been struck, too, with the large proportion of gray-haired men; and inquiries have brought out the fact, that with you the hair commonly begins to turn some ten years earlier than with us. Moreover, in every circle I have met men who had themselves suffered from nervous collapse due to stress of business, or named friends who had either killed themselves by overwork, or had been permanently incapacitated, or had wasted long periods in endeavours to recover health. I do but echo the opinion of all the observant persons I have spoken to, that immense injury is being done by this high-pressure life—the physique is being undermined. That subtle thinker and poet whom you have lately had to mourn, Emerson, says, in his essay on the Gentleman, that the first requisite is that he shall be a good animal. The requisite is a general one—it extends to the man, to the father, to the citizen. We hear a great deal about "the vile body"; and many are encouraged by the phrase to transgress the laws of health. But Nature quietly suppresses those who treat thus disrespectfully one of her highest products, and leaves the world to be peopled by the descendants of those who are not so foolish.
>
> HERBERT SPENCER, *Essays Scientific, Political and Speculative*

Discuss the passage with regard to sources of evidence, reliability of the sources, types of reasoning, and correctness of procedure.

3. In 1910 a book entitled *Bacon Is Shakespeare*, by Sir Edwin Durning-Lawrence, re-argued the popular contention stated in the title, using

a cryptogram as the basis of deduction. The cryptic word, Sir Edwin found in the fifth act of *Love's Labour's Lost* where a clown, mocking the pretentious language of a Schoolmaster and a Curate, says of them to Moth, a page boy:

> O, they have liv'd long on the alms-basket
> of words. I marvel thy master hath not
> eaten thee for a word; for thou art not
> so long by the head as honorificabilitudinitatibus

From this magnificent word, Sir Edwin constructed this anagram in Latin:

HI LUDI F. BACONIS NATI TUITI ORBI
(These plays, the offspring of F. Bacon, are preserved for the world.)

and then concluded:

> This explanation of the real meaning to be derived from the long word Honorificabilitudinitatibus seems to be so convincing as to scarcely require further proof.

To convince any who still doubted, Sir Edwin went on to point out that by giving each letter a numerical value (A,1; B,2; C,3— omitting some letters and counting W as two V's), the value of the word turned out to be 287. Since the word appeared on page 136 of the First Folio, and since it is the 151st word in the act (if italicized words and the first word are not counted), an addition gives 287. This number is a revelation because it makes clear

> that the Great Author [Bacon, not Shakespeare, of course] intended to reveal himself 287 years after 1623, the date when the First Folio was published, that is in the present year, 1910. . . .

Apply the test for inductive and deductive reasoning to the statements and data given above.

4. The following passage brings several kinds of "proof" to the support of an explicitly stated proposition. Locate the proposition and label, according to source or procedure, the "proofs" adduced to demonstrate its truth.

> The natural world in its infinite variety charms us all from infancy to old age, but its power lies not alone in its charm. "Go to the ant, thou sluggard; consider her ways and be wise," says the writer of Proverbs, and his advice comes not amiss. In nature man sees the pattern and type of life as it should be lived. The flower lends its sweetness to the bee; the mothering bird patiently teaches her fledglings to fly; the rain showers its blessings on the parched earth, and the sun bestows its beneficence on the grass. Each sunbeam, each raindrop, each bird, bee, and flower is a strand in the intricate tapestry of divinely ordered Nature. How

proper, then, that man, the fairest creature of all, should become, as it were, a mirror of that tapestry, imitating in his every act the benevolence of the inferior world and reflecting in his life the entire design of the natural order! From the timeless time in which God said, "Let there be light!" man has been ordained the ultimate creation of the natural world. Though he put his world, even himself, in bondage to the machine, yet his true nature is one with the nature of the elements. As they are inspirited masses of atoms, particles made animate, or soul-bearing, by the suffusing presence of purpose and plan, so man embodies an order beyond his knowing. Unguided, he gropes his way toward chaos; tutored by nature, he fulfills in himself the eternal harmony of the universe.

5. List the unsupported propositions in the passage above and indicate the evidence that would be required to prove or disprove them. Prepare a counterargument (a) using the same kinds of "proof" as those used in the original passage, and (b) using other kinds of "proof."

6. What steps would you take to test the truth of the following propositions?

   a. that women are superior to men
   b. that fluorine prevents tooth decay
   c. that God exists
   d. that international socialism is inevitable
   e. that Lee's defeat at Gettysburg was caused by faulty military strategy
   f. that a religious revival is taking place in America
   g. that in the long run popular opinion is more reliable than the opinion of experts
   h. that seeding clouds produces rain
   i. that eighteen-year-olds should be allowed to vote
   j. that a new vaccine will prevent multiple sclerosis
   k. that Western civilization is decaying
   l. that movies are better than ever

7. Which of the conclusions in the following syllogisms are *true?* Which are *valid?*

   a. Cats are animals, and all animals need food; therefore cats need food.
   b. Dogs are reptiles, and reptiles are warm-blooded; therefore dogs are warm-blooded.
   c. Fish are vegetarians, and vegetarians eat nothing but bread; therefore fish eat nothing but bread.
   d. Birds build nests, and sparrows build nests; therefore sparrows are birds.
   e. Snakes are harmful and snakes are popular; therefore harmful things are popular.
   f. Horses are becoming stronger, and anything that becomes stronger needs more to eat; therefore horses need more to eat.
   g. Laws are legislated; there are laws of nature; therefore there must be a legislator of nature.

⊂⊃ *Persuading*

FOR CENTURIES students of language have speculated industriously about the relationship between words and concepts, between words and the "real" world, between words and the intentions of their users, between words and the effects they have upon their hearers or readers. In recent times, some have suggested that language originated in gesture and in unstructured sounds expressing emotional responses; others, that it arose from early magical and myth-making attempts to coerce and control the nonhuman world. One group of linguists, those called "mentalists," believes that words refer only to mental events, to occurrences in the mind which are completely nonphysical; another group, those called "mechanists," insists that no such mental events occur and that words are really no more than signs of complex bodily processes; both groups, it is apparent, think of language as primarily related to the speaker's or writer's experience and only secondarily, if at all, to the process known as "communication." In contrast, other investigators think that the real importance of language lies not in its power to define and realize the speaker-writer's situation or condition but in its function as a transmitter, as a device for conveying some state of mind from one person to another. That state of mind they construe to be composed of three elements: the concept represented by the words used, the speaker's or writer's intention in representing it as he does, and the consciousness of various ways in which that verbal representation may be interpreted by the hearer or reader. Even so complex a concept of language as this three-part one surely does not provide an adequate account of the nature of language itself. Yet the concept has a certain utility, and it is adopted here as a means of beginning the discussion of a fourth procedure in which language is very important. To that procedure we give the name *persuading*.

Previous chapters have already dealt at some length with the process of selecting words adequate to represent accurately and fully the object or idea which a writer has in mind. This chapter turns to problems raised by the writer's desire to represent an object or idea in a particular light, that is to say, with his desire to persuade others to take a particular view of it.

THE UBIQUITY OF PERSUASION

Now, in a broad sense of the term, all communication is persuasive, a fact which Kenneth Burke has compressed into the effective statement, "Style is ingratiation." The generalization does not mean, of course, that a writer is always consciously intent on cajoling or convincing. Yet the fact that a writer must choose among words and combinations of words does mean that there must be a ground of choice, and that ground is essentially their capacity to "persuade," in the sense indicated above. Although a communication may be apparently only explanatory or descriptive in purpose, it is at the same time an attempt to lead others to see or understand something as the writer sees or understands it. Strictly speaking, there is no such thing as "objective" writing. A writer's words refer to events, ideas, things, and their qualities, true enough, but it is to events, ideas, things, and qualities as they are known to the writer. His use is always one man's use (though not necessarily different from every man's use, for all that), and his communication is the act of getting others to accept that use, even if only temporarily.

The fundamental persuasiveness of the act of communicating is enhanced by the nature of words themselves, and since it is with words (with words-in-order, to be precise) that a writer conducts his communication, a treatment of persuasion may well begin from them.

THE SOURCES OF CONNOTATIVE MEANING

The discussions of defining and asserting have already required that some attention be given to the expressive or emotive effect of words, to what are commonly called their "connotations." Now it is necessary to examine closely the properties of words and the conditions of their use which combine to make such a phenomenon as connotation occur.

First, it is important to remember that words are arbitrary, that— to use the words of John Locke—there is no "natural connection . . . between particular articulate sounds and certain ideas, for then there would be but one language amongst all men." Yet, though words are arbitrary, they are not all alike in their referential character, and since it is partly with the character of words that persuasion is concerned, some way must be found of distinguishing among words on that basis. In the first place, it is clear that the concepts to which some words refer are much broader than those to which others refer. The referent of "pay," for instance, is large enough to *include* the referents of "salary," "wages," and "stipend." It is the work of the definer to sort these referents into categories and subcategories even though, in ordinary discourse, we often use one word rather than another without very careful attention to the distinctions at which a good definer would arrive.

There is more to the matter than getting the definitions straight, however. We may be able to make absolutely airtight distinctions between the words "fat," "stout," and "obese" and still hesitate about which word to use in referring to a person who is overweight. The point of interest here is the ground on which a choice among those adjectives might be made. To speak of a "fat" bank roll is certainly to say nothing in dispraise of it, but to refer to a woman as "fat" may be very uncomplimentary indeed. In part, the difference is that fatness is generally thought, in our culture, to be a good characteristic of bank rolls and a bad one of persons. But if the fatness of the woman is a fact, and if the fact must be mentioned, we still may choose to avoid using the word "fat" about a woman and decide to substitute for it the word "stout," or even "plump."

In rhetoric, "stout" and "plump" are sometimes referred to as "euphemisms" for the word "fat," but to call them "euphemisms" is not to explain their character or to explain our choice. What is it that makes one word more or less palatable than another?

Now, for a few words in the English language, there does appear actually to be something in the character of the word itself that affects its meaning. Those words take on distinct coloration because they contain sounds which, for reasons not fully understood, generally occur in words of a particular connotative tendency. Thus, when William Faulkner named one of the families in his novels "Snopes," he helped to establish its unsavory character, even before he depicted it, by using the sound "sn-" in its name. The English language has a remarkably large number of sn- words having unpleasant associations—*snoop, sneak, snide, snort, snare, snag, snarl, snob, snout, snap, snitch*—and "Snopes" catches some of the unpleasantness by aural contagion.

The number of words that have such indigenous bias is not great, but its smallness should not obscure the fact that the *sound* of a word may be a part of its persuasive capacity. Indeed, those words which we call "onomatopœic" because they are attempts to reproduce "natural" sounds—"crunch," "murmur," "buzz," and so on—are effective largely because of their sound. Advertisers constantly play upon our responsiveness to the sound of words, and poets, of course, do so, too. But, except in single words or brief phrases, neither can rely primarily on sound to convey meaning, or even to stimulate feeling. Not until idea joins sound, as it soon comes to do even in onomatopœic words, is the persuasive capacity of the word fully realized.

Two much more important sources of the persuasive effect of words are (1) the context in which they are habitually used and (2) the total character of the concepts to which they refer. A word that is "borrowed" from one situation and applied to another carries over to the new situation some of the associations of the one it has left. Thus, the word "scientific" is frequently employed to provide the stamp of approval even though nothing that remotely resembles scientific study may be involved. That particular use of connotative effect, of course, is bad, and it may be dangerous. The indiscriminate labeling of things with terms used largely for their associated meanings is the practice of charlatans and demagogues. But the exploitation of associated meanings must not be condemned simply because it is abused. To go back to an earlier example, we may choose the word "stout" rather than the word "fat" out of the best of motives, knowing almost without thinking about it that "fat" has accumulated associations which make it unflattering when it is used to describe a person and that "stout" is for some reason rather free of such associations.

Consider again, for example, some of the words which refer to money received in exchange for services rendered: *wages, pay, salary, fee, hire, stipend, emolument, remuneration, honorarium, pittance, screw, dole.* As noted above, "pay" is probably the broadest of the lot, and were "hire" in more common use today than it is, the two words might be treated as the class-words for this series. "Wages" are generally paid weekly or daily and therefore are considered to be the return for manual or mechanical and perhaps intermittent work, which is most often paid on that basis. "Salary," on the other hand, is a fixed sum frequently paid only once a month or once every two weeks; generally speaking it is (or used to be) a larger amount than wages, though a policeman's salary today will fall considerably below a mason's wages. The word is undoubtedly used in some instances to lend prestige to relatively low-paying work, though its origin (from *salario,* a sum of money given to Roman soldiers for the purchase of salt) offers no support for that usage. A "fee" is the sum received for special and usually professional services—an architect's pay for designing a building, a doctor's pay for treating a patient, a lawyer's pay for drawing a contract; or for services whose cost is set by law or tradition—a notary's fee, a bailiff's fee, and so on. "Fee," too, may suggest a certain dignity simply because it is associated with the work of officials and of specially trained people, groups which continue to have prestige whether or not the prestige is matched by financial returns. The prestige of the work rubs off on the words by which its pay is designated.

The clearly honorific words (*stipend, emolument, remuneration,* and *honorarium*) are both seriously and ironically used. Where seriously, they often seem to be self-conscious efforts to take the supposed crassness out of exchanging money for services rendered. Of the four, only "honorarium" is etymologically grounded in a sense of *noblesse oblige,* and it is different from the others in that it generally refers to an unusual service, the value of which is not at all to be measured by the amount of the sum paid. A "stipend" is the least inflated and pretentious of the terms, but its association with permanence (it is generally used of pay calculated by the month or year) lends it a dignity greater than that owned by "salary." "Emolument" and "remuneration" are both so Latinate and uncommon that their use for "pay" nearly always signifies prestige. A certain Micawberishness about them, and about others in this group as well, makes them quick subjects for irony and for mockery of false gentility. Thus a medical intern, scraping along on almost no pay at all, may refer to his salary as "emolument." Or to give the slender monthly sum something nearer its due, he may exaggerate in the opposite direction and use a pejorative term for it. Of the pejorative terms listed (*pittance, screw, dole*), one—"screw"—is used only in England; its derivation is uncertain, but its use is confined largely to workingmen and, even among them, it is slangy. Both "pittance" and "dole" are deprecatory when used in half-humorous or sardonic reference to pay, probably because both are associated with the charity dispensed to the sick, the infirm, and the unemployed. "Pittance" has the same etymology as "pity"; "dole" comes from the verb "to deal" and therefore suggests a general distribution of money or goods, not one reckoned according to services performed or according to worth.

Now it is hard to say whether the connotative "aura" of some of these words used to designate money received in exchange for services is the product of context or of what is called above "the total character of the things" to which the words refer. Perhaps it is the product of both. The connotations of such a word as "wages" do undoubtedly implicate the situations to which the word is relevant (daily or hourly rates for work that may be intermittent) and the attributes of the actual amounts paid (barely enough to live on; not much, considering the hours you have to stand on your feet to earn it; good enough while it lasts but you never know how long it will; and so on). In fact, the connotative, or suggestive, effect of the word will probably reach even to the attributes of the work performed for wages and of the people who perform it. This may seem to be a great deal to expect of a word, and indeed it is more than one should expect, though not more than one should be prepared to take into account in making a choice among several words that come to mind.

There are, of course, no rules by which one can determine the connotative aura of a particular word; one must simply know. Such knowing is chiefly the result of a broad experience with words, and wide reading is perhaps the surest avenue to such experience. It takes more than wide reading, however, to make a person aware of still another way in which single words may persuade, a way which is often summed up in the word "metaphor." For an appreciation of the power of metaphor, the reading must be not only wide but perceptive and thoughtful.

THE METAPHORICAL GROUND

Metaphor is one of the most fundamental of linguistic activities; some have even suggested that most language is, at bottom, metaphorical. However that may be, it is certainly true that all developed language is deeply indebted to metaphor and that all good writing reflects the writer's consciousness of the metaphorical vitality of the words he uses.

As defined in the early study of poetry, "metaphor" usually means "a comparison without the use of 'like' or 'as.'" "He fights like a lion in battle" is said to be a simile; "He is a lion in battle," a metaphor. As "metaphor" is used in the discussion of language, it is a broader term, comprising all those linguistic activities by which the attributes of one thing are imputed to a different thing. To take an example close at hand, the previous paragraph speaks of developed language as "deeply indebted to metaphor." A debt is something owed by one person to another; to say that language owes a debt to metaphor is to personify language and to speak metaphorically. More obvious metaphors (a child's observation, for instance, that the sun is "smily") are easy to detect and fairly easy to use; submerged metaphors like the one just examined are likely to conceal their very real persuasive effect under the bland façade of ordinariness.

The way in which overt and submerged metaphors do their work becomes apparent if we consider carefully a passage of prose which is written with both kinds in mind.

"The style is the man"; but the social and rhetorical influences adulterate and debase it, until not one man in a thousand achieves his birthright, or claims his second self. The fire of the soul burns all too feeble, and warms itself by the reflected heat from the society around it. We give back words of tepid greeting, without improvement. We talk to our fellows in the phrases we learn from them, which come to mean less and less as they grow worn with use. Then we exaggerate and distort, heaping epithet upon epithet in the endeavour to get a little warmth out of the smouldering pile. The quiet cynicism of our everyday demeanour is open and shameless, we callously anticipate objections founded on the well-known vacuity of our seeming emotions, and assure our friends that we are "truly" grieved or "sincerely" rejoiced at their hap—as if joy or grief that really exists were some rare and precious brand of joy or grief. In its trivial conversational uses so simple and pure a thing as joy becomes a sandwich-man—humanity degraded to an advertisement. The poor dejected word shuffles along through the mud in the service of the sleek

trader who employs it, and not until it meets with a poet is it rehabilitated
and restored to dignity.

WALTER RALEIGH, "Social and Rhetorical Corruptions," in *Style*

This passage is so heavily metaphorical that meaning is as often obscured as revealed in it, but its dense figurativeness provides ample
illustration of the ways in which metaphors work to persuade, and for
that reason it is valuable for our purposes here. The *statement* of the
passage is approximately this: "Conventional and unconsidered use of
language destroys the capacity of words to express a man's thoughts
and feelings." The expression of that statement is developed, in large
part, by two metaphorical procedures: (1) *reification,* the treatment of
abstractions as though they were things ("influences adulterate and debase"), and (2) *personification,* the treatment of things as though
they were persons ("the poor dejected word shuffles along"). Two
strong metaphors dominate: men's thoughts and feelings as "the fire
of soul" which "burns . . . and warms," and joy as a "sandwich-man."
Of these two, the first is continuously elaborated in other metaphorical
expressions of slightly reduced intensity, the "smouldering pile" of epithets, the "tepid" greeting, and so on. Still further down on the scale
of intensity, or of obviousness, other metaphors continue the transformation of abstract into concrete, of inanimate into animate: the
"heaping" of epithets, the way in which we "callously" anticipate objections which are "founded" on the "vacuity" of our emotions, the pro-
gressive meaninglessness of words "worn" with use, the eventual "re-
habilitation" and "restoration" of a word when it "meets with" a poet.

The overt metaphors strike eye and ear at once and, if they are
fresh and apt, persuade us to consider their subject in a particular
light. The submerged metaphors, though they make less noticeable impression on us, affect our consideration fully as much for the reason
that we assent to them without thought or examination. An overt metaphor may induce us to accept a new way of looking at a matter, but
it does so over a certain amount of resistance simply because the new
way runs counter to habit. A good writer is likely, therefore, to be
sparing in his use of strong figures of speech. And, because he knows
that submerged metaphors have a persuasive effect out of proportion
to their quiet presence, he will treat them with a great deal of respect.

Metaphor is, then, a very important instrument for directing the
persuasive energy of language, probably the most effective single instrument when it comes to controlling the connotations of a particular
word. It may seem that the associative aura of words is being treated
here too much as though it had a demonic capacity to make effective
communication almost impossible. Therefore it may be wise to point
out that, in addition to the connotative spread already noted, there is
another with which the writer must deal. Besides the indigenous bias

of a few words (the sn- words mentioned above) and the general connotative aura of most words, there are "meanings" for words which are
either entirely private or limited to a small number of people. Such
specialized meanings (or "subjective intensions," as Cohen and Nagel
call them) no writer can completely predict. The adjective "fat" annoys a large number of people; used as a verb, the word "contact" may
raise the hackles of only a few beleaguered purists; and the noun
"asparagus" may revolt only a neurotic John Doe, who once became
violently ill after eating asparagus and cannot forget the experience.
Even could he predict such connotations, the writer can do nothing
directly about them. Indirectly, however, he can still manage to control such random associations by the way in which he makes sure that
this word, and no other, is the one that serves his purpose at the moment. If the word, or the image, is exactly right for his purpose, its
context will in large measure protect it from taking on associations
other than those he desires it to evoke.

If individual words and phrases have persuasive effect, it is obvious
that sentences do, too, and attention is paid to the effects of syntax in
later parts of this book. At this point, it is enough to reiterate the statement that all language is persuasive and requires constant alertness in
those who use it.

THE ETHICS OF PERSUASION

To insist on the persuasiveness of language is to raise an ethical
problem which has always engaged the attention of writers and which
has been one of the main preoccupations of modern semanticists, or
students of the meaning of words. Although what has been said so far
in this chapter may often seem to imply that words have an autonomous
life, wielding power independent of their users, that proposition is itself more metaphorical than not. *People* use words, and it is their way
of using them that is largely responsible for their persuasiveness.

The traditional term for the use of language to persuade is "rhetoric," and the fact that an ethical problem is associated with that use is
apparent in the disrepute into which the term has often fallen. In the
sixteenth century, Montaigne decried persuasive practices in these words:

> . . . Aristo wisely defines rhetoric as "a science to persuade the people";
> Socrates and Plato as "the art of deceiving and flattering." And they who
> deny the general definition verify it throughout in their precepts.
> The Mohammedans forbade their children to be instructed in the art,
> on account of its uselessness.
> And the Athenians, having perceived how pernicious was the practice
> of it, though it was held in high esteem in their city, ordained that the

principal part, the appeal to the passions, should be abolished, together with the exordiums and perorations.

It is a tool invented for handling and stirring up a mob and an unruly community; and it is a tool that is only employed for sick states, like medicine. . . .   *Of the Vanity of Words*

Montaigne, of course, is speaking here of the abuse of language, of the deliberate attempt to use words so that they will stifle the reason rather than encourage it to exert itself. It is against rhetoric of that kind that popular books on semantics wage their chief battles, and nothing said so far in this book should lead the reader to think that the act of persuasion is automatically a good act or, conversely, that it is automatically a bad act, either. At the bottom of most popular semanticists' worry about "slanting" and "prejudicial language" there would seem to be a serious misconception about words. It is not the words that are bad or good but the intentions of those who use them. Once stated, the objection seems so obvious as not to need statement at all, but the misconception is too common to be entirely ignored. The ethical problem is a serious one, of course, but it should not be confused with description of language itself.

It would be possible to provide a more elaborate description of the persuasive effect of words than appears in this chapter, but economy of space dictates that we turn to other considerations about that matter, considerations which have to do with a larger relationship of the writer to his reader and to his subject matter.

THE WRITER'S PRESENCE

Behind the words stands the user, and literary art is at bottom a manifestation of the devices by which the user of words turns them to his purposes. "Style is ingratiation," and ingratiation is the act of winning favor, of persuading. Discussion of all the techniques of literary art, then, is relevant to this chapter, and were it a book instead of a chapter they might be examined one by one for their peculiarities and for their contributions to the act of using words to influence thought and action. Instead, the chapter must deal in more summary fashion with the ways in which writers learn to manipulate language so that the full compass of their meaning lies before the reader's eyes.

The writer's "presence" in what he writes is to be taken for granted. No matter how much he may wish to dissociate himself from his text, of course he cannot. He uses the meanings of words as they are known to him; he represents the world as his senses make it possible for him to conceive it. Even the most fantastic creature of his imagination or the character most unlike his own day-to-day self is material from his autobiography. A man can only express what he can conceive (and not all of that), and what he conceives is a part of himself.

Above this necessary sense in which the writer is present in his work, there is another which is sometimes identical with the necessary one and sometimes very different. Even in expository prose, where no deliberate activity of the creative imagination may be required, the writer more or less consciously stands revealed in his work. One reason is that he writes out of some feeling or conviction about his material; he has an attitude toward it, and the nature as well as the strength of that attitude will affect his choice of words, his syntax, his organization. Another reason is that he frequently assumes a certain audience for his work. That audience is the person or group of persons to whom or for whom he is writing and with whom he already has, or hopes to establish, a relationship stable enough so that the lines of communication can be kept clear. The most obvious situations in which the writer singles out his audience come quickly to mind: letters above all, public addresses and private conversations, pieces written for special occasions, pieces written for magazines with known predilections and clientele, and so on. But even for those writings whose audience is generalized or unknown, the skilled writer usually tries to have someone or some *kind* of person in mind with whom he wishes to ingratiate himself. One of the most noticeable characteristics of amateur writing is its apparent ignorance of or indifference to the reader. Such ignorance or indifference can be fatal to the persuasiveness of a piece of writing, and the competent writer is therefore always concerned to draw his reader into active participation with him in the examination of whatever subject matter he treats.

TONE

In the main, the writer establishes the character of his putative reader and his own relationship toward that reader by adopting a manner suitable to that relationship. The term commonly used to describe that maneuver is *tone*. In an eighteenth-century novel or essay the author frequently addressed the reader outright, but that literary convention is rarely used today. Instead, a writer today relies principally on choice of vocabulary, on selection of images and examples, and on syntax to indicate the kind of person he assumes his reader to be and the relationship he wants to have with him. And the relationship he has in mind will also serve him as a means of knowing how much he must explain and what he need not explain at all, where and how strongly he should place emphasis, by what means and how fully he should elaborate. Although it is not always easy to put one's finger on the devices by which a writer achieves tone, even the unskilled reader is generally able to detect the tone that is being used. Though perhaps unconsciously, he may resent being patronized or coddled, resist being bullied, or feel satisfaction at being treated as an equal. Such responses indicate that tone is not *entirely* a matter of calculation by the writer. Rather it is a reflection both of what the writer is, as a thinking and feeling person, and of the role he chooses to play in a particular piece of writing. Often tone does not so much announce itself as make itself felt in sentence after sentence through patterns of words, images, allusions, and epithets, patterns showing a consistent habit of speech and through it a consistent way of looking at the world and of letting the reader look at it, too.

How swiftly it is possible for an author to establish tone, a series of brief excerpts will show more quickly than further discussion.

> It is not to be avoided—a book on the Victorian novelists must begin with Dickens. Not that he needs praising. He is the one novelist of his school whose books have not grown at all dusty on the shelves, whose popularity has suffered no sensible decline. Nor that there is much new to be said about him; Mr. Santayana and Mr. Chesterton, to say nothing of lesser critics, have seen to that.   DAVID CECIL, *Early Victorian Novelists*

> After a few hundred of the more pressing post-war problems have been solved, it might not be a bad idea to launch a movement to put the legal profession on Basic English. Even if it could be got back to just plain English that would be so much velvet.
> FRANK SULLIVAN, *A Rock in Every Snowball*

> It is an easy phrase, "the art of living," and one which, like a cliché, is rather of the tongue than of the mind, yet in a general way we know well enough what we mean to signify by it.
> JAMES TRUSLOW ADAMS, *Our Business Civilization*

> Listening to music is such a muddle that one scarcely knows how to start describing it. The first point to get clear in my own case is that during the greater part of every performance I do not attend. The nice sounds make me think of something else.
> E. M. FORSTER, "Not Listening to Music"

> I like a country where it's nobody's damned business what magazines anyone reads, what he thinks, whom he had cocktails with. I like a country where we do not have to stuff the chimneys against listening ears and where what we say does not go into the FBI files along with a note from S-17 that I may have another wife in California.
> BERNARD DE VOTO, "Due Notice to the FBI"

> One Christmas was so much like another, in those years around the sea-corner now and out of all sound except the distant speaking of the voices I sometimes hear a moment before sleep, that I can never remember whether it snowed for six days and six nights when I was twelve or whether it snowed for twelve days and twelve nights when I was six.
> DYLAN THOMAS, *A Child's Christmas in Wales*

By his tone, the writer establishes the grounds on which communication between him and his writer is to be conducted. In *most* expository writing the tone will be that which the writer unaffectedly holds toward his assumed reader or readers. There will be occasions, however, which may require that the writer adopt one tone rather than another, as when he is addressing an audience of varied ages, varied educational backgrounds, varied interests, and so on. Because his actual social relationship with a mixed group varies from one member to another, his tone would change were he to address each one separately. Since that is precisely what he is not doing, he must adopt a tone which will be appropriate for the group. In practice, this is very hard to do, and public speakers and writers for "popular" periodicals may perhaps be excused some of their flatulence on that account. Compared with them, a student writing a critical paper is in a favored position: he usually has an audience of one for his work and a social situation—teacher-student—of fairly clear-cut protocol. Some feeling of rebellion against the confinement imposed by so limited an audience and so formal a relationship is natural, but the confinement is in fact no more repressive in this situation than in another, though obviously of a different kind.

PERSPECTIVE

There is something of make-believe in tone, just as there is in all art, no matter how deeply it is concerned to display the truth of things. A second manifestation of this make-believe, and a second means the writer has of making his identity felt in his work, is apparent in the stance he takes before his subject matter itself. No matter what the real situation is, he can appear to be detached or intimately concerned, actually in contact with the things he describes, or removed from them by thousands of miles or by centuries. He may profess to see them as they appear to others or greatly distorted, as in the mirrors of an amusement arcade. These are essentially choices of *perspective*.

The simplest perspective is probably that of *direct confrontation*. The writer stands before his subject, walks around it, studies it. The tone he adopts when he is using such a perspective may be cordial and comradely, that of "Come and look with me" or perhaps rather distant or even patronizing, that of "Stay there and I'll tell you what there is to be seen." In unskilled writing, the first tone is likely to take the form of exhortation ("Let us look now at . . .") and the second, the form of passive and impersonal constructions ("The matter can be considered . . ."). Yet neither is a necessary consequence of the perspective and tone because the same effects can be achieved without awkwardness by the skilled writer simply through careful choice of language and careful management of structure.

Instead of looking at the subject directly and in the round, the author may choose to take an oblique view of it, as though he were standing to one side with an eye (and perhaps a mind) half closed. By this means he sees the subject, as it were, in relief, and perhaps in profile. Angularities which seemed a part of the general harmony when the object was viewed in the round now are stark and even incongruous. The purpose of such perspective, of course, is emphasis, and its ground is a conscious bias, in the radical sense of that word. The writer views the subject from an announced or implied vantage point in sensation or emotion or thought. By that oblique viewing he brings clearly into view some aspect of the object which has heretofore been hidden. It is clear that this procedure has to do with something more than the manipulation of words, though it is through words that it will necessarily achieve its end. What actually happens is that a writer transforms the properties of whatever he is discussing, either by actually misrepresenting them or by misrepresenting their relationship with each other: an idiosyncrasy is exaggerated, something detestable is praised or something praiseworthy is condemned, the inconsequential is made important and the important inconsequential. Through these deliberate distortions the writer realizes his purpose of persuading the reader to re-examine a subject under his direction.

To speak of a writer's "perspective" and of his "tone" as partly make-believe may be somewhat misleading. A better way to describe what is meant by those terms is perhaps to say that they are conscious and artful means of conveying insight and feeling. To "distort" an object and to "assume" a tone are, therefore, not falsifications but revelations.

The actual means by which perspective is accomplished are several, and each is different from the other not only in nature but in purpose. One very effective way of persuading a reader to disapprove of something is to make a parody of it. In essence, a *parody* is simply an exaggeration, though not all exaggerations are by any means parodies. Underneath this device there is the assumption that almost any human proceeding has a certain amount of absurdity at its core. By seizing upon distinctive characteristics of the proceeding and stretching them, the parodist attempts to make that absurdity evident, and through it, to discredit the proceeding itself. The schoolboy who entertains his fellows with an artful imitation of the manner and speech of his teacher is a parodist; so, too, in a hackneyed fashion, is the after-dinner speaker at the suburban country club who begins with the phrase, "Friends, Roamers, and Country Gentlemen. . . ." These examples suggest another requirement of parody: it must have as its subject something that is well known, or the exaggeration will not be apparent. In fiction, parody is common; in expository writing, its use is less frequent but not for that reason ineffective. It may, in fact, be the most economical means of presenting a criticism, as in this excerpt from a book review.

> The new book which Mr. ——— has written about the Constitution is a very different kind of book. You can read it without thinking. If you have got tired trying to read the other kind of books, you will be glad of the nice restful book that Mr. ——— has written. It runs along like a story in a very interesting way. Most of the story is about how the Constitution got made. This is really history, but it is written in a very lively way like a novel, with a great many characters, almost all male, and plenty of conversation and a very exciting plot. Many of the chapters have names like those in a novel such as "The Opening of the Battle," "The Crisis," "The Dawn," "Nearing the End," "The Curtain Falls," and others. Besides the story there are many quotations from Shakespeare, Beethoven, Horace, Isaiah, Euripides, Beard, and other famous men. Many of these quotations are quite old, but some of them seem fairly new. They help to make the book a real high-class book. There is not much more to say about the part of the book that tells how the Constitution got made, except that it is fun and easy to read and seems pretty true to life.
>
> THOMAS REED POWELL, "Constitutional Metaphors"

Although the writer has not announced his intention to make fun of the style and content of the book he is reviewing, it is quickly apparent that he is doing so. The repetition of excessively simple sentences, the patronizing colloquialisms, the patent emptiness of much that is said— all of these are criticisms conveyed by parody.

A more elaborate device of persuasion than parody is *satire*. Where parody is largely concerned with the manner of an action (and, of course, with whatever that manner implies about the actor), satire deals with the action itself. Through selection, exaggeration, and meaningful juxtaposition, it attempts to expose and to bring into ridicule whatever is unnatural or unwise or evil. It plays primarily upon the difference between the state of something and its ideal condition and is therefore commonly concerned to lay bare the hypocrisy of human action, as when it shows the claim of service for the common good to be subterfuge for the satisfaction of private interest, or the assertion of righteous indignation to be a public disguise for wounded vanity.

The satirist, of course, may be himself a literal hypocrite, in the sense that he may pretend to approve what he actually detests. When he gives such approval, however, he does it in such a way that his detestation is apparent to all but the most obtuse. One of his favorite devices is to shift the apparent time or place of the action; another, to rename characters and places; a third, to analogize from one action to another. Thus, George Orwell's novel *1984* is really concerned with the political tendencies he discerned as threatening in 1948; and Aldous Huxley's *Brave New World,* another anti-Utopia, is really an account of a coming world "brave" only in its disregard of human values. Another way to develop a satire is to create a series of situations parallel to the ones to be criticized and then to present the created situations in such a fashion as to make their absurdity, or their wrongness, obvious. When, in *A Modest Proposal,* Swift advocated that babies be fattened for human consumption as a means of alleviating the twin problems of overpopulation and poverty in Ireland, he did so in most solemn and reasonable vein, and some actually took him to mean what he said. Here the satiric device is to treat matter-of-factly that which is horrible beyond imagining, an oblique way of presenting the callous attitude of the English Parliament of the time toward the oppressed and famine-stricken Irish people who were subject to its authority. Still another way is to pretend to ignorance about the premises on which certain actions are based, a procedure much more effective than might at first be imagined. If a bird, for instance, were endowed with a highly developed power to reason but were completely ignorant of human behavior, what would it make of a tennis game? or of a church service? It would note the actions as well as any other intelligent being, but the meaningfulness and the relatedness of the actions it would have to guess at or reach by continued observation and a laborious inductive process. Either means is certain to be full of errors and false leads, and it is such errors and false leads that the satirist relies on to reveal the oddities of those things with which the reader has always thought himself perfectly well acquainted. And, finally, the most obvious means of the satirist is direct contradiction: by what he does a character contradicts the precepts he preaches; a situation belies what is predicted or postulated of it.

The writer of expository prose will find the devices of satire most useful when his general intent is to encourage change, for satire is essentially the vehicle of reform. By making faults ridiculous, it seeks to provide enlightenment, to stimulate disapproval, and to make correction mandatory: in its commitment to reform, it is more clearly an instrument of social action than parody, which mocks as much in fun as in hope of improvement. Because reform is the goal of satire, the subject matter must be, either directly or by implication, the behavior of human beings. La Fontaine's fables, for instance, have animals as their evident subject matter, but the correspondence of the animals' actions and speech in the fables to the actions and speech of human beings is so patent that every adult reader knows that the fables are really criticisms of human behavior.

The peculiar power of satire to persuade lies in its manipulation of different, and often contradictory, emotions. Though the faults which it attacks may be, and generally are, faults which the reader commits or has committed, the fact that he is brought to laugh at them, and thus at himself, destroys some of his power to resist the attack and to refute the demand for reform. As with all rhetorical devices, miscalculation in the use of satire—too gross an exaggeration, too obvious a contradiction, too blatant an absurdity—destroys effectiveness. Such miscalculation, it might be noted, is not always simply an awkwardness in the handling of the device but often a symptom of some intellectual dishonesty—of an attempt to misrepresent the reality as well as the appearance of the object.

Both parody and satire are formal structures; or, to use the metaphor of perspective, they are distortions which result from presenting the object obliquely so that details become magnified or dislocated. *Irony* is not so much an arrangement of situations as an attitude toward them and a device for conveying meaning by saying the opposite of what is meant. There is another difference. Satire and parody work on materials which are well enough known so that the falsification of them is apparent to nearly everyone. Irony, on the other hand, is an exclusive practice: it assumes a fairly large audience which may take words to mean only what they say and a small audience, the one it is addressing, which will understand them to be only a façade for another meaning. Irony is subtle and often delicate; it compares with satire as the sting of a whiplash compares with the pain of a thorough drubbing. Moreover, its purpose is often less clearly therapeutic than is that of satire. Irony notes the discrepancy between what things are and what they appear to be, or between what they are and what they ought to be, and it displays the writer's acuity and his amusement or contempt, but it does not always make a demand for reform. There is a kind of Olympian irony which affects to look on most human action with an indulgent smile, and a tragic irony which has no smile at all but a degree of compassion for the futility of the human condition. Whatever the kind, the ironist must in a sense look down on his subject, see it in a broader relationship than that available to most men, and then communicate what he has seen by such slight alterations in his language as will lead the initiated reader to know that the words he reads are to be understood as though they were preceded by "not."

The master ironist of the English language is probably the historian Edward Gibbon, and it is fitting that this discussion of irony close with a few illustrations from his *Decline and Fall of the Roman Empire*. A thoroughgoing eighteenth-century rationalist, Gibbon found religious controversy especially distasteful, referring to it as "the exquisite rancour of theological hatred," just as he both hated and feared the claims of supernatural intervention in the affairs of man, to which he gave the name "holy romances." Of the miraculous acts of St. James, the apostle, he writes:

> The gravest historians have celebrated his exploits; the miraculous shrine of Compostella displayed his power; and the sword of a military order, assisted by the terrors of the Inquisition, was sufficient to remove every objection of profane criticism.

Though much of his irony is directed against religion, and against Christianity in particular, Gibbon hated what he believed to be fraud or base servility wherever he found it. He speaks, for instance, of Herod and his sycophants in these words:

> . . . the greatest part of his life was spent in philosophic retirement at Athens and his adjacent villas, perpetually surrounded by sophists, who acknowledged without reluctance the superiority of a rich and generous rival.

As these examples show, irony is a devastating instrument of persuasion, for its agreeable surface deflects the expostulations even of those whom its implications have wounded. It thus invites the reader to participation with the writer by guaranteeing him safety even as it offers him the flattery of being among the elect who discern the real intent of what is said.

To include all literary devices, all figurative forms of speech, and even the accidental encrustations on words as elements of persuasion may be to stretch the category until it is an *omnium gatherum* into which all left-overs may find a resting place. Yet such catholicity has one virtue, and it is a virtue especially important to the concept of persuasion: to realize that all use of language is persuasive is to recognize that no user can safely be indifferent to his choice of words, his syntax, or his literary demeanor. Even as expositor of the slightest matter, he employs an instrument which has effects, produces reactions. Though he cannot predict reactions with certainty, he can in large measure control them if he is aware of the many ways in which language moves readers and if he then trains himself to use language wisely and well.

EXERCISES

1. For each of the italicized words in the following sentences, indicate denotations and connotations.

   a. Every generation reaps what its predecessor has sown; our *harvest* is bitter rice.
   b. *Gulliver's Travels* is a *mordant* satire on most of mankind.
   c. Darwin was *savagely* attacked for his treatise on the evolution of man from *lower* forms of life.

d. Montesquieu's descriptions of eastern culture in the *Lettres Persanes* are more nearly *romance* than report.

e. He was a false-swearer, a low conniver and cheat, a veritable *lackey* of a man.

2. Select the word or phrase in each passage whose connotations are inappropriate in this context and provide an appropriate substitute.

a. The whole statement has the ring of truth. She has spoken precisely and firmly throughout; there is even a kind of radical zeal in what she says.

b. Great men are often models for our action, and we do well to mimic them.

c. She was singularly fair of aspect, her face charming and entirely regular save for a slight bump on the left brow.

d. A good critic does not belabor his point but rams it home with the skill of a fencing-master.

e. Gore spurted from the artery like water from a fountain.

3. Examine a series of advertisements to discover how persuasion is effected by appeals to prestige, pity, money, popularity, prejudice, and so on. Reduce each advertisement to its informational content.

4. Compare two newspaper accounts of the same incident (one from a tabloid, one from a newspaper, like the New York *Times,* whose reputation for uncolored reporting is well established). Do the contents of the two reports differ? How is emphasis achieved? Can you find specific instances in which the selection of words casts different light on the topic?

5. Compare these two accounts of an episode in the French Revolution.

> Early in October it began to be feared that the king was yielding again to the influences at the court which were hostile to reform, and a great mob from Paris invaded the gardens and palace at Versailles. The king was saved from the mob by the National Guard, but he was obliged to follow the advice of La Fayette and take up his residence, with his family, in Paris.
>
> GEORGE BURTON ADAMS, *The Growth of the French Nation*

> The dull dawn of a new morning, drizzly and chill, had but broken over Versailles, when it pleased destiny that a bodyguard should look out of window, on the right wing of the chateau, to see what prospect there was in heaven and in earth. Rascality male and female is prowling in view of him. His fasting stomach is, with good cause, sour; he perhaps cannot forbear a passing malison on them; least of all can he forbear answering such.
>
> Ill words breed worse: till the worst word come; and then the ill deed. Did the maledicent bodyguard, getting (as was too inevitable) better malediction than he gave, load his musketoon, and threaten to

fire; nay actually fire? Were wise who wist! It stands asserted; to us not credibly. But be this as it may, menaced rascality, in whinnying scorn, is shaking at all grates; the fastening of one (some write, it was a chain merely) gives way; rascality is in the grand court, whinnying louder still.

The maledicent bodyguard, more bodyguards than he do now give fire; a man's arm is shattered. Lecointre will depose that "the Sieur Cardine, a national guard without arms, was stabbed." But see, sure enough, poor Jerôme l'Héritier, an unarmed national guard he too, "cabinet-maker, a saddler's son, of Paris," with the down of youthhood still on his chin, he reels deathstricken; rushes to the pavement, scattering it with his blood and brains! Alleleu! Wilder than Irish wakes rises the howl; of pity, of infinite revenge. In few moments, the grate of the inner and inmost court, which they name Court of Marble, this too is forced, or surprised, and bursts open: the court of marble too is overflowed; up the grand staircase, up all stairs and entrances rushes the living deluge! Deshuttes and Varigny, the two sentry bodyguards, are trodden down, are massacred with a hundred pikes. Women snatch their cutlasses, or any weapon, and storm in, Menadic; other women lift the corpse of shot Jerôme; lay it down in the marble steps; there shall the livid face and smashed head, dumb forever, *speak*.   THOMAS CARLYLE, *The French Revolution*

What rhetorical figure is employed in each of these expressions?

> rascality
> down of youthhood
> living deluge
> Menadic

What is the precise descriptive achievement of the term "rascality" as it is coupled with verbs and reused in the passage?

6. Without making any direct reference to the relationship between writer and reader, write separate versions, as indicated, of the following:

   a. a letter of protest (to a close friend, to a subordinate, to a superior)
   b. an introduction to a talk to be given (before a high school audience, before a group of businessmen, before a group whom you suspect to hold an opinion of the subject quite different from yours)
   c. an announcement for the attention (of subway riders, of resort dwellers, of bed-patients in a hospital)
   d. the opening paragraph of an essay on the poetry of a modern poet to be published (in the Sunday supplement of a good newspaper, in a scholarly journal, in a popular magazine)

7. Write an ironic sentence which will convey

   a. disapproval of the motives which led the city council to grant permission for pari-mutuel betting at the local race track
   b. disapproval of the principles on which a group of citizens based their argument against that permission

   c. doubt about the salubriousness of a much-publicized climate

   d. dissatisfaction with the outcome of a recent election

   e. displeasure at the fashion among college students of growing beards

8. The first passage below is an excerpt from a novel; the second is a parody of it. After examining both with care discuss the stylistic characteristics which the parodist chooses to make fun of.

> The fact that she "knew"—knew and yet neither chaffed him nor betrayed him—had in a short time begun to constitute between them a goodly bond, which became more marked when, within the year that followed their afternoon at Weatherend, the opportunities for meeting multiplied. The event that thus promoted these occasions was the death of the ancient lady her great-aunt, under whose wing, since losing her mother, she had to such an extent found shelter, and who, though but the widowed mother of the new successor to the property, had succeeded—thanks to a high tone and a high temper—in not forfeiting the supreme position at the great house.
>
> It was with the sense of a, for him, very memorable something that he peered now into the immediate future, and tried, not without compunction, to take that period up where he had, prospectively, left it. . . . The consciousness of dubiety was, for our friend, not, this morning, quite yet clean-cut enough to outline the figures on what she had called his "horizon," between which and himself the twilight was indeed of a quality somewhat intimidating.

9. Make a parody of your own on the style of this excerpt.

> Toward evening the rain ceased; and rising up I went out a short distance to the neighboring stream, where I sat on a stone, and casting off my sandals, laved my bruised feet in the cool running water. The western half of the sky was blue again with that tender lucid blue seen after rain, but the leaves still glittered with water, and the wet trunks looked almost black under the green foliage. The rare loveliness of the scene touched and lightened my heart.

The first four chapters of this book provide a discussion of as many characteristic uses to which words and word-structures are frequently put in expository writing. Without being either entirely theoretical or entirely analytical, these chapters are nonetheless primarily concerned with the nature, rather than with the exploitation, of those characteristics. The second part of the book reverses emphasis: it does not disavow the theoretical and the analytic, but it gives its main attention to the practical matters of actual composition. It does not attempt to provide a complete account of English grammar or an exhaustive rehearsal of every rhetorical figure. Rather, it tries to deal thoughtfully only with those matters of composition, whether grammatical or rhetorical, which most frequently arise in students' expository writing. Throughout it eschews the hard and fast rule, except where rules —or conventions, as they might more properly be called—are the only explainable grounds for standard practice. In place of rules, it offers such reasoning about the effects of each locution or structure as seems to the author sound. Because the author, like his readers, comes from a place and a time, his preferences will undoubtedly be more apparent than he wishes they would. And, the subject being what it is, he will undoubtedly fail, by omission or commission, to please any reader all of the time. The second part of the book will serve its purpose well enough, however, if it proves to be an enlightening and useful guide to those who take their thinking seriously enough to desire its expression in a form capable of adequately containing and effectively transmitting it.

Part Two

☞ The Grammar and Rhetoric

of the Sentence

What grammarians say should be has perhaps less influence on
what shall be than even the more modest of them realize; usage
evolves itself little distorted by their likes & dislikes.
FOWLER, *Modern English Usage*

IN THE PAST FIFTY YEARS more and more people (linguists, then
teachers, then their pupils) have come to regard grammar as a matter
of record, not of rule. They speak of it as *descriptive* rather than
prescriptive, and they have ample historical justification for doing so.
Just as Aristotle's *Poetics* is an account of the drama *as it was* in his day
(with observations by the author and some expression of preference),
so grammar is generally considered today to be an account of what is
acceptable and accepted in the language of contemporary society. It is
a fact that a good many of the "rules" generally considered sacrosanct
are themselves of recent origin. So it is with the "shall-will" distinction
for the future tense, the insistence on the apostrophe for the possessive of nouns, the distinction between "farther" and "further." But it
must not be forgotten—and the defenders of the descriptive point of
view sometimes do forget—that rules also have validity, that they
often represent a codification of experience. Sometimes their purpose is
purely pedagogical: to provide a kind of shorthand for passing on to
the uninstructed certain information about a given tongue; sometimes
their purpose is to improve language for its native users, to improve it
by reducing the danger of ambiguity (as in the case of the possessive
apostrophe, noted above) or by increasing the subtlety of inflection and
meaning. In the end, only a judicious balance between the two positions
is defensible. James Boswell, the biographer of Samuel Johnson, sometimes wrote (to himself) in his journals at the end of an exciting day,
"You was the great man today." The use of "was" with the second person was common in the eighteenth century and served to separate the
singular from the plural "you." Less than two hundred years later, however, a biographer of Walt Whitman could, with some justification, re-

proach the American poet with "a rather meager education" for writing, in a letter to his mother, "I wish you was here." What happened in those two centuries was that the intervention of grammarians fastened "was" to the first and third persons only. There can be little doubt that another two centuries will make respectable the currently unacceptable "he-she-it don't" and "alright." Some of the currently popular (but not standard) forms will take longer to come into formal usage or may never get there at all: the prejudice against "ain't" and against such double negatives as "can't hardly" is so great that there is little likelihood of their early absorption. The point to be made is that forms of language alter. Changes usually come first in speech; they make their way into personal letters and diaries, then into creative expression (the dialogue of realistic drama and fiction, for example), and later into more somber studies and documents. The proliferation of ephemeral printed material in newspapers and popular periodicals hastens change; so also do the unceasing flood of words from radio and television and the constant mixing of cultures that results from easy, fast transportation. Formal education retards the process and in so doing performs a distinguished service to language, helping it to hold fast to what is good. Yet, even in a country like ours which boasts of universal education, change goes on. All the time there are new words pushing into general use, old forms disappearing (or, curiously enough, if they are old enough, reappearing), a vast unchartable mutation delightful to lexicographers and infinitely upsetting to the native learner, the foreign visitor, and the lover of things-as-they-are.

Where, then, is the student to turn for guidance when in doubt? The answer is not an easy one; on the other hand, it is not nearly so complex as the preceding paragraph may lead him to fear. In the first place, he can always play safe, that is, observe the "rules" in any good handbook. His language may seem stiff at times but it will always be acceptable and even respected. The one danger in this strict adherence to the guide books of language is the development of a kind of linguistic snobbery, a "purism" that too often leads the adherer to social and moral judgments on his fellows based solely on the degree of their respect for what are, after all, matters not necessarily of character or of conscience. If the student chooses this "safe" way, the history of language obligates him not to be unduly proud of his choice: he has picked the conservative gray flannel, knowing that it will serve him for nearly every occasion, in preference to a garment somewhat less adaptable but more self-expressive.

If he adopts a purely descriptive standard, if he determines that any form now in use is good enough by virtue of its existence, he will find his sensitivity to nuance gradually dulled and his capacity to communicate markedly diminished: by this extremism, he impairs the power language has to sharpen his own intellectual processes and he impairs the power it has to provide contact with the thoughts and actions of others. If he is intellectually curious and naturally inventive and adventurous, he may, however, wish to free himself somewhat from the kind of minimum standard that a handbook provides. In that case, his course will be risky though exhilarating, like Odysseus' venture between the twin dangers of Scylla and Charybdis. The sea between these destroyers is not an easy one to sail (the student who chooses this way must know more, not less, than the handbooks tell), but it leads to the open sea. Much of the richness of language lies beyond the rules, and it is there that this combination of historical knowledge and intelligent respect for current standards occurs. Fortunately the student ambitious enough to want some acquaintance with language greater than that which the rule books give has today many good sources at hand. The *Oxford English Dictionary* traces changes in form and meaning, providing dates and examples in profusion. Mencken's *The American Language* is packed with information about the development of English in this country. Its style is at times witty, at times indignant and scornful, its learning is generally sound, and its scope broad. Fowler's *English Usage,* though British and sometimes overly finical, and Eric Partridge's *Usage and Abusage* are volumes that every student should have on his desk alongside his dictionary. With these reliable resources at hand, almost any student with enough diligence to turn pages and enough interest to watch for the questionable spots in his own writing can venture with confidence into what someone on the staff of the *New Yorker* has called "the brier patch of English usage."

Since the sentence is the basic unit of discourse, examination of specific matters of grammar and of rhetoric can begin with it. The characteristic structure of the English sentence is that described in the familiar formula: subject-verb-object. The order seems "natural" and even inevitable to an English-speaking person, but a moment's reflection will show that other languages may have other patterns. In Latin, for example, the sentence equivalent to "The boy loves the girl" might theoretically be juggled about in a number of ways without in the least affecting its primary meaning: *Puer amat puellam; puer puellam amat; puellam puer amat; amat puer puellam; amat puellam puer.* Such a shifting of words in the English sentence produces a change in meaning, or meaninglessness. The reason is obvious enough: English relies on word order to make meaning clear because English nouns and verbs and modifiers have few inflections. Although there are at least three cases for nouns in English (whether or not there are more depends on the mode of analysis), two of them are indistinguishable in form; although there are three persons for verbs, the verb form is often

identical for all three. Pronouns are more highly inflected than nouns, but adjectives and adverbs have changes of form only to indicate degree (comparative or superlative), never to make clear their association with one of several words to which they may possibly be attached. Word order must take care of the modifying relationship, then, as it does to a large degree of the subject-object, subject-verb, and verb-object relationships.

Because word order is so important in English syntax, one leading modern grammarian (Charles Fries, in *The Structure of English*) has attempted to analyze our syntax as largely "positional" in nature. Although his analysis encounters some difficulties which are not very satisfactorily resolved, it is clearly sound in its major premise: that the study of English grammar must be a different thing from the study of Latin grammar, the traditional model for it. To pay a great deal of attention to accidence (inflected forms) and to slight syntax is to ignore the principal difference, and for that reason this discussion begins with the interplay among units within a sentence rather than with the various forms words take in order to indicate person, number, time, mood, and aspect.

The Latin sentences cited above were said to be unaffected in their primary meaning whatever the order of the words. Another word for "primary" in this context might be "discursive" or even "logical." In addition to this primary, or discursive, or logical meaning of a sentence there is another, secondary only in the sense that it is another, not a lesser, meaning—the rhetorical. A good Latinist would reject some of the sentences as unconventional, some as uneuphonious, and would classify others as prosaic or poetic in rhetorical climate; yet he would at the same time agree that the "logic" of one structure is equivalent to that of another. The discursive and rhetorical meanings are both important, for it is the juncture of the two—the "what" of the sentence and its "how" —that produces the single experience which we call *"the* meaning." Consider these sentences:

1. The richest man is the one who has the cheapest pleasures.
2. He who has the cheapest pleasures is the richest.
3. That man is richest whose pleasures are the cheapest.

The three sentences have a common vocabulary and say the same thing; yet there are distinguishable differences among them. The first uses the syntax of contemporary prose, adjectives preceding the nouns they modify, the relative clause ("who has . . .") following directly its referent ("one"). The second substitutes a pronoun for the noun "man" and attaches the relative clause to it in a fashion which sounds slightly stiff and overformal to the modern ear. The third (a statement by Thoreau in his *Journal,* March 11, 1856) places the relative clause apart from its referent. Apparently Thoreau's intention is to take advantage of the heightened contrast which comes from balancing "richest" against "cheapest" in identical positions in their respective clauses, and to use the emphatic position at the end of the sentence for the word which is the key to this unconventional assertion. His sentence is meant to ring in our ears, to take on some of the power of the proverb, and it succeeds in doing just that.

So simple a matter as the arrangement of clauses or the substitution of a noun for a pronoun is, then, a proper consideration for the careful writer. The precise effect of various word patterns he will learn to appreciate only as he extends his reading and as he practices achieving specific effects in what he writes. Such a prognosis may not seem particularly helpful to the present reader, however, if his concern in the matter is already acute. For that reason, some positive suggestions are clearly in order.

INDEPENDENT CLAUSES

One of the readily discernible characteristics of good modern writing is a tendency to shorten the sentence, sometimes to a single independent clause, a tendency carried to an extreme in the "tough" novel of our day. Whatever the complex historical and psychological causes of this shortening of the sentence may be, it is possible to credit it with the virtue of directness and, often, of succinctness.
Compare

Jake strode into the room. The door banged behind him, hard. He stopped short in the middle of the room. "Hullo," he said. "What's that?"

with

Jake strode into the room, banging the door hard behind him, and stopped short in the middle of the room. "Hullo," he said, "What's that?"

or

After Jake strode into the room, banging the door behind him, he stopped short in the middle of the room and said, "Hullo! What's that?"

There is a vigor, a suggestion of abrupt action, in the first passage that is only partially conveyed by the others where the participial phrase ("banging . . ."), by subordinating one action, has the effect of reducing the separateness and therefore the abruptness of the actions.

Constant use of the short independent clause as a complete sentence has the fault, however, of its virtue. Because each clause produces a solid thump, the ear soon loses the power to distinguish between thumps. The result is a sense of sameness and of disjunction between successive sentences. Nonetheless, this simple kind of structure is a valuable one. The writer who habitually gets wound up in sentences of tortuous complexity will find temporary use of it an effective curative.

DEPENDENT CLAUSES

The grammatical character of the dependent clause is familiar to many for whom its rhetorical functions are quite mythical. Yet the uses of dependent clauses are so many and so important to the effect of a sentence that indifference to them is fatal to effective expression. One of those functions is the indication of logical relationship. The sentences which follow need to have relationships more clearly defined:

> The Bodleian manuscript is obviously a copy of the original. It has several interpolations. The interpolations may be the work of a Benedictine monk.

Converting the second and third sentences into a dependent clause draws the information together and places emphasis on the predication of the first sentence:

> The Bodleian manuscript, which has several interpolations possibly the work of a Benedictine monk, is obviously a copy of the original.

An alternative arrangement draws the information together and places emphasis on "interpolation":

> The Bodleian manuscript, obviously a copy of the original, has several interpolations possibly the work of a Benedictine monk.

A second rhetorical function of the dependent clause is to induce anticipation. Each of these clauses

> When Louis refused a third time to hear its emissaries

> If you add copper sulfate instead of sodium

arouses the reader's desire to know the consequence of the action described. Conversely, the feeling of the vitality of action often declines when the dependent clause follows:

> The council decided to turn directly to the people when Louis refused a third time to hear its emissaries.

> The solution may explode if you add copper sulfate instead of sodium.

The nature of the consequence will to some degree determine the placement of the dependent clause. If the conclusion of the second sentence, for instance, were "may turn green," it would be rhetorically preferable to begin with the independent clause. Since "may explode" is an adequate satisfaction of the tension created by an opening dependent clause, however, that sentence is better written thus:

If you add copper sulfate instead of sodium, the solution may explode.

The same is true of the first example, which is better written:

> When Louis refused a third time to hear its emissaries, the council decided to turn directly to the people.

Besides providing unity and a sense of anticipation, the dependent clause may help in the *control of emphasis*. Curiously enough, it may function either to increase or to decrease the weight placed on a term. In the sentence

> Inexperienced workers naturally make more mistakes

the term "inexperienced" may be given more prominence by conversion:

> Workers who are inexperienced make more mistakes.

But a desirable de-emphasis results from creating a dependent clause in this instance:

> The sighting of the new star was made possible only by the development of a more powerful telescope, and the star was later named Pluto.

> The sighting of the new star, which was later named Pluto, was made possible only by the development of a more powerful telescope.

In the examples given here, the dependent clause achieves emphasis by expansion of an adjective into a dependent clause and de-emphasis by the reduction of an independent clause to dependency. The obvious inference from the examples is not sound for all possible situations, of course, but it is good enough as a rough generalization to warrant notice.

One caution concludes this brief discussion of dependent clauses: a writer must know the precise effect of the subordinating conjunctions with which such clauses begin. (A list of the common ones appears later, in the discussion of transitions.) Very frequently, the unintended implication that sends the reader in the wrong direction comes from nothing more than the faulty use of a subordinating conjunction, as in the passage below:

> The usual European explanation for American shyness is that Americans almost by definition have no interest in any sort of intellectual endeavor. Kluckhohn offers a more subtle interpretation *although* it is a valid one.

PARTICIPIAL PHRASES

Probably more students are familiar with the classic blunder in the use of participial phrases than with the particular effects achievable by correct use of them. To move from the familiar to the unfamiliar, then, is to begin with that cardinal error, the *dangling participle*. Considering the prominence it has in most handbooks of grammar, it is remarkable how persistently it continues to disgrace the writing not only of students but of others who might reasonably be expected to avoid it. Part of the persistence is due, no doubt, to its innocence and convenience. Only in such "boners" as

> Wearing a red shirt, the bull attacked the unfortunate man

does it offend, and amuse, the general reader. And were it not for the confusion a dangling participle often causes, it would not deserve further attention. That it does cause confusion is evident in a sentence like this:

> Defending liberty with such vigor, my opinion is that Milton in his *Areopagitica* is the leading libertarian of his time.

Who or what is "defending"? The answer can be puzzled out, of course, but one writes to inform a reader, not to puzzle him. The construction of such a sentence is, therefore, indefensible. Such confusion can usually be avoided by keeping a simple rule in mind: the participial modifier should come as close as possible to the word it modifies. Not:

> Having no grounds for his argument, it seems to me that Alcibiades decided to rely on rhetoric in order to defend his position.

But this:

> It seems to me that, having no grounds for his argument, Alciabides decided to rely on rhetoric in order to defend his position.

Wherever possible it is wise to avoid separating subject and predicate-verb by the participial expression:

> Alcibiades, having no grounds for his argument, decided to rely on rhetoric in order to defend his position.

> CORRECTED: Having no grounds for his argument, Alcibiades decided to rely on rhetoric in order to defend his position.

The earlier sentence about Milton is so awkward that relief can be found only in complete revision:

> Milton's vigorous defense of freedom in the *Areopagetica* makes him, in my opinion, the leading libertarian of his time.

So much for the abuse of the participle. What of its effective use? The principal utility of the participle seems to lie in its power to create a sense of *simultaneity*.

> Cassius spoke cautiously to Brutus, measured each word with care, and increased his fervor at each sign of impatience in Brutus' face.

CORRECTED: Cassius spoke cautiously to Brutus, measuring each word with care and increasing his fervor at each sign of impatience in Brutus' face.

In these examples, "spoke" indicates an action which *includes* the other verbs. Turning "measured" and "increased" into participles makes the inclusion clear and gives the reader an almost graphic realization that the actions of measuring and increasing go on during the speaking and are a part of it.

Moreover, participles make it possible to establish clearly the relationship of two periods of time within a single sentence:

Although he tried repeatedly to do so, Coleridge could never recapture the vision of "Kubla Khan" which came to him in a dream that was interrupted by the untimely intrusion of a visitor.

CORRECTED: Although he tried repeatedly to do so, Coleridge could never recapture the vision of "Kubla Khan," the product of a dream interrupted by the untimely intrusion of a visitor.

Participles, present and past, also serve as instruments of *unification*. In the sentence about the sighting of a new star, revised several pages back, a further improvement might be made by reducing the dependent clause to a participial phrase:

The sighting of the new star, later named Pluto, was made possible only by. . . .

Such use of the participial phrase is almost too common to warrant mention, and its abuses—largely those of misplacement—are relatively infrequent. The use of the participle in so-called "absolute" constructions, however, is less common though fully as useful as a unifying device:

He climbed out of the ring, his ears nearly deafened by the roar of the crowd around him.

Its oars rising and falling rhythmically, the first shell swept around the bend of the river and into the final stretch.

Here the participial constructions attach relevant information to the main clauses and thus unify the action described in them.

PREPOSITIONAL PHRASES

Mention has already been made of the important role which the position of words plays in conveying the meaning of a sentence. The need for a considerable fixity of position in English is obvious, for without it the relationships between the various nouns in a sentence and between the nouns and verbs would quickly become obscure. If position were all that English could rely on to establish relationship, however, it would be a very inflexible language. That it is not falls partly to the credit of the preposition. Although position is principally responsible for our understanding the relationships in a sentence like this

> He gave the girl the money

it is through prepositions that relationships are conveyed in sentences like this

> The girl in the bank put her pen on the counter.

A simple test of the importance of prepositions is to block out all of them in a brief passage of prose and then try to understand the meaning without them:

> Genuine crises are rare. Various times, civil and religious disputes have filled the air lasting and deafening clamor, yet leading vital transformations. The political and social foundations State were never shaken or even called question. Hence they cannot be regarded genuine crises. We find examples this firstly the Wars the Roses England, which the people trooped one two factions nobility and the Court, and secondly the French Wars Religion, where actual fact the main issue lay the followers two noble houses, and the question was whether the King would maintain his position independently either, or which he would join.

While it is possible to guess at the prepositions omitted in many places, especially where idioms are involved ("called *in* question," for instance), the nature of the relationship between nouns and between nouns and verbs becomes ambiguous in many others. It is those relationships which the preposition clarifies when it is properly and accurately used.

As its name implies, the preposition is not used alone; it always has an object which is, grammatically, a noun or a pronoun or some word acting as surrogate for a noun or pronoun:

> We are going *to* his house.
>
> He delights in *singing*.
>
> He came *from New York*.
>
> *Where* did he come *from?*

This combination, known as the prepositional phrase, is generally used as a modifier (adjectival or adverbial) within the sentence:

> The man *on the horse* is a polo player. (adjectival)
>
> He strikes the ball *with a mallet*. (adverbial)

Its use as subject or object of the verb is either elliptic or awkward or both:

> *In the air* is better than *on the ground*.
>
> *At my house* will be satisfactory.

Considering the many functions of the prepositional phrase in its adjectival and adverbial roles, it seems wise, therefore, to separate it entirely from the subject-object functions, and formal writing generally respects that separation.

As modifiers, prepositional phrases act like one-word adjectives and adverbs. They name attributes of nouns (the girl *in blue*) when they are adjectival, and like one-word adjectives usually follow the nouns they modify. When they are adverbial, they express one of the usual adverbial relationships: those of time, place, direction, derivation, condition, consequence, exclusion or inclusion, means, manner, or agency; like one-word adverbs they usually precede the adjectives they modify and may either precede or follow the verbs they modify. The word "usually" is needed for any statement about the placement of prepositional phrases: because they are supplements to the "main line" of the sentence—subject-verb-object—they are relatively instable and quite susceptible to the demands of emphasis, rhythm, and euphony as well as to those of logical relationship.

The difference between the two following sentences is one of emphasis:

He put down his knapsack in the middle of the room.

In the middle of the room he put down his knapsack.

The difference between these is one of clarity:

They poured the syrup which they had spent all afternoon boiling out of the bucket.

They poured out of the bucket the syrup which they had spent all afternoon boiling.

And between the sentence immediately above and this one, the difference is one of rhythm and euphony:

The syrup which they had spent all afternoon boiling they now poured out of the bucket.

Problems of placement do not yield readily to solutions by rule. A writer has to be alert to detect the possibilities of confusion from bad placement and sensitive to the sound of language to detect those placements which offend the natural rhythm of English or throw emphasis where it is not wanted. While the same alertness and sensitivity would certainly prevent other abuses of the prepositional phrase, it is possible to make concrete suggestions for a few, not as a substitute for alertness and sensitivity but as an aid where they may not be sufficiently acute to be a guide.

a. There are much worse sins than leaving a preposition at the end of a sentence. In speech even the most fastidious users of language are likely to do so on occasion; in formal writing the preposition is usually joined firmly to its object, however. Some of the uses objected to by the overly cautious are not really abuses of prepositional unity at all but are simply emphatic placements of adverbs so closely attached to the verbs they modify that they constitute a part of the verb: "That is treatment he is not willing to *put up with*." It was a secretary's correction of such a locution that is said to have led Winston Churchill to write in the margin, "This is the kind of nonsense up with which I will not put."

b. Much worse than the "dangling" preposition is the overuse of compound prepositions, especially of those whose metaphorical ground has been obscured by time: *on the basis that, in terms of, in consideration of the fact that,* and so on. A paragraph full of such prepositional structures so far divorces the active words of the sentence that a kind of miasma begins to rise from it, covering its movement and its meaning:

> In respect to the terms of the agreement made on the basis of a consideration of the factors in the case, we are of the opinion that to act in the sense of the terms in this instance without more examination concerning the possible effects on the ground of damage to other parties in the situation would not be in the interests of anyone.

c. Any *succession* of prepositional phrases is likely to confuse a reader because it presents a string of qualifiers separated from the words they qualify. Even when the meaning is not obscured by such a succession, the elegance of the sentence may be injured (see Euphony below).

d. Occasionally the practice of separating a preposition from its object leads a writer to repeat it unintentionally:

> The shrubs along the road *in* which he had for the last two hours been crouching *in* were thick enough to conceal him completely.

To expose such a repetition is to condemn it.

e. The most serious misuse of prepositional phrases, and probably the most common, is that arising from indifference to meaning. "With," for instance, has become a jack-of-all-prepositional-trades; "in" and "into" are carelessly interchanged; "by" is used to mean "beside"; "off of" is substituted for "off" in defiance of logic. There is nothing harder for a foreigner to get used to than the prepositions in our language when they are correctly used; considering the cavalier treatment some of them habitually receive, it is not surprising that they are frequently confusing even to natives. Only a laborious catalogue would make it possible to establish the significance of each English preposition, and a complete catalogue, if it included all current usages, would undoubtedly show so much overlapping that most distinctions would become questionable. The best single piece of advice may be this: since prepositions are relational in their function, thinking whenever possible about their relational inten-

tion in physical terms may prevent misuse. It ought certainly to eliminate such sentences as these:

With such people all you can do is hope they will change.

He sings *with* a high voice.

If you want to succeed *with* some other means, you are free to try.

He came back to the house *with* his hat lost.

He earns his living *with* the sweat of his brow.

INFINITIVE AND GERUND PHRASES

The infinitive phrase is a convenient but not very flexible structure.
Its most natural use is as object of a verb or as appositive:

He wants *to spend his vacation in Bermuda.*

His plan *to do so* was foiled by an accident.

As subject of the verb, the infinitive phrase is rather formal and not common to speech, in which it is likely to be replaced by a gerund.

To see is to believe. (*Seeing* is believing.)

The gerund, or verbal noun, is used as nouns are most commonly
used—as subject or object of a verb, as object of a preposition:

Climbing the mountain is more fun than *descending* it.

He thinks his success comes from *waiting.*

They tried *running* in pairs but soon gave up *trying.*

Both the infinitive phrase and the gerund phrase provide ways of maintaining the vitality and movement implicit in a verb at the same time as
they make the action figure as the thing talked about in the sentence.
Their grammatical peculiarities, though perplexing when analyzed,
cause little difficulty except in connection with the agent of the action
they imply. Despite the fact that they function as nouns, they retain
some of their verbal character, grammatically speaking. Thus, although
they may themselves be subjects or objects of a verb, they also have
subjects and objects; and the form of their subjects is often mishandled.
The logic of the distinctions may be omitted here, but the distinctions
themselves need brief mention:

a. The subject of an infinitive is in the objective case:

She wants *him* to go alone.

b. The subject of the action implied in a gerund is in the possessive case:

She approves *his* trying to go alone.

They like Mary's singing.

The so-called dangling or detached infinitive—

To treat first matters first, the ship is too slow for our needs

—is frowned upon by some, but its only disadvantage seems to lie in the possibility of confusion. In the example given above, no one is likely to think that the infinitive phrase modifies "ship"; in the one that follows the construction is less defensible because it does create some ambiguity:

This is a means, to do him justice, by which some good may be accomplished.

BALANCED PHRASING

By the time students reach college, some have developed an ear sensitive to the poise and cadence of language, perhaps the result of direct instruction, but more likely the fruit of wide and attentive reading. Those who already have it are possessed of a principal means to rhetorical power. Those who do not can develop a rudimentary command of it by considering the various effects which the shifting of verbal structures can produce.

Since the dominant pattern of English is the simple one described above (subject-verb-object), it is not strange that *inversion* commands immediate attention. Its usual effect is to emphasize or dramatize the word which is moved out of its ordinary place, as in these examples:

Had Napoleon acted, Moscow might not have been burned.
(*Instead of* If Napoleon had acted. . . .)

Undaunted, he faced the angry mob. (*Instead of* He faced the angry mob undaunted.)

In the first sentence, the writer throws weight on what is actually a dependent clause by inverting the subject and a part of the predicate verb; in the second, he does the same for the participial adjective by moving it so that it precedes the pronoun it modifies. Both of these illustrations show a kind of redressing of balance, a corrective to the normal syntax which provides inadequate emphasis for the word or clause of primary importance in this context.

A less spectacular kind of balance is created by repetition of pattern, by what is known as *parallel structure*. In simplest form, this is no more than maintaining one part of speech in a series, a device that produces some of the most memorable phrases in our language:

Life, liberty, and the pursuit of happiness.

Read, mark, and consider.

The world, the flesh, and the devil.

The single rule governing such structures is that each part provide an identical grammatical pattern, even though elements in it, as in this oft-quoted excerpt from Bacon's essay, "Of Studies," may be omitted:

Reading maketh a full man; conference, a ready man; writing, an exact man.

Actually it is possible to vary one part of each phrase slightly without damage to the parallelism if the varying is of a kind not to distract:

Histories make men wise; poets, witty; the mathematics, subtile; natural philosophy, deep; moral, grave; logic and rhetoric, able to contend.

In this illustration, "histories," "poets," and "the mathematics" are not identical, in that the first represents the product of study, the second the producer, and the third the study itself. We can understand, perhaps, why Bacon deviated from the strict pattern (which he observes with fidelity elsewhere in the essay) if we try to rephrase the sentence more rigidly:

History makes men wise; poetry, witty; the mathematics, subtile.

In our reconstruction "history" is ambiguous since, particularly before the pattern is established, it may be taken to mean "the study of history" or "the events of the past"; and "poetry, witty" offends the ear.

There is something valuable to be learned from this example. Parallelism is wonderfully effective but it must not be used insensitively. Overused (as it is, indeed, in Bacon's essay), it becomes monotonous. Used without attention to other considerations, it may damage the sentence it balances by offending on some other score. When parallelism governs sentences, they are likely to be sharply rhetorical. The speeches of Brutus and Antony at Caesar's burial, speeches which most schoolboys know by heart, are examples of the power that word arrangement has to move the listener. When parallelism works in combination with other structures, it is, though less rhetorical, no less effective. In this sentence, for example, the parallelism of the phrases following the colon brings them together into a unit which, in turn, strikes a just balance with the phrase preceding the colon:

Rousseau's *Confessions* is a chronicle of self-pity: for the dereliction of parents, the infidelity of friends, the hostility of the world.

LOOSE AND PERIODIC SENTENCES

The terms "loose" and "periodic" as characterizers of a sentence refer to its syntax, specifically to the way in which principal and subordinate elements are arranged. In a *loose* sentence, the main clause is completed early and the qualifying elements follow.

> The *Prelude* is an autobiographical poem in which Wordsworth tried to represent the origin and growth of poetic feeling from the dim impressions of infancy through the highly formative experiences of youth into the troubled and frustrated years of young manhood.

In general, the loose sentence is relaxed and informal precisely because it makes use of the natural structure of the language, proceeding from subject (with modifiers, if any) to object (in this example, with a modifier of considerable complexity and length). The *periodic* sentence "shapes" its structure more formally, placing modifiers so that the predication of the sentence, and therefore its direction and intent, is not clear until at or near the end.

> Through the dim impressions of infancy, the highly formative experiences of youth, and the troubled and frustrated years of young manhood, Wordsworth's autobiographical poem, *The Prelude,* tries to represent the origin and growth of poetic feeling.

The purpose of the periodic sentence is twofold: (a) it increases the tension of a sentence by withholding all or part of the predication, and (b) it brings modifiers into prominence by gathering them within the area where the tension has been created. It is useful, then, wherever control of the reader's attention is vitally important. Because it involves some infringement on the natural course of the sentence, however, the periodic device is quickly noticed, and its prolonged use, as in Henry James's novels, marks a style as clearly idiosyncratic. Whether or not the idiosyncrasy is desirable depends largely on whether or not the kinds of interruptions introduced are suitable to the matter and purpose of the piece. A sentence as hesitant and tortured as this one is certainly ill-suited to strong assertion:

> He knew with the suddenness of insight to which he had grown accustomed in his new mental state that these, the infertile flowers of a life too long spent in what had been, from whatever point of view one chose to examine it, a manner excessively solitary, were not now, and never had been, the sort of tributes to lay at the feet, if so pagan and oriental a tradition of worship were not presumptuous and uncharacteristic for him to consider, of his beloved, and too long neglected, friend.

Nor are the balanced periods of this sentence suitable for quiet and tentative statement of opinion:

> This man, long the consort of criminals and enemy of the law-abiding, a petty tyrant of back alleys made powerful by the corruption of those in high places and relentless by his insatiable greed and vanity, has again demonstrated his cunning as well as the indifference of those charged with the public welfare by seizing in our time of greatest need the very resources on which we most depended for our sustenance.

The point of these examples is that the periodic sentence is a flexible instrument, adaptable to thunderous indictment as well as to introspection. But whatever its content and whatever its tone, it draws attention to the informative detail incidental to the principal assertion. The loose sentence is like a kite, its tail of dependencies fluttering at the end; the periodic sentence is like a ceremony in which the rolling out of the red carpet prepares for the entrance of the chief dignitary.

RHYTHM

The effects which the structural devices discussed above have on a reader are partly the result of the meaning conveyed within each and partly the result of the rhythm, or cadence, of the structure itself. Although it is not possible, short of writing a treatise on the subject, to present an adequate account of prose rhythms in English, it is worth while to note that there are such rhythms and that they do affect the total meaning of a prose passage. The words generally used to describe various rhythms are largely metaphorical—such words as "leisurely," "crabbed," "sonorous," and "labored"—and hard to define in specific terms. The fact that English is an *accented* language, however, and that words commonly have only one major accent suggests that these adjectives must refer, in some measure, to the succession of accented and unaccented syllables.

In poetry we are accustomed to "scanning" lines according to accentual patterns, and there is no reason that one cannot scan prose in the same fashion. Many scholars and critics have indeed done just that, but their findings do not as yet provide enough evidence to make it possible for a writer to rely on the effect he may produce from a particular succession of accents—not that a writer is likely to go about the business by sounding on his fingers anyway. The inadequacy of the analyses made so far is attributable to many causes: as noted above, rhythm accounts for only a part of the total meaning of a sentence and it is hard to separate that part from the rest; even could it be separated, so little has been known until recently about the role of pitch in conveying meaning that a further separation between the effects of rhythm and of pitch must still be made; and, finally, modern prosodists are convinced that, beneath the accents indigenous to each word there are other kinds of accents which arise from the association of words into meaningful utterances, subaccents which may be quite as important to the rhythm of poetry and prose as those which would be indicated by a traditional scanning. The most that can be said in such brief space may take the form of two general observations: (1) a long succession of monosyllabic words creates some sense of the unrelatedness of parts, perhaps because so large a number of the subordinating conjunctions and prepositions in English are dis- or trisyllabic; (2) attempts to imitate the regularity of poetic meters are nearly always detrimental to prose.

EUPHONY

Like rhythm, euphony is a characteristic of prose to which no good writer is indifferent but one about which very little advice can be given. The exploitation of sound is particularly noticeable in poetry, of course, where it often serves for emphasis and for confirming the relationship of words in the poem as well as for more special effects. In prose, the attempt to make "linkèd harmonies" is seldom worth the effort it requires. At the same time, there are conjunctions of sound which a fastidious writer of prose will avoid: a series of words ending in -ion ("The notion that there could be provision of equal portions of the spoils for every nation is so serious an evasion of intelligent speculation that . . ."); a succeeding pair ending in -ing ("He stayed through the meeting seeming not to care what . . ."); a succession of polysyllables of any termination ("The prodigious celerity and ingenuity characteristic of reactions stimulated by . . ."); accidental alliteration ("They knocked not noticeably louder than anyone else, but . . ."), especially of sibilants ("Since separating silver from baser metals is scarcely as easy a process as . . ."); successive prepositional phrases beginning with the same preposition ("At the middle of the bottom of the lower half of the sheet of graph paper he put . . ."). The generalization deducible from such specific cases is that repetition of sound is often dangerous in prose. Again, the generalization is subject to many exceptions and has no value except as a general caution. Of so-called harsh or uneuphonious sounds, nothing need be said save that they have their uses and are perhaps less likely to be abused, in the long run, than those which are thought to be "sweet."

CONSISTENCY IN VIEWPOINT

The devices so far discussed generally do their work of providing balance in a sentence by calculated management and are therefore more the mark of the studied than of the natural style. Even in the free flow of language, however, balance is desirable and necessary. There, it comes primarily from consistency in viewpoint, a matter which may be examined under five separate headings.

Person. There are, grammatically speaking, three persons in English: the first person (speaker), the second person (person spoken to), and the third person (person spoken about). Consistency demands that there be no unmeaningful shifts in person, and that sentences be so constructed as to eliminate ambiguity of person. To write

Everyone likes pleasure, but you shouldn't be its slave

is to move, for no adequate reason, from the third person ("Everyone") to the second ("you"). A proper choice of pronoun for the second clause not only corrects the grammatical error but improves the rhetorical quality of the sentence:

Everyone likes pleasure, but no one should be its slave.

The phrase above, "for no adequate reason," is meant to catch the eye. As a matter of fact, there is *a* reason for the shift in the illustrative sentence, even though it is not an "adequate" reason. Modern English actually uses *two* persons for the indefinite pronoun rather than the traditional *one.* In colloquial speech we commonly use "you" to indicate the indefinite, saying, "When you try to figure out a problem like this, you invariably discover the depth of your ignorance." The "you" of this sentence is not the person-spoken-to but the person-spoken-about. Actually, the person-spoken-about in this situation seems to make a more intimate inclusion of the speaker himself and of the person-spoken-to than does the indefinite "one." In more formal discourse, we adopt a generic noun ("a man," "a person") or an indefinite pronoun ("anyone," "someone"); more and more rarely, in American English, does the once-traditional form "one" appear. No matter which form is used, however, the rule of consistency stands; it is bad to shift persons unmeaningfully.

Number. Like shifts in person, shifts in number generally stem either from carelessness or from the confusion that still marks the activity of the indefinite pronouns in English. That a student, after years of the study of English, should write

The practice of simony, like that of granting indulgences, were common in the medieval church

is inexcusable; that one should get tripped up in a sentence like

> Everyone has their own way of doing things

is, considering the double suggestion in "everyone," not entirely surprising. A careful grammarian would point out that "one" is singular and is so considered by the writer since he employs a singular form of the verb; pragmatists point out that "every-" obviously implies more than one and has good cause to assert its plurality in the adjective "their" even if it does not do so in the verb. The debate about these pronouns rages wherever English is taught and differences in use occur wherever it is spoken, but the practice of treating what the textbooks consider to be singular pronouns as though they are plural if the sense of plurality can be inferred appears to be increasing and now occurs even in the speech of educated people. It is not, however, commonly encountered in the serious writing of those people, and it is on such ground that a stand affirming the rightness of the singular concept of the indefinite pronouns *everyone, anyone, no one* must rest:

> Everyone has his own way of doing things.

Maintaining consistency in number is necessary not only within the sentence but also in the sequence of sentences. If not absolutely wrong, it is at least confusing to write:

> *Soldiers* highly trained in the convention of traditional warfare *are* often terrified by the irregular. *This soldier* cannot accommodate *himself* to the tactic which *he has* never encountered. So it was with the Roman *troops* when *they* faced the unorthodox attacks of the barbarians from the North.

Tense. Consistency in the use of tenses does not limit the writer to the use of a single tense within a sentence or passage, but it does limit him to a sequence. The most common errors in tense found on students' papers come from failure to understand the relationships indicated in this grouping:

I	II
present tense	past tense
perfect tense	past perfect tense
future tense	conditional tense
auxiliaries: may	auxiliaries: might
can	could
shall, will	should, would
has, have	had

Crossing the tenses of one group with the other may disturb the time balance in a sentence:

> If Arnold *had not used* the phrase "sweetness and light" so frequently, the importance he *attaches* to it *would be* less apparent than he *wanted* it to be.

CORRECTED: If Arnold *had not used* the phrase "sweetness and light" so frequently, the importance he *attached* to it *would have been* less apparent than he *wanted* it to be.

The ramifications of tense order are many but the little chart above is a simple and handy guide for the most common perplexities of this sort.

One further note about tense is relevant here. The present tense is a particularly lively one in English. It not only indicates current action:

I *see* your books are new

and habitual action:

I *hear* the opera every Christmas

and future action:

He *goes* to Paris next spring

but is also useful in animating the past, particularly in narrative passages:

Lincoln *strides* into the committee room, his face rigid with anger

and in presenting textual analysis:

In this episode, Homer *introduces* the goddess who is to watch over the fortunes of Telemachus and Odysseus throughout their adventures.

The use of the present tense in textual analysis is so important to the writer of critical essays that it deserves emphasis. If he is referring to a source, and his interest is in the content of the source, not the historical situation in which it appeared, he should use the present tense:

Professor Wilson *suggests* that "solid" is actually a misreading for "*sordid*" in Hamlet's famous lament, "O that this too too solid flesh would melt!"

This use of the present tense is proper whether or not the author is still alive:

Goethe's interest in Faust-the-man *is* greatest of all in the last act of Part II where care overwhelms the proud humanitarian Faust has become.

Both of these illustrations use the present tense because emphasis is on the text and the text is, in some sense, always alive.

Where emphasis is on the author and the historical situation in which statements are made, the situation changes:

A few months ago, Professor Wilson *suggested,* in an article in *PMLA*, that. . . .

As he grew older Goethe's interest in Faust-the-man *deepened.*

The historical situation and the ever-presentness of the text may, and frequently will, occur together:

Crèvecœur *was* the first to attempt a definition of the independent spirit of the colonists. His popular book *depicts* the emergence of. . . .

Mood.   Traditional textbooks list three moods for English: the indicative, the subjunctive, the imperative. These they distinguish as referring to definite action (indicative), probable or desired or predicted action, or action contrary to fact (subjunctive), and command (imperative). The indicative and imperative moods are firmly fixed in the language:

> According to report, Carlyle *rewrote* his history of the French revolution from memory after the manuscript was accidentally destroyed. (indicative)

> Bertrand Russell's advice is this: in matters of thought *distrust* all authority. (imperative)

Of the subjunctive, however, there seem to be only vestigial remains. The contrary-to-fact condition still exerts influence on the verb *to be,* as in

> If Ptolemy *were* right, there would be no way to account for the behavior of heavenly bodies in galaxies distinct from our own

but, even there, ordinarily only in the past tense. The action denoting probability or wish or prediction may be subjunctive, but there is today very little use of the "subjunctive" form of the verb, save as that term is applied to the use of certain auxiliaries (as in "*may be* subjunctive" in this sentence).

The demise of the subjunctive need not concern us here. The one point to be made is that undiscriminating shift of mood within a sentence is a troubling matter to the reader because it requires him to follow a shift in attitude-toward-action for which he is not prepared. Such shifts are particularly annoying when they are from the imperative to either of the other moods. This sentence is bad for that reason:

> It *may be* that Toynbee *is* right about repetition in history, but *take* the similar idea of Spengler and you *will see* how different the conclusions from such an idea *can be.*

> CORRECTED: It *may be* that Toynbee *is* right about repetition in history, but Spengler *had* a similar idea and *reached* a very different conclusion.

Voice.   Some modern grammarians are as dubious about there being two "voices" in English as about there being a "subjunctive," and they prefer to talk of a "passive construction" rather than a "passive voice" since the verbs used for such a construction do not alter their form. Whichever term one chooses, it is clear that there are two patterns in our language which differ in the relationship of their grammatical subject to the predicate verb.

In the active voice, the grammatical subject indicates the doer-of-action:

James I created a new dynasty in England.

In the passive voice, the grammatical subject indicates the receiver-of-action:

Charles II was beheaded in 1649.

Both voices have their usefulness, naturally, or they would not exist. For some reason (one on which psychologists would do well to spend some energy) the passive voice has a remarkable attraction for the semi-educated and the officious. There may be some connection between its use and legal phraseology, one borrowing the other's linguistic mannerism in the hope that legal dignity and authority will accompany the borrowing. Whatever the source, it turns out ugly instructions like this one from the Office of Price Stabilization, an order once prominently displayed in places of business for the edification of all who read:

Quality and Quantity Are Required To Be Maintained.

On second thought, it may be the impersonality of such an expression that pleases the bureaucrat. *Who* requires it? *Of whom* is it required? The iron hand wears here a velvet glove, but it is a shoddy velvet glove indeed. Because stuffiness and impersonality are the enemies of a good style, a writer does well to avoid the passive whenever he can do so without awkwardness.

The problems of *person* and *voice* often combine to annoy the writer of expository prose. If he is describing or explaining an activity or condition in which human participation is implicit, he has these choices: (1) to create a semifictitious personage to whom he can refer ("the writer" is the one often used in this book); (2) to reify abstractions, making them the subjects of active verbs ("Such an analysis requires careful examination . . ."); (3) to use the "editorial *we*" ("If we examine this analysis carefully, we see that . . ."); (4) to avoid "we" by using "one" ("If one examines this analysis carefully, one sees that . . ."); (5) to employ direct address ("You must examine such an analysis . . ."); (6) to resort to impersonal constructions ("From an examination of such an analysis it becomes apparent that . . ."); or (7) to use the passive voice ("If such an analysis is carefully examined . . ."). There is no rule of thumb for deciding among them, and within a long piece of prose a writer will ordinarily use several. Such differences as are discernible alter from context to context, and generalizations about them are likely therefore to be somewhat misleading. Nonetheless, a few recommendations are warrantable if they are accompanied by the warning about blind acceptance which is proper to most generalizations about the use of language:

a. A semifictitious *persona* often becomes a trap for the writer simply because he has no real existence as a flesh-and-blood being, even in the writer's imagination. Gradually he is transformed from a generalized being into a prototype to which all vices or virtues can with impunity be attributed. The reader, meeting this bloodless character on page after page, develops an independence from him rather than the identification with him which was the author's aim in introducing him in the first place.

b. Making abstractions act as vital agents in a sentence is, on the whole, a good practice, principally because it is forceful and economical. The active verbs brighten and give movement to matter which might otherwise be heavy and static. The danger in this procedure is that the abstractions will become so independent that they obscure their derivation from separate events, that is, from the "facts" which are their ground and reason for being.

c. The "editorial *we*" and the formal "one" are both such obvious conveniences that they have little vital juice in them. "We," particularly, is a convention which has lost much of its original weight. The true "editorial *we*," like the "royal *we*," is meant to convey the power of concerted action. The critical essay which uses "we" to mean "the author" is probably making the best of a bad situation: the writer wants to avoid the intrusion of himself-as-a-person which takes place if he uses the pronoun "I," and he wants also to avoid the awkwardness and heaviness of passive and impersonal constructions. There is one "we" which seems to have a better argument for existence, that which a writer uses when he *joins* the reader in speculation; if misused, it is likely to sound patronizing ("We don't want to make that sort of error, do we?"), but judiciously and honestly used it helps to strengthen the communication between writer and reader.

d. Direct address is proper for commands but likely to be annoyingly avuncular or magisterial when it is used to point out the application of statement to the reader's own life. When "you" is a substitute for the third person indefinite pronoun, it does not carry those overtones, but it is still rather colloquial for formal expository prose.

e. Impersonal constructions and the passive voice depend on the static verbs of equivalence (copulative verbs) and therefore have a certain rigidity about them. Moreover, as noted above, they tend to obscure the *real* agent of whatever relationships are predicated. Certainly they are not always to be avoided; neither are they to be preferred if alternatives readily present themselves.

The grammar and rhetoric of the sentence are, of course, to some extent also the grammar and rhetoric of the paragraph and of the essay or book. Increased dimension raises additional problems for the writer, however, and at the same time offers him scope for more complex effects. Those problems and effects are the subject of the following chapter.

⟘ Logic and Strategy in the
Paragraph and Essay

ALTHOUGH THE COMPOSITION of an essay must proceed by sentences, it is only in a discussion of paragraphs that one comes close to its vital elements, the thought which is its substance and the assessment of situation which guide the presentation of that thought. What we want to express is a sort of intricate tapestry in our minds, and when we come to express it we are faced with the physical necessity of drawing the threads out, one after another, into separate sentences and, at the same time, with the knowledge that as fast as they are drawn out they must be rewoven to make a facsimile of the tapestry of thought which they are supposed to represent. The metaphor does not do full justice to the complexity of the process because it does not indicate how shabbily and inadequately sentences represent the thoughts from which they spring unless great craft is brought to their organization, to the reweaving of the tapestry into something like its original form. It may serve, however, to suggest that logic, for all its importance, is an insufficient instrument for composition, and it may serve also to give art its due as the only means by which a writer can hope to produce any satisfactory account of his thought.

Logic and strategy, the rational ordering of substance and the artistic "making whole," work together, logic massing the battalions of substance in order, and strategy deploying them to the best advantage. Without the battalions there can be no deployment, of course; but without deployment, without the art of assembling and dissembling, the power of substance is blunted. It is the necessary dependence of one on the other that makes discussions of the "organization" of paragraphs seem so unreal, "outlines" so empty, and "devices" for gaining coherence, unity, and emphasis so artificial. The distance between analysis and creation is always great; yet an artist is necessarily an analyst and that may be justification enough for analysis as a means to execution. If analysis is understood to be descriptive, and only tentatively so at that, and not taken as a prescription to be followed without reflection, it can be of use to the amateur writer as an insight into what he has been doing all along. Even if, like M. Jourdain's discovery that all his life he had been speaking prose without knowing that he did so, it simply makes him proud of his accomplishment, it will have served some purpose. If it increases his ability to see how others have manipulated their materials for best effect, it will be a guide to good models. And, finally, if it teaches him a few tactical maneuvers, it will have been effort well spent.

The caution with which the analysis of the paragraph has been approached so far is itself a strategy. The matter is a complex one, far too complex for a half-dozen ready-made rules. And the readers of this book, it is assumed, are themselves well enough acquainted with language so that they are inclined to resist, more or less consciously, any generalizations about so complex a matter. The strategy of the first two paragraphs of the chapter is designed to reassure the reader at the same time as it makes a case for doing what is to be done. The two rather elaborate metaphors and the allusion to a well-known incident in a French comedy represent an effort to make early contact with the reader. The pronoun "we" appears in the second sentence and is intended to act as a further bond between reader and writer, a "we" of common experience quite different from the "we" of concerted authority or of omniscience.

Beneath these surface deployments, substance exerts its pressure. The substance of the first paragraph might be represented in these words:

> The writing of a paragraph or an essay is a matter of using literary art to fashion the substance of thought into some verbal equivalent of its original complexity.

And that of the second in these words:

> The matter and the manner of a composition are so dependent on each other that separate analysis of each falsifies both. Analysis is nonetheless justified because it does increase appreciation and may increase skill in execution.

If the paragraphs can be so succinctly summarized, is the effort of elaborating them through various means a wasteful and wasted one? Not any more than saying "The President appeals to the people for their support in this time of peril" instead of "Support the President" is wasteful and wasted. Both modes of expression are useful; each expresses more than it says because the strategy assumes much about the relationship between speaker and listener (or writer and reader) and is calculated to stir a particular kind of response. Yet the two are substantively equivalent. The difference between an order and a plea is obvious enough, and their respective strategies are equally obvious; but, obvious or not, strategy is always a part of expression, and the tough-

minded realist who wants to cut out all the fripperies and get down to
the facts is simply announcing that he prefers one strategy to another,
Whether or not his strategy is the better one depends not on "getting
down to the facts" but on the complexity of his thought and feeling, the
purpose of his expression, and the character of his audience. Unless he
talks, or writes, in a vacuum, he relies on strategy in the use of language just as he relies on gesture, facial expression, and the cut of his
clothes to convey the manner of man he is.

THE TOPIC SENTENCE

The topic sentence is a more or less fictitious entity. Sometimes it
makes a real appearance, but fully as often it is something in the atmosphere of the paragraph, a core of meaning like those sentences abstracted above from the opening paragraphs of this chapter. The schoolboy notion of a topic sentence as the big firecracker from which a string
of little firecrackers is suspended, each due to go off with a tiny "pop"
when the big one is ignited, has little relationship to the truth. An accomplished writer of prose is much too well aware of the weaving required for a good representation of his thought to lay it out, thread by
thread, with no regard for the original design. But accomplished writers
no longer need to read analyses of this kind, so it is wise to consider,
even in half-fictional terms, the problems of those who do.

Paragraphs can be written, of course, in firecracker order. For some
purposes, that may be their best order. An explanation of process, for
example, is most efficient if the steps of the process are chronologically
catalogued:

> An omelet requires strictly fresh ingredients and a skilled hand. The yolks
> and whites of the eggs are separated first and the yolks beaten slightly
> with a fork until they are well blended. To the blended yolks is then
> added. . . .

Even in this simple process, a strategy is apparent, and a part of that
strategy is the opening sentence which serves as a kind of warning and
summary-in-advance.

A more helpful view of the topic sentence comes from abandoning
any attempt to select a single complete grammatical utterance in the
paragraph as it is finally written and from considering instead sentences
like the "abstracted" sentences presented above. These are actually central propositions which it is the business of the paragraph to develop
as their nature and their purpose make necessary. They correspond to
the topical headings of an outline save that here they are presented, as
they usually are not presented in outlines, in complete sentences. To
facilitate discussion at this point, it will be useful to examine a core or
"abstracted" sentence which is short and uncomplicated. What is said of

it will be relevant to more complicated sentences but will require less dealing with specific detail.

The battlement speech in *Macbeth* expresses perfectly the despair that follows discovery in a tragedy.

This sentence—call it "topic" or "core" or what one will—is clearly one which could provide the ground for much more than a single paragraph, and it is useful here for that very reason. To see what its possibilities for expansion are, one may begin with a grammatical analysis:

SUBJECT The battlement speech in *Macbeth*
VERB   expresses perfectly
OBJECT   the despair that follows discovery in a tragedy.

Now the subject of a sentence is always the "given" of the proposition. It is the thing of which something is to be predicated and is therefore above suspicion, so to speak, for the moment. Its being above suspicion does not mean, however, that it is necessarily self-explanatory, and a certain amount of information may be needed in this example to identify the speech, as a preliminary to satisfaction of other obligations implicit in the sentence. The verb makes the first step beyond what is to be taken for granted in the proposition, and in this instance that step is a big one. The meaning of "expresses" as it is used here must be explained and, one would expect, illustrated as well; but it cannot be adequately elaborated apart from its object, which requires some attention to the generalization that despair follows discovery in a tragedy as well as elucidation of the terms "despair," "tragedy," and particularly "discovery." Since verb and object are both, as parts of a proposition, that which is "to be proved," they can be linked in the single term "predicate" and the sentence redivided in this fashion:

SUBJECT   The battlement speech in *Macbeth*
PREDICATE expresses perfectly the despair that follows discovery in a
      tragedy.

Now what is gained by this division? Simply a separation of two distinct obligations which the writer takes upon himself when he writes the sentence: (1) to explain the subject, and (2) to explain and defend ("prove" in the sense used earlier in this book) the predication. If the core sentence is to be expanded only into a paragraph, the writer will limit explanation and defense accordingly; if it is to be expanded into an essay, he will plan to take one paragraph or several for each of his obligations. If it is into several paragraphs that the expansion is to fall, each of those paragraphs, too, will have its core sentence, and each core sentence will likewise be divisible into subject and predicate, laying upon the writer obligations like those already illustrated.

So long as he fulfills his obligations, the writer is free to devise whatever strategy he thinks most likely to suit his matter, his purpose, and his reader. For that reason, what is conventionally called the "topic sentence" may be broken into parts or, if kept intact, may be placed at one of several places in the paragraph, or so transformed by rhetoric that its presence comes more through the "sense" of the paragraph than through any explicit statement. A paragraph picked almost at random from the writing of an English essayist and novelist will illustrate the point:

> No, I distrust Great Men. They produce a desert of uniformity around them and often a pool of blood too, and I always feel a little man's pleasure when they come a cropper. Every now and then one reads in the newspapers some such statement as: "The *coup d'état* appears to have failed, and Admiral Toma's whereabouts is at present unknown." Admiral Toma had probably every qualification for being a Great Man—an iron will, personal magnetism, dash, flair, sexlessness—but fate was against him, so he retires to unknown whereabouts instead of parading history with his peers. He fails with a completeness which no artist and no lover can experience, because with them the process of creation is itself an achievement, whereas with him the only possible achievement is success.
>
> E. M. FORSTER, *Two Cheers for Democracy*

The paragraph is not so much an expansion of any stated proposition as the progress through several propositions which, taken together, culminate in a core of meaning, a something which we might say the paragraph is "about":

> Those men who are conventionally called "great," unlike those who act out of love or out of the desire to create, leave nothing behind them if they fail.

The author's assertion of distrust, his many ironic turns of phrase, his fictitious Admiral Toma: all are stratagems, and it is to them that the richness of the paragraph is almost entirely indebted.

The sentence which comes closest to being a "topic sentence" in the paragraph just quoted is the last one. In another paragraph, it might be the second or a middle sentence. The location of the topic sentence, then, if indeed it is ever stated in so many words, will vary. The paragraph may move from or toward it, or it may rise to it and fall away from it like a wave sweeping the shore.

DEVICES OF EXPANSION

Whatever the location of the core sentence, its work is carried on by the other sentences of the paragraph. The division of that work—explanation of subject, explanation and defense of predication—has already been presented. Now it is important to examine the means by which writers do the explaining and the defending. The warning which appears again and again in this book deserves repetition at this point: to describe the devices of expansion is not to suggest that writers think of them as devices or that they consciously "fill out" each statement as though they were stuffing a pillowcase with feathers. To repeat, the expansion is (a) a necessary explanation of the core substance and (b) a part of the strategy by which the author contrives to render his full meaning. It is not separate from the core of the paragraph but is actually the medium through which the core of meaning is transmitted. Treating each device in isolation falsifies the actual situation somewhat, but it is the most convenient and useful procedure and is therefore the one chosen.

The most common device of expansion is *restatement*. Despite the dangers of repetition, the simple fact is that a certain amount of repetition is necessary in the use of language, not only for the sake of emphasis, but quite as much for the full expression of whatever is to be said. Restatement is not a completely literal repetition, of course, and that is why it succeeds. It is a second or a third attempt to weave a design from the strands of thought; if the first does not succeed, one of the later ones may, or all of them together will give a fuller reproduction than any one. Note how restatement works in this paragraph:

> Each generation takes a special pleasure in removing the household gods of its parents from their pedestals and consigning them to the cupboard. The prophet or pioneer, after being at first declared to be unintelligible or absurd, has a brief spell of popularity, after which he is said to be conventional, and then antiquated. We may find more than one reason for this. A movement has more to fear from its disciples than from its critics. The great man is linked to his age by his weakest side; and his epigoni, who are not great men, caricature his message and make it ridiculous. Besides, every movement is a reaction, and generates counter-reactions. The pendulum swings backwards and forwards. Every institution not only carries within it the seeds of its own dissolution, but prepares the way for its most hated rival.   w. r. inge, *Outspoken Essays*

One would not characterize this paragraph as repetitive; yet it is full of restatement: the second sentence is the first sentence looked at in different perspective; the "pendulum" sentence uses a metaphor to restate the one which precedes it; and the final sentence, which is as close to being the topic sentence of the paragraph as any, is an accumulation and repetition of parts of the first, the fourth, and the fifth sentences. Good restatement enriches and colors explanation and is therefore invaluable as a means of conveying the complexity of thought.

Example provides the most obvious means of expansion, and just because it is obvious it is uniquely suited to the job of clarifying the obscure and of making the general specific and the abstract concrete. Although they do not constitute formal proof—one swallow does not make a summer, as the saying goes—examples are really attempts at proof because they display the phenomenal evidence which is the ground for general statements. For that reason, they must be treated with respect; a faulty example is bad not simply because it is in itself inappropriate but because its failure detracts from the authority of the generalization it is supposed to support.

Whether or not an example needs to have attention called to its character as example depends on its context and its length. An example which is only a phrase or single sentence will generally not need any indicator of its presence:

> The most enlightened members of the state—*the scribes, the councilors, and the wise men of the inner temple*—have for a long time predicted this event.

> Men of lofty vision and deep conviction are often regarded with suspicion by their fellow men. *Socrates was condemned to die for corrupting the youth of Athens; Jesus was crucified for blasphemy.* Yet vision and conviction, being themselves incorruptible, have their way in the world.

Examples of greater length are sometimes treated more formally; either they are set off from the main body of the text, as the examples above are set off, or they are preceded by a signal of some sort:

> The life of a President is so exacting that it must be relieved by regular periods of physical exertion. Every President within recent memory has found need for the stimulation of muscle tone and the relaxation of nervous tension which come from a vigorous hour or so of brisk activity. Mr. Eisenhower, *for example,* plays golf several days a week; Mr. Truman used to take a fast morning walk; Roosevelt swam daily in the White House pool, and his predecessor, Hoover was an ardent fisherman.

> The fable has a double tradition in Western literature. From Æsop it inherits a certain moral solemnity; from La Fontaine, the habit of ironical reflection on the disparity between appearance and reality and between precept and practice in human affairs. Although the fable is no longer so popular as it once was, its modern practitioners have found it a useful instrument for satire of man and morality alike. *The two modern fabulists who come most quickly to mind*—Edward Lear and James Thurber—are both swift to detect the ludicrous in action and precept, but neither is so blunt as La Fontaine in exposing it.

The use of *supporting data* for statements, like that of examples, is a convenient and obvious means of clarifying and documenting whatever is predicated. The kind of data will be determined, of course, by the nature of the statement, and no illustrations are necessary here: statistics, tables, graphs, enumerations, diagrams, and citations of text, for instance, are all relevant. The means of handling such material within an essay are as varied as the nature of the material, and generalization about procedures is therefore difficult. The practice of relegating extensive documentation to footnotes or appendices is, in the main, a wise one, particularly if the exposition in the text itself does not depend on such documentation for its clarity. Where clarity is at stake, the supporting data should remain in the text and there be exposed as economically and attached as organically as possible.

Both example and supporting data are largely substantive, though they have strategic value, too. Some other devices of expansion have less to do with support, or proof, of assertions than with their illumination. Among them, *anecdote* is one of the most valuable. Now it is clear that an anecdote is, in one sense, also an attempt to insist on the soundness of a statement by showing its representation in experience. But the sense of the particular and informal which is part of an anecdote detracts from its value as documentation at the same time as it adds to its value as illustration. Whether the anecdote is historical or contemporary, about the actions of someone well known or about the writer's personal experience, it adds the power that storytelling has for all readers. Abstractions, after all, are the dried leaves of event; to use anecdote as an expansion of a general statement is therefore to do no more than bring it back to life.

Like anecdote, *quotation* and *allusion* are more dramatic than substantive in character. They are different from anecdote, however, in being oblique aids to clarity and completeness. They suggest the rightness or the meaningfulness of preceding statements by proposing corollaries in the experience of writer and reader, corollaries which are called to mind by a familiar phrase or by mention of some figure or event which has taken on a particular character in the public consciousness. To describe Woodrow Wilson as "America's Robespierre" is to clarify and, at the same time, to add information so extensive that it would take pages of exposition to equal it. The problem which rises from the use of illusion is readily apparent from the example: if the allusion is within the reader's range of experience, it may be wonderfully effective; if it is outside that range, it may be annoying and will certainly do little to clarify. To some extent, the same thing may be said of the use of quotations, especially when they are presented elliptically:

> The medieval warning, *De gustibus* . . . , is more pertinent to fashions in clothing than to styles in art.

Many quotations, however, are so much a part of the public treasury that a writer may be almost sure of his reader's familiarity with them. The problem with them is that their very familiarity may annoy. A writer must simply steer his way carefully between obscurity and triteness if he chooses to amplify meaning by the use of allusion and quotation; moreover, if he is wise, he will be sparing of both, for a text which relies on these two devices very heavily is likely to look like a connoisseur's display of dainties rather than a firm and rich elucidation of thought.

ORDER

The classical structure of the oration was for a long time the model for ordering expository prose. Its three main divisions provide a scheme which is at once handsome and comprehensive: introduction (*exordio*), body (*præcognitio, partitio, explicatio, amplificatio, applicatio*), and conclusion (*peroratio*). There is a brief rhetorical opening; then a careful statement and dissection of the thesis, followed by an analysis of each part, an elaboration and a direct application to the life of the listener; finally, a summation designed to bring the weight of the thesis to bear on the listeners' feeling and on their desire for action. Implicit in the scheme is a recognition that reason is paramount but that it must be linked with feeling before it will produce action. And implicit also is the condition of argument—an assertion whose truth it is the purpose of the exposition to prove beyond question. Everything is taken care of in the most orderly fashion: terms are defined, possible ambiguities eliminated, implications and assumptions explained, proofs adduced, and examples provided. Beneath the formal structure an almost infinite variety is possible in the organization or order of matters in each part. One section may proceed by classification, another by contrasts, a third by chronology, and so on. Yet, whatever the internal variety, the enclosing structure remains firm and almost relentless.

The formal pattern of the classical oration is no longer in fashion, not even in sermons, which for a long time continued to exploit it after it had largely disappeared from general use. In its place—partly, no doubt, from analogy with discoveries in the natural sciences—there has grown a tendency to make even expository writing "express" in its form the nature of its substance. It is not easy to say how form and substance can be made one, and it may be an exaggeration to speak of equivalence where only appropriateness is possible. Yet, whatever the formula, it is certainly true that some material, used for a particular purpose, is better dealt with in one form than in another. A particular argument, for instance, may achieve its greatest clarity and power in the form of a dialogue; one sort of proof may be most appropriately presented by the orderly tracing of cause and effect, another by the uninterrupted accumulation of supporting data; classification may best suit analysis; or chronology, narration. No general rule is possible, of course, for writers' intentions vary so widely that only ingenious combinations of form are sufficient to satisfy them. It is possible, however, to describe several kinds of organization and to point out uses and abuses of each.

Order by *classification* is the most obvious means of organization for expository prose, and it comes closest to the oratorical pattern mentioned above. The proposition which is the core of the essay (e.g., "Washington's policy of avoiding 'foreign entanglements' is no longer possible for any civilized country") is first divided, as suggested above, into "subject" and "predicate." The subject ("Washington's policy of avoiding 'foreign entanglements'") is explained by reference to his Farewell Address and, in order that the policy may be accurately represented, by some account of the events during his tenure of office. Then the predicate ("is no longer possible for any civilized country") is developed—in this case, "proved"—by a presentation of arguments classified, let us say, as "economic," "political," and "moral." The classification itself arises from an initial listing of arguments and from the observation of similarities among those arguments. A decision about which of the three classes to present first depends in part on the strength of the evidence for each and in part on the particular emphasis a writer wishes to provide. A contributor to the *Christian Century*, for instance, might discuss all three classes but elaborate only "moral" intensively, placing it third in the series so that it might come as a climax to the whole line of argument. A political analyst in the New York *Times* might subordinate "moral" and "economic"; an editorialist for *New Masses* would undoubtedly make "economic" the climactic classification. Classification always depends in part on the observer's way of looking at a matter, so it is not surprising at all that various writers will classify and develop the same matter differently. Nor is it undesirable that they do so. The important thing is that the classifications, whatever they are, be borne out by the material and that they be sufficient to encompass it.

It is clear that order by classification requires that the subject matter be such as to lend itself to categories, to more or less watertight compartments. Classification is the handmaiden of analysis when analysis is concerned with what is static. To use it as the order for explaining a process is therefore inadvisable, for it reduces emphasis on action, which is the heart of process.

A second, and also common, order is that of *cause and effect*. Where classification throws emphasis on substance, cause and effect throws it on the active relationship between substances, on the alteration which results from their coming into contact with each other. Obviously, then, it is particularly useful for the explanation of process. At its simplest, this kind of order may seem to present no problems: cause precedes effect in fact and should therefore precede it in report on fact. Yet even to explain the chain of events which turns water into ice requires attention to more than one cause—to pressure as well as to temperature. Perhaps it is the term itself that misleads one into thinking of cause and effect as simple; "causes and effects" would be far more accurate, for few things happen in this world as the result of a single cause and few causes have only a single effect. This multiplicity and variety require that the writer select among causes and effects those relevant to his purposes (all are relevant to the action itself), and it is in the act of selection that trouble is likely to occur.

In the *Brothers Karamazov* Father Zossima argues that every man is responsible for everything, that responsibility is total because all events are inevitably interconnected. The opposite contention has been advanced by a modern English statesman of deep religious convictions who argues that each man's responsibility ceases at the point of action precisely because his action is only one of the innumerable actions which together produce an effect. Whichever conclusion one comes to, this much is clear: the writer who uses cause and effect as a principle of order must be alert to causes and effects which do not at once meet the eye; he must be ready to explore for more of both and should perhaps begin from the assumption that apparent causes and effects may or may not be the most important or even the real ones. Once he has made his selection, he can proceed from one to the other in either direction, making the choice of direction depend on whether he wants emphasis to fall on causes or effects. If he finds, and decides to deal with, a plurality of causes and effects, he will also find the order of cause and effect insufficient and will almost certainly have to call on another principle of order to act in subordinate capacity. Think, for example, of the problem of explaining the causes of so simple an event as a summer shower. Does one begin with today's wind and heat or with the warm front which began to develop last week in Texas and the breakup of an ice pack in Greenland? For practical purposes the writer must restrict the causes and effects he considers according to their proximity to the event and according to their necessity; those which are distant and, though relevant, either not absolutely necessary to the effect or not of major importance, he must perforce ignore or skim over lightly. Those which are immediate and essential he retains or brings to the fore, marshaling them in such fashion as to make their relationships apparent.

The dominant connection which he must exploit in this procedure is a hybrid, a cross between "therefore" and "thereafter" which unites time and cause. Since he will find that the use of a word to indicate the one relationship is often enough to suggest the other, he will not need to reiterate signals at every step. On the other hand, the fact that succession often implies dependence and derivation sometimes leads a writer into the fallacy known as *post hoc ergo propter hoc*, the assumption that because one event follows another it is the consequence of the one it follows. The fallacy suggests the advisability of caution in the use of cause and effect as an order of development.

Where relationships are purely associative, of course, that order is manifestly improper; but even where they are derivative, it may be misleading. Unless the lines of causation and response can be clearly
sorted and exposed, it may be better to limit oneself to simple succession, carefully avoiding any indication of another relationship. The
cumulative effect will be much the same, and the particular links of
the chain will not then be subject to criticism.

In human experience, events seem to be inevitably related in time,
whatever their other relationships may be. It is natural, therefore, that
chronology should be an important principle of organization, even in
nonnarrative prose. Its importance is enhanced, however, by the fact
that all writing and speaking are also involved in duration so that
even in pure description of a static object chronology is implicated:
"What shall I describe *first?*" the novice asks. There would seem, then,
to be two kinds of chronological order, that which records the actual
progression of events (real chronology), and that which creates a progression which is not an action of the object but one of the observer (subjective chronology). Real chronology may be manipulated
for effect, the writer beginning, as Horace advised poets to do, in the
middle of things; or at the beginning, or at the end. Subjective, or
psychological, chronology is already a manipulation of the fact, generally a manipulation for the sake of emphasis: the writer begins by
describing the nose because it is the nose to which he wishes to give
prominence, or he holds back from describing the nose until the end
of his account for the very same reason. Most expository prose stays
within the sphere of real chronology, but the informal essay and, in
recent years, even the speculative essay have shown a disposition to
take liberties with it, to fuse the time of conscious, rational experience
with the time of memory and feeling in which conventional order is in-
verted, distorted, or reduced to simultaneity. The effects achieved by
such freedom are its best defense; for the purpose of this discussion
it may be wise to note that they are achievable only, like syncopation
in music, when a strong sense of real chronology lies behind them. The
amateur writer does well, then, to make sure that he can manipulate
the patterns of ordinary chronology before he attempts to represent
the extraordinary chronologies of subjective experience.

Aristotle noted that the ability to detect likenesses is one of the
sure signs of intelligence, and it is on this ability (which, of course,
implies the ability to detect differences) that he based his system of
classification and his theory of definition. The habit of creating order by
comparison and by *contrast* seems, as a matter of fact, to be almost as
natural to man as thought itself. Metaphor lies at the root of language
and is fundamentally comparative in nature, exposing a likeness which
is not patent but which is nonetheless real. To some degree all com-

parisons are useful in the same way—they call attention to characteristics which might otherwise escape the eye. An exposition of the concept of piety in The Book of Job may be greatly enriched by a comparative exposition of the same concept in Aeschylus' *Prometheus Bound,* the details of one revealing the absence or transformation of those details in the other. A discussion of a republican government's right of eminent domain profits from comparison of that right with a king's prerogative of entry and use for defense of the realm, the extent and power of the former becoming apparent only when the much more limited royal authority is described. Besides calling attention to detail, comparisons are particularly useful when the purpose of an exposition is to aggrandize or to demean; setting two objects or events against each other makes one into a touchstone or foil, a standard by which the other can be measured.

Managing a comparison is not easy, whether its purpose is simply to describe likenesses and differences or to solicit approval of one matter at the expense of another. If the explanation of each is developed separately, the force of comparison is diminished; if the objects or events are developed concurrently, each characteristic being balanced immediately against its foil or counterpart, the comparison becomes an annoying seesaw. Somehow the sense of integrity and the force of relationship must both be retained, a feat best accomplished by a judicious use of both procedures, coupled with another ordering device, perhaps that of classification. To return to the "piety" example mentioned above: the comparison might begin with a brief account of the cultural context of each of the works, using their approximate dates of composition as the initial links between them, then touching on the differences in the cultural context, and finally drawing the two together again on the subject matter of the essay—the embodiment in each of a concept of piety. At this point there comes an opportunity for further unifying by definition and by classification: determining the meaning of "piety" for this essay and stating the considerations relevant to exploration of the concept in these two works. The "body" of the essay may well continue the alternation between union and division: for each of the considerations to be developed, a sentence or more to point out the relevance of that consideration to both the Greek and the Hebrew work, then a point-by-point comparison of passages which illustrate the similarity or difference. And so on until the entire ground is covered.

Most comparisons, of course, are a compound of likenesses and differences, and the order of presentation is affected by the general rule of emphasis: the subordinate precedes the principal. This is true of a whole essay as well as of paragraphs or sections within it. By the same token, the place for concession or qualification is early rather than late. In the example given, if the differences between the two concepts of piety outweigh the likenesses, it is with the likenesses that the essay should begin. The essay thus falls "naturally" into two major divisions; within each, subdivisions will more or less imitate the arrangement of the larger unit to which they belong.

Because comparison implies a balancing, this kind of order provides opportunities for rhetorical parallels of all kinds, an opportunity not really satisfied by bare connectives like "on the other hand" and "in contrast." How adroit a writer must be to manage comparisons effectively one can best learn from observation.

> The uppermost idea with Hellenism is to see things as they really are; the uppermost idea with Hebraism is conduct and obedience. Nothing can do away with this ineffaceable difference. The Greek quarrel with the body and its desires is that they hinder right thinking; the Hebrew quarrel with them is that they hinder right acting. "He that keepeth the law, happy is he"; "Blessed is the man that feareth the Eternal, that delighteth greatly in His commandments";—that is the Hebrew notion of felicity; and, pursued with passion and tenacity, this notion would not let the Hebrew rest till, as is well known, he had at last got out of the law a network of prescriptions to enwrap his whole life, to govern every moment of it, every impulse, every action. The Greek notion of felicity, on the other hand, is perfectly conveyed in these words of a great French moralist: *"C'est le bonheur des hommes"*—when? when they abhor that which is evil? no;— when they exercise themselves in the law of the Lord day and night? no; —when they die daily? no;—when they walk about the New Jerusalem with palms in their hands? no;—but when they think aright, when their thought hits: *"quand ils pensent juste."* . . . The governing idea of Hellenism is *spontaneity of consciousness;* that of Hebraism, *strictness of conscience.*   MATTHEW ARNOLD, *Hebraism and Hellenism*

The four principles of organization discussed so far rely more or less heavily on a fifth, that of *climax*, or order of importance. It is no secret that emphasis, in a sentence as in a paragraph or an essay, is stronger at the beginning and at or near the end than in the middle. The order of the English sentence is partly responsible for that fact, no doubt, but more responsible is the human habit of expectation. Impressive climaxes and satisfying resolutions depend on the preparation that precedes them, and for that reason the usual order of matter is from the less to the more important. Now, as in chronological order, a writer may achieve special effect by doing the unexpected, by using an anticlimactic order. In general, however, that practice is useful only for surprise or for brief and violent emphasis, and it imposes upon its user the problem of retaining the reader's attention and of developing a stable perspective on the subject matter once the opening cannon has been fired.

Few essays of any length rely on a single organizing strategy for the good reason that readers expect a measure of variety in prose just as they expect a measure of uniformity in verse. Moreover, a flexible strategy makes it impossible for a writer to exploit the full resources of whatever material he has at hand. And, finally, a single principle of order is seldom sufficient to provide for the complexity of the matter it is intended to control. The professional writer is able to shift from one kind of order to another without taking thought. The tyro may have to lay out his strategy well in advance and follow its successive maneuvers scrupulously to avoid a rout. For him an *outline* is important and often essential.

THE OUTLINE

As the underlying metaphor implies, an outline describes the circumference of an essay and of each of its various parts. If, then, the earlier contention about topic sentences is sound, an outline is the orderly presentation of main assertions, those which are to be expanded by various devices. To make it any less than that is to respect form and to ignore substance. An outline for the projected essay on piety, for example, is little short of useless in this state:

> I. Introduction
> II. Body
>   A. Similarities
>   1. Idea of God
>   2. Idea of man
>   3. Idea of punishment
>   B. Differences
>   1. Idea of God
>   2. Idea of man
>   3. Idea of relationship
>   4. Idea of afterlife
>
>   .   .   .
>
>   .   .   .
>
> III. Conclusion

Yet that is what "outline" means to many who have been taught to look upon it as a kind of ritual preliminary to writing. A good outline is not a ritual; it springs from thought and should capitalize on its origin. In its early state it may be no more than a series of assertions, set down (elliptically, perhaps) just as they occur to the writer:

1. Job and Prometheus know their inferiority in power
2. Job habitually dutiful, Pr. habitually resentful
3. Greeks thought of afterlife as a dark continuation of existence, not punishment or reward
4. Job patient under affliction, rationalizing at first
5. Both fall from high to low estate: Pr. for deliberate acts of rebellion, Job not

6. Hebrew idea of Sheol (afterlife) as a comfortable extension of life after death
7. Both pieces probably written in 5th century B.C.
8. Hebrew and Gr. culture separate but both East Asian
9. Hebrew culture more isolated than Greek
10. *PB* a religious drama; Job half drama, half poem?
11. *PB* not a speculation but a demonstration of agreed-upon concepts
    . . .

One assertion suggests another and the accumulation soon suggests the possible combinations and the appropriate means of organization. From the list an outline grows which not only guides the writing of the essay but stimulates it and provides a clearly focused test for its achievement. An outline developed from such a series of assertions is immediately useful to the writer; with it before him, he can work swiftly and efficiently, explaining and expanding each assertion, "filling in" the outline with the corroborative and illustrative data he has accumulated by research and reflection.

THESIS: The treatments of piety and impiety in *Job* and *Prometheus Bound* reflect the most important differences between traditional Hebraic and early Greek religious belief.

1. Although Hebraic culture is more isolated than Greek, both are East Asian.
2. Fatalism, strong sense of human inferiority, common to both; so also a vigorous tradition of the hero and saviour of a group or people.
3. Hebraic view of afterlife (Sheol), like Greek Hades, reflects uncertainty about judgment hereafter for acts committed here. Importance of justice vs. rule of inscrutable God.
4. Main difference between concept of single God and of a pantheon; distance between Job and God greater than that between Prometheus and Zeus.
5. Difference reflected in the two works.
   a. Job habitually dutiful; Prometheus independent.
   b. Job patient under affliction; Pr. resentful.
   c. Job finally distrustful of reasoning; Pr. full of reasoning on his own account.
6. Idea of a "testing" of Job consistent with relationship (See 4); Prometheus' ordeal not a test but a punishment.
7. Forms of the two works also reflect difference.
   a. *Job* part drama, part poem of speculation; its drama full of suspense (wagers, tests, peril, victory, reward).
   b. *P B* a religious drama designed to illustrate orthodox concepts; drama ritualized, outcome foreknown.
8. Form and content together develop attitude toward piety in each work.
   a. *Job*—piety is waiting patiently to understand will of God.
   b. *P B*—(by negative illustration) piety is obedience.

There is another use of the outline which must not be overlooked. Besides serving as a guide to composition, it may be a tool for reorganizing what has already been composed. Some writers like to release the pressure of thought within them by writing it out without preliminary concern for neat and efficient order. When they have temporarily exhausted their resources, they turn a critical eye on what they have produced, summarizing it in outline form just as it occurs and then rearranging sections for clearer directions and sounder emphasis. The procedure is attractive in so far as it allows a writer to rely on the rush of thought as long as it lasts; it is perhaps less attractive in the later stage, when by rewriting and reorganizing it he must make up for the inadequacies of what he has produced. An early outline will reduce the amount of reconstruction necessary when the first draft is completed though it may not eliminate all reconstruction and certainly will not eliminate some amount of rewriting. Most people who have something to write use outlines both at the head and the tail of their work, even when they do not write them down. The form in which they cast the outline, if they do write it down, is of relatively small importance so long as the principal assertions are precisely stated and then arranged so that their relationships are made clear and so that the whole plan displays a steady forward movement.

COHERENCE

The three traditional goddesses of rhetoric—unity, coherence, and emphasis—are, suitably, the deities which all of the matters discussed in this section are supposed to serve. Of the three, *coherence* calls for special attention. Although sheer bulk may impose emphasis and a rough unity on the matter of an exposition, it is no aid—and is often a detriment—to coherence. Now coherence can be best defined by reference to its etymology; literally, it means a "sticking together," and in rhetoric it is the term used to designate the connectedness between parts large and small. While it is clear that coherence will be affected by the degree to which the materials of an essay are congruous (a discussion of three battles of the Civil War would achieve some coherence simply as a by-product of the unity of its subject matter), congruity is not alone sufficient.

The basic means of achieving coherence is by rational *arrangement* of material, a matter already adequately discussed. A second means is by the judicious use of *connectors*, a matter treated at the end of this chapter under the heading "transitions." Both means are largely structural, that is, concerned with the manipulation of blocks of expository matter. Within the blocks, of whatever size, and controlling their internal chemistry several other means of achieving coherence may come into action. *Repetition*, for instance, whether of a key word or of the pattern of phrases, clauses, and sentences (parallel structure), calls attention to the relationship between parts and thus increases coherence. The use of a *key metaphor,* whose terms are introduced obliquely and unostentatiously over a long passage of prose, may draw the whole passage together most subtly. More effective and less "literary" than either repetition or the use of a key metaphor, however, is the development of coherence by control of *agent-and-action.*

In one sense, an essay—or a paragraph of an essay—is a dramatic incident. A subject—personal or impersonal—performs an action which begins, proceeds to climax, and ends. The essay remains coherent as long as the actor and the action make their presence constantly felt; it becomes disconnected and diffuse when their presence is obscured. This theatrical metaphor shows its relevance most clearly, of course, when the subject is personal:

> With regard to this system, Ammianus has but two general comments to offer, and, of these, the first concerns the Roman aristocracy. In a number of striking passages, which have been used by Gibbon as the basis for a brilliant portrayal of contemporary imperial society, Ammianus lets himself go in a scathing indictment of this class. With Juvenalian scorn he stigmatizes the aimless frivolity of lives made possible only through swollen incomes derived from the exploitation of the provincials and consecrated to no purpose worthier than the ostentatious display of wealth and pride. He describes the incessant round of amusements, bathing, driving, hunting, yachting, and the exchange of hospitality, whereby the worthless aristocrats of his day sought to conceal the futility of their existence. He points with disgust to their moral and spiritual shortcomings, their cowardice and effeminacy, their avarice and wastefulness, their quickness to borrow, their slowness to repay; above all to the childish superstition which prompts them to resort, on the slightest pretext, to diviners and soothsayers who prey upon their fears. This superstition he attributes to the lack of any serious principles of conduct, a defect for which they have themselves to blame, inasmuch as they have turned from the cultivation of the mind, rejecting the heritage of philosophy through which alone such principles may be attained, in order to immerse themselves in mere sensationalism. Accordingly, among their retainers, the crooner has replaced the philosopher, the teacher of histrionics that of oratory; they seal their libraries like tombs, but construct for themselves hydraulic organs.
>
> CHARLES NORRIS COCHRANE, *Christianity and Classical Culture*

Any subject may be treated as though it were personal and thus become the dominant presence in its development. Obviously, a slavish sequence of "he did" or "it did" sentences will be as annoying as a series of abrupt movements on stage, and it is to avoid abruptness that Mr. Cochrane varies the structure and length of sentences so carefully in the excerpt just presented. But there is no need for a slavish sequence in the first place. The actor may be given many names, by use of synonym and paraphrase; a series of actions may be so attached that only one mention of the actor is necessary for all; artful manipulation of syntax can place the actor at other than initial positions in the sentence without altering his grammatical and logical authority. All that is necessary is that the central figure and the central action dominate.

Now there is no denying that this formula for coherence is oversimple. It is nonetheless a useful one, often useful for actual composition, nearly always useful for clearing up passages which have become muddled and directionless. Its weakness is that it operates from a fixed element, the actor, and this limits flexibility and movement. Some of that weakness is easily overcome by taking liberties with the "actor." For instance, in this opening paragraph from an essay about the English novelist E. M. Forster, "novel" is the actor for the first two sentences and "novelist," for the ones which follow:

> The English novel has traditionally admitted of no exact definition, no generic purity. Written by all sorts and conditions of men, as was the poetic drama of the Elizabethans, it has been designed for as many kinds of readers. The responsibility of the nineteenth-century novelist was to offer his readers a "story"; apart from that, and within the bounds of Victorian taste, he might provide what *extras* he would—sociological, psychological, moral. Sweeping his puppets aside, he might preach the new ethics, expound the nature of things, prophesy the future actions of his characters or the future of human character; returning again to his puppets, he was free to pass in and out of their minds, now seeing through this pair of subsidiary eyes, now through that, now exerting the omniscience of his own sight.   AUSTIN WARREN, *Rage for Order*

In the end, coherence is always a quality of thought rather than a manner of expression. The confused mind cannot produce coherent prose. On the other hand, the deliberate effort to make an obscure or muddled passage coherent by the use of rhetorical procedures often helps to reduce the mental confusion in which it originated.

INTRODUCTIONS

The frustrating experience of trying to find "a way to begin" is common to amateur and professional writer alike. At bottom it is usually a compound of dread and perplexity: dread of the labor involved in translating thought into language, and perplexity about which spring to touch first in order to set the machinery of composition going. Most writers resign themselves to the fact that they will begin a half-dozen times, throwing away one effort after another, until something satisfies enough so that writing can continue. Not infrequently, the sentence or paragraph which succeeded will later be abandoned entirely or completely altered, but if it has served its purpose the loss is a gain of one kind.

Because most serious writing goes through several stages, what is said about composition may apply to one stage but not to all. That is particularly true of introductions. It is more important to a writer that he get started than that his introduction be, at the outset, all that he wants it to be. Later, when he is revising, he can afford the energy to polish up the handle on the big front door of his essay, and these remarks are therefore directed to that final stage of his work.

A cursory glance at the articles in any popular magazine, of whatever repute, will disclose several strategies for introducing the subject and for engaging the reader's attention. The more "popular" the magazine, the greater will be the effort to relate the text to the reader's casual experience and the less will be the effort to make him rise out of his casual concerns into the particular world of the article before him. Ordinarily, the superficiality and sensationalism of an introduction will be consistent with the quality and manner of the exposition which follows it. For the writer of serious expository prose, directed in the main at those who may be assumed to have an initial readiness to be informed, it is therefore not necessary to provide further discussion of the opening maneuvers of less sober writing.

The aim of the introductory sentence or paragraph of a critical essay should be to get things moving: to indicate the topic of discussion, to give information about the limitations to be placed on that topic, and to set, or at least hint at, the tone of what is to follow. All this should be done as compactly as possible. Purely mechanical interposition of the writer is the sure mark of the amateur. This does not necessarily mean that use of the first person is bad, although it is true that "I" is a difficult pronoun to manage in many ways. Consider this example:

> I firmly believe that the honor system should be substituted for the present proctored examination system. I shall attempt in the following paragraphs to convince the reader of this.

Now, the first "I" is without question justifiable because this is an expression of opinion, and the writer wants the reader to know that it is his own opinion he is expressing. He could have done so, of course, by writing, "An honor system should be substituted for the present proctored examination system," and before he is done, having hunted for phrases to keep the "I" going—"in my opinion," "it seems to me," "as I see it"—he may wish he had. But "I firmly believe" is not entirely bad and even has the advantage of directness and simplicity on its side.

The same cannot be said for the second sentence. Here the writer enters though his presence has no value. At the moment he should be getting on to defend his revolutionary proposal, he is holding up a placard which reads, "This way to the main works."

The series of introductory sentences below illustrates clearly the process of improvement in the making of introductions which a student might practice in his own writing.

1. In the following paragraphs I shall compare and contrast views on American society as they were expressed by two foreigners writing about one hundred and fifty years apart.

2. Although one hundred and fifty years separate their views on American Society, there are many similarities between the observations of Crèvecœur and Müller-Freienfels.

3. Although their observations are separated by one hundred and fifty years of extensive social change, both Crèvecœur and Müller-Freienfels see that the most distinguishing characteristic of American society is the leveling process.

CONCLUSIONS

There are two common faults in the concluding sections of students' papers. One is the reintroduction of the mechanical "I."

> Thus I have shown how one can obtain a synthesis of Martius yellow in shorter time by a reduction of the number of steps in the initial process.

The other might be called the "pious hope." It usually appears in some such form as this:

> If more men today would capture the great vision of St. Augustine's *City of God,* there would perhaps be no need for a United Nations.

The faults point to their own correction. A conclusion should be no more general than the essay it concludes; its job is to restate, as adroitly as possible, the principal matter and the tone of the preceding text. Rewritten, the examples given above might read:

> This eliminates a third step in the initial process for synthesizing Martius yellow and reduces the time for the whole operation to two hours and thirty-five minutes.

> The *City of God* is all of these things—history and theology, philosophical speculation and textual criticism—but above all it is a vision of the world redeemed by a "new Adam," Jesus Christ.

TRANSITIONAL WORDS AND PHRASES

If there is one difficulty that harasses students more than any other, it is the linking together of sentences and paragraphs. In large part, good transitional structures are a corollary of good organization; the author who is completely in command of his work, who knows just where he is going as he writes, will have no trouble with transitions. But the unhappy fact is that students generally do not have—nor can they be expected to have—such command, and they are therefore continually bothered by their awareness that what they have written doesn't hang together quite as it should and that they don't know just how to make it do so.

Although the artificial taking apart of the process of writing sharply reduces the effect of any exercises based upon such a separation, that is perhaps less true of transitions than of any other expository matter analyzed thus far. It is possible to deal with them apart from a text and to achieve thereby not only command of transitions but, surprisingly enough, the ability to discover and correct flaws of organization.

Literally, "transition" means "a crossing"; in the practice of exposition, the transition acts as a bridge between sentences, between groups of sentences, between paragraphs and sections. Moreover, it is a bridge with a direction sign: it not only takes the reader across but it tells him where he is going and where he has been. Explicitly, *a transition reveals relationship.* The possible relationships are many: cause to effect, general to particular or particular to general, supplementation, restriction, concession, and so on. The writer can readily decide which relationship exists between units by asking such questions as these:

> What do I want to accomplish in the sentence I am about to write? Am I simply adding information to that already given? Am I presenting conflicting matter? Do I wish to make a concession? prove a point? present a reason for something's being so? show the next step in a process? Is this sentence to be illustrative only or will it further the discussion? Does it define? assert? support?

Once the relationship is known, a proper connective can be selected. To make that selection one must know the precise effect of conjunctions and other transitional words and phrases. Curiously enough, even the most common ones suffer misinterpretation and should, for that reason, be listed here.

and moreover furthermore	These expressions indicate that what follows is supplementary to what precedes. They should, therefore, link matters of like kind and grammatical form.
but however yet	These mark a change in direction or the introduction of material which conflicts with what has gone before. Since opposition is intended, they, too, should link matters of like kind and grammatical form.
still nevertheless notwithstanding	The sense of an opposing current is conveyed by these words, also, but they generally come after some sort of concession has been made.
although though while	These words are concessive. They always require a balancing principal statement.

for because	Both introduce the *reason for* another statement or condition.
then since as	As conjunctions, these three words may be used to show cause or they may simply indicate a relationship in time.
in order that so that	These show purpose.
provided that in case that	These restrict.
as if as though even if	These suggest some amount of uncertainty in the statement to follow.

Complete command of these connectives is a requisite of good writing, but they will not alone give all that is needed for free and forward movement of discourse. In fact, overuse of them can easily become an impediment to the easy flow of good prose. A page spattered with *however*'s and *for*'s and *then*'s is as unsightly as a garment held together with safety pins. The kind of transition that does best service is the unobtrusive one, the one that comes from making the language of the text provide its own connections, the transition known—for want of a less pretentious word—as the "organic transition." It is not nearly so mystical as it sounds, and a little practice will give any student confidence in its use.

To create an organic transition, a writer may think of it as looking in two directions at once: back to what has been said and forward to what is to be said. The trick—and it is a kind of trick—of delivering that sense of double awareness lies simply in picking up a word or a phrase or the main idea of the preceding passage and touching it lightly, with or without some change, in the connecting term. Examples will make that procedure clearer than will further explanation.

The student who wrote the following paragraph has used both formal and organic transitions within the paragraph.

> For several reasons the convention is sometimes considered better than the primary system. *In the first place,* it is obvious, from the small number of voters in primary elections, that the public generally cares little about them. *Moreover,* the convention system allows selection of candidates so that the ticket is balanced to give all groups representation. *This kind of selection* has the *additional* advantage of providing a guarantee against the nomination of "crackpot" candidates and of sharply curtailing campaign expenditures, itself an important matter if one realizes that, in politics, support is always accompanied by the expectation of favors and patronage. *All these* are valuable considerations. *Yet,* in the face of the one great objection to conventions—machine domination—they lose their importance.

This kind of selection uses a key word in the preceding sentence and leaves to *additional* the work of showing that this statement is supplementary to its predecessor. *All these* gathers the four arguments advanced in favor of party conventions, and the sentence it introduces reinforces the tone of approval.

> . . . and throughout the first chapter of *Walden* there is a note of impatience, sometimes an almost feverish desire to get the world to shake itself clear of clutter and complication, to give up the velvet cushion for a pumpkin, to stop the trains from running, the newspapers from pouring out their daily rush of words, the housewives from adding to the useless piles of stuff in the attic, and their farmer husbands from adding shed to outhouse and barn to shed and mortgage to all. The *impatience and the fever* well up in a great cry, "Simplify! Simplify! Simplify!"
>
> But simplification was the one thing the world had no intention even to consider. The steam engine had come, and soon there would be. . . .

In the foregoing passage, a good part of the unity of the paragraph is achieved by the series of parallel phrases. The repetition of "impatience" and "fever" add to the unity by drawing the examples together in the generalization originally proposed; and the turning of "Simplify" into a noun gives the following paragraph an emphatic but unmechanical link with the paragraph just concluded.

The more skilled the writer, the more subtle and varied will be the devices he employs for binding sentences and paragraphs together. The relationships conveyed by those devices will nonetheless be the same as those mentioned earlier, and a student can for that reason properly begin with them and with the rudimentary transitions as a means of coming to realize which connections between statements are common. Once he has those connections firmly in mind, he can learn to handle the many devices for making a paragraph or an essay appear as inevitable in its progress as a river.

⊂ Diction

Otto Jespersen, a great grammarian of the English language, is said to have remarked that the direction of change in a language is from ditch to castle. Since he made that remark (if he did) there have been many efforts by serious students of language to make sociological classifications of one kind or another. Thus, within the great classes of origin (Indo-European, Hittite, and so on) and within the national and regional classes (French, Germanic, Arabic), additional classes have been sorted out on the basis of characteristic vocabulary, syntax, and conformity to traditional or "approved" usages. Obviously these classes are of very different kind from the one grounded on the historical development of linguistic forms, and they lack the neatness and reliability of those earlier classifications. Yet they have a particular interest for the writer because they attempt to distinguish, among the various patterns of speech in a given language, those patterns which are distinctive indicators of the economic status, the cultural experience, and the social position of the speaker. An analogy to this kind of classification can be found in the highbrow-middlebrow-lowbrow metaphor used a few years ago to describe social habits and tastes in clothing, cigarettes, movies, magazines, and alcohol.

Of course, people have undoubtedly made social distinctions about the forms of language since culture began. Attempts to teach young people to speak and write "correctly" imply established forms and corruptions of them, and the forms considered "established" are necessarily those which the teachers themselves are accustomed to using. If this were the complete story, however, there would be little difficulty in determining correct language: the language which the tradition-bearers (teachers, priests, hereditary chieftains) learned from the tradition-bearers who preceded them would continue to be the correct language. In isolated and strictly hierarchical societies, if there are any left, that may still be the case. But most societies have experienced frequent disruption of hierarchies and almost none are really isolated today. Certainly, as far as Western culture is concerned, it is not possible to consider any society of the past three thousand years as either rigidly hierarchical or culturally isolated. Wherever a society is at all mobile and flexible, its language will undergo change; and wherever language undergoes change, some of the changes which occur will develop in small groups and come to be identified with them. Quite naturally, those who receive formal education in their youth will be exposed to the traditions of language-as-it-has-been-used, and those who do not will derive their norms of language from the speech they hear about them.

Now, while it is true that formal education often tends to perpetuate forms and distinctions which have lost currency even among educated people, it is also true that it preserves forms and distinctions which have developed in the language as aids to clarity, precision, and beauty. The thesis that it is only in the language of the uneducated that one finds language richly used is absurd. One has only to listen to the conversation in a crowded subway car or to read the banal and nerveless monologues of Ring Lardner's characters to explode that myth. The language of the uneducated is, on the whole, imprecise, redundant, awkward, and limited in the degree of complexity it can express. It may be more graphic and is often more emphatic than the language of the educated, but there is no evidence to show that either of these qualities proceeds out of real inventiveness or out of keen perception. Language is a reflector of being, and it simply does not make sense to impute mysterious refinements in language to those who have little refinement in their lives. Dullness and poverty of mind are not special prerogatives of the uneducated, of course, any more than sensitivity and brilliance are prerogatives of those who have had a university education. But the gradations of language—from accurate to less accurate and from powerful to ineffective—are more likely to match the gradation from much to little education than the reverse.

The point is not that educated people are "better" or "worse" than uneducated people, but simply that they use language more effectively. Since that is true, it is reasonable that the "Standard English" taught in the schools should be the English used by well-educated people. In a democratic society, and particularly in one which has universal education, "Standard English" will be less the characteristic of economic status or social class than of formal education, and therefore, of occupation, since those who are formally educated make up the bulk of the "professional" classes, and those who are not, the bulk of the "working" class. The sociological "levels of language" which one may distinguish in such a society as ours, therefore, are roughly parallel to the amount of formal education required for various occupations. Since the metaphor "levels" suggests a fixity and separateness which falsify the actual situation, it might be better to think of the differences in usage in a geological metaphor as strata which blur at their upper and lower edges into contiguous layers, all essentially more alike than different.

For the readers of this book, it is less important to make fine distinctions among strata than to examine that stratum which is particularly appropriate to their purposes. Except for a few preliminary observations about peripheral aspects of Standard English, therefore, this chapter will confine itself to the proprieties of English as it is spoken and written among the well educated.

The term "diction" refers to the *kinds* of words a writer uses. The lingo of sports columnists, the sonorous phraseology of Supreme Court justices, the slang of the schoolboy, the elliptic language of informal conversation, and the abstruse terminology of the philosopher—all are kinds of diction and all have validity. One canon by which they are measured is that of *appropriateness:* lofty abstractions do not suit an account of yesterday's baseball game any better than slang suits a judgment of minority rights. Every language provides this variety of diction and every language also imposes on it this restriction of *propriety* and one other, that of *accuracy.*

These two restrictions need careful attention because failure to apply them accounts for much of the clumsiness and ineffectiveness that mar students' writing.

IDIOM

As a language develops, constructions establish themselves firmly in it, some of them reflections of logical relationships, others apparently quite arbitrary. We say that we "catch cold" from sitting in a draft although the sense of "catching" is certainly not in our mind, as it might well be in the expression "catch your cold." We speak of "limping *along*," "*bearing up* under hardship," "*trying our hand* at something new," and "*getting by without* effort." All are idioms and our ability to use them correctly comes from familiarity with them rather than from rule. Only with one group of idioms—those containing nouns or verbs which have prepositional prefixes—is there a general rule, and even it is not always reliable. Roughly speaking (an idiom), however, such nouns and verbs will employ a following English preposition which is the counterpart of the preposition within them. These faulty expressions occurred on native students' papers and may be considered, therefore, to be worth (an idiom) general attention:

immune from the attacks	*im*=to;	immune *to*
involved with these issues	*in*=in;	involved *in*
he aspired for power	*a*=to;	aspired *to*
Judge Fuld dissented with the opinion of the others	*dis*=from	dissented *from*

When there is no prefix in the noun or verb, the choice of preposition is more difficult. These expressions are wrong because the proper sense is not conveyed by the preposition chosen:

The qualifications which they have *toward* commenting on society (for)

There is no justification *in* destroying it (for)

He should not be heedless *to* the will of . . . (of)

These simply contravene established usage:

on *most* all the issues (almost)

We are not going to keep a man out of office *due to* his previous experience ("because of"; "due to" is used only where there is a noun which "due" may attach itself to. The barrier is breaking on this form, and soon "due to" may be completely in charge of the field; for the present, however, its use is particularly offensive to many who will tolerate outright solecism more willingly.)

to try *and* defend such a statement (Logic would seem to give one meaning to the phrase when it is written with "to" and another meaning when it is written with "and"; but language is notoriously illogical at times, and this is one of them. This phrase is common now, but it still annoys many readers, especially those who are conscientious about their own use of language.)

the *amount* of people in our country ("Amount" refers to unnumbered quantity; use "number.")

This flexibility is one of the *reasons why he won.* (Despite Tennyson's famous poem, many people, including admirers of Tennyson, find this in some sense redundant and insist on "reason that.")

I believe a close analysis proves *differently.* (For information on such bewildered attempts to reduce the behavior of adjectives and adverbs to infrangible rules, see Fowler's comment on UNIDIOMATIC -LY, then further his comments under IDIOM and CAST-IRON IDIOM.)

A final set of idiomatic lapses, these dealing with verbs:

to *judge on* the wisdom of (a direct object is demanded)

He *accuses* that technology is the sole despot of life. (charges)

He *places* many compliments *on* the British. (Why not "He compliments the British"?)

Democracy *infuses* the people with a desire for change. (If the verb is to be used here at all, it must take "desire" as its direct object: "Democracy infuses in the people a desire for change"; one may wonder, however, whether desire can be "poured into" people, even figuratively speaking.)

These examples make one thing clear. Correct idiomatic expression depends on *knowing;* nothing short of knowing will suffice. For those who do not know or who are in doubt, there are, of course, references that help. A good desk dictionary will sometimes provide the information needed (*Webster's New World Dictionary* is particularly helpful in this respect); textbooks of grammar generally contain glossaries of usage which list common idiomatic expressions; Fowler's *Modern English Usage,* though keyed to British locutions, is remarkably detailed; and Mencken's *The American Language* provides a superbly indexed and authoritative analysis of usage in the English spoken on our side of the Atlantic.

COLLOQUIALISM

The term "colloquialism" comes from a Latin word meaning "to speak" and is used to refer to the informal expressions of ordinary conversation. It differs from idiom in being thus restricted to the casual and informal and has, therefore, less importance in a consideration of expository style. Several pages back, in discussing the use of the indefinite pronouns, it was noted that "you"—the second person—often takes over the work of the indefinite pronoun; this is particularly true in *colloquial* usage. In conversation, we generalize with it:

> You don't have to be a genius to go to college.

We use it for giving directions:

> After you get the mixture boiling, you add enough water to fill the vessel half-way to the brim.

No one questions the usefulness and appropriateness of "you" in such contexts. In serious prose, however, it is out of place for the same reason that any number of expressions common in speech are improper in written exposition; they alter tone and very often reduce, rather than increase, clarity. A writer who mixes colloquialisms and formal diction unsettles his reader and thereby impedes communication, as in this passage:

> Mark Twain's greatest book, *Adventures of Huckleberry Finn,* catches to perfection the deep rootlessness and unconventionality of the nineteenth-century American man. And we still understand Huck well because his blood runs in our veins. Many of us long silently to loosen the ties of family and ordered society; *maybe* some even feel that nothing but complete emancipation will *fill the bill.* What Huck offers us is a vision of the ever-youthful wanderer, studying the depths of the silent world of the understanding and *all the time* growing without ever growing up.

The division between serious written prose and speech is not, perhaps, so great as it once was, but there is a division still. The student who develops a sensitivity to the distinction will find his reward in the control he has over the response of the person who reads what he has written.

SLANG

Colloquialisms last; slang does not. Those expressions which come striding into our daily speech with all the gusto of a Texan visiting Boston overwhelm us for a time and then leave us wondering, after they have disappeared, at the power they had as long as they lasted. The slang of our fathers is a dead language; the slang we use will be meaningless to our children. Who says, "Twenty-three skiddoo" today? Just as many as will say "Dig that square" tomorrow. The prose we write may not be deathless, but it deserves the most enduring diction we can manage. Slang has little place in it.

DIALECT

Unlike slang and colloquialisms, which are likely to be pervasive, dialect is regional. It is, moreover, fairly stable so long as the region where it is used has limited contact with other regions. Dialectical expressions have the charm of strangeness but, like slang and colloquialism, are generally inappropriate in serious prose. No one is likely to consider very carefully the statements of a person who writes

> Helen was still right pretty but Menelaus was too tuckered out by fighting to pay her any mind.

Correct use of idiom depends on *knowing* the patterns within a language. Correct use of dialect, slang, and colloquialism depends rather on *feeling* their appropriateness or inappropriateness for a given context. The general rule is to avoid them in serious exposition. The only qualification of that rule seems to be this: a writer may use any one of the three to create *carefully calculated effects* of surprise, emphasis, irony, or humor.

FAULTS OF STYLE

Diction is an important consideration in style but it is not the only one. An earlier part of this book dealt with some of the others in positive fashion, showing how good effects can be achieved. Since one of the principles of learning is that we profit by error, it may not be inappropriate now to re-examine some of the considerations discussed earlier from another point of view—the negative and critical one.

Redundancy. The English language inherited from both Romance and Anglo-Saxon sources the characteristic of repetition as a means of emphasis—repetition sometimes of a single word or phrase, sometimes of a meaning in different words. Thus, the conventional expression "wear and tear" indicates nothing more than "wear" but achieves a kind of reinforcement from the addition of "tear." Consciously used, repetition has great rhetorical power. Recall

> To-morrow, and to-morrow, and to-morrow
> Creeps in this petty pace from day to day . . . .

> . . . Love is not love
> Which alters when it alteration finds
> Or bends with the remover to remove.

There are kinds of repetition, however, that come from no conscious use by the writer but are the result entirely of his ignorance of the full force of a word or his inattention to what he is doing. Such ignorance and inattention produce what is called redundancy or pleonasm. The reader can check his susceptibility to such fault by proving himself on the sentences given below, all of them taken from papers written by students. The "horrible examples" appear in group A; the error in each is revealed in group B.

A

1. A hero is usually distinguished in bravery, fortitude, and courage.
2. The deliberate, planned lie is generally less successful than the spontaneous one.
3. Hatred of the Church blinds the eyes of Mark Twain to much that was good in medieval society.
4. He is an author contemporary with the modern time.
5. These two contrasting attitudes toward war present an ever-dangerous peril.
6. The general trends of the two essays head in the same direction.
7. This is something foreign to the common populus of the U. S.
8. Neither the big magnates of the corporations nor the specialized experts and trained technicians realize fully what is at stake.
9. First comes their need for future re-election.

B

1. The three nouns are not quite identical ("bravery" is derived from a word meaning "fierceness"; "fortitude," from a word meaning "strength"; "courage," from a word meaning "heart"); but the characteristic they refer to here is probably a single one. Unless the writer has a reputation for nuance, his reader will undoubtedly take this for mere wordiness.
2. How are "deliberate" and "planned" other than synonymous here? It is conceivable that, in speech (see "Oral and Written Expression"), a certain emphasis might be achieved by this repetition. If the same force is desired in writing, however, some change must be made. Such a simple change as

this might do the trick: "The deliberate, the planned lie . . ."; or better: "The deliberate lie—planned with care and executed with calculation— is . . . ."

3. ". . . blinds the eyes . . ."! What else?

4. The verb is in the present tense, so there is no need that "contemporary" be reinforced by "with the modern time." "Contemporary" can, of course, be used with times other than modern: as in "St. Francis, the founder of medieval mystical piety, was a contemporary of St. Dominic, the founder of the Inquisition."

5. When a peril ceases to be "ever-dangerous," it ceases to be a peril. This is a matter of not knowing the meaning of "peril"; a little acquaintance with Latin would have helped.

6. Everything, it seems, has a "trend" nowadays (see "Jargon") and the mere use of the word is enough to repel many readers. What, then, of trends that "head in the same direction"?

7. Latin again. The populus (populace) is everyone and there's no one more "common" than that.

8. By derivation, magnates are big; by necessity, experts are specialized; and by definition, technicians are trained. In this example, the writer doesn't seem to care that his reputation with his reader is also "at stake."

9. "Re-" is a supple prefix (it can mean either "back" or "again") but it's hard to see how a "re-election" can be anything but "future."

"Elegant variation." Fear of repetition occasionally leads students to avoid it at too great cost. They escape the frying pan of monotony only to fall into the fire of overingeniousness and affectation. A right balance between repetition and variation is not a matter for prescription, but examples may help to suggest the nature of the disease and the character of a cure.

> *Prohibition* seems to be a stimulant to most people. Even if they have no inclination toward doing what is *forbidden,* they feel an urge to resist *proscription* for the sake of resistance; or they assume that what is *interdicted* must be worth investigating or it would not have been *disallowed* in the first place. And the more strict the *ban,* the more subtle will be their efforts to outwit it.

In this illustration, the effort to avoid repeating "prohibition" is so noticeable that a reader is more likely to concentrate on the writer's ingenuity (or his capacity for using a book of synonyms) than on what he is saying. Such a laborious procedure is bad not only because it distracts the reader and lends an air of pomposity to the passage but because it fails to make effective use of the key word. The passage is better on all three counts if the writer shows moderation in the use of synonyms.

> *Prohibition* seems to be a stimulant to most people. Even if they have no inclination toward doing what is *forbidden,* they feel an urge to resist *prohibition* for the sake of resistance; or they assume that what is *pro-*

hibited must be worth investigating or it would not have been *forbidden* in the first place. And the more strict the *prohibition*, the more subtle will be their efforts to outwit it.

Elegant variation may actually cause misunderstanding as well as distraction and annoyance, as in this example:

> *Power* is the basis of political action. Whether *control* is exerted by elected or self-appointed or hereditary officials, *authority* conditions and manipulates action at will.

Are we to understand the italicized words as synonyms, or is some distinction suggested? If the former, then surely the passage will be more effective if written thus:

> *Power* is the basis of political action. Whether *it* is exerted by elected or self-appointed or hereditary officials, *power* conditions and manipulates action at will.

It is not fair, however, to condemn a practice because of its abuse. Repetition is too valuable an aid in good expression to discard because the incompetent use it without discrimination. A better procedure is to look to the ideas; if *they* are not idly repeated, one need have little worry about the repetition of words. To show how effective sheer repetition may be, this discussion of attempts to avoid it closes with a passage well known in English literature. It is the work of an author whose deliberate use of repetition consorted magnificently with his deliberate limitation of emphasis to a few great ideas and made his voice a dominant one in the culture of half a century.

> The pursuit of perfection, then, is the pursuit of sweetness and light. He who works for sweetness and light, works to make reason and the will of God prevail. He who works for machinery, he who works for hatred, works only for confusion. Culture looks beyond machinery, culture hates hatred; culture has one great passion, the passion for sweetness and light. It has one even yet greater!—the passion for making them *prevail*. It is not satisfied till we *all* come to a perfect man; it knows that the sweetness and light of the few must be imperfect until the raw and unkindled masses of humanity are touched with sweetness and light. If I have not shrunk from saying that we must work for sweetness and light, so neither have I shrunk from saying that we must have a broad basis, must have sweetness and light for as many as possible. Again and again I have insisted how those are the happy moments of humanity, how those are the marking epochs of a people's life, how those are the flowering times for literature and art and all the creative power of genius, when there is a *national* glow of life and thought, when the whole of society is in the fullest measure permeated by thought, sensible to beauty, intelligent and alive. Only it must be *real* thought and *real* beauty; *real* sweetness and *real* light. Plenty of people will try to give the masses, as they call them, an intellectual food prepared

and adapted in the way they think proper for the actual condition of the masses. The ordinary popular literature is an example of this way of working on the masses. Plenty of people will try to indoctrinate the masses with the set of ideas and judgments constituting the creed of their own profession or party. Our religious and political organizations give an example of this way of working on the masses. I condemn neither way; but culture works differently. It does not try to teach down to the level of the inferior classes; it does not try to win them for this or that sect of its own, with ready-made judgments and watchwords. It seeks to do away with classes; to make the best that has been thought and known in the world current everywhere; to make all men live in an atmosphere of sweetness and light, where they may use ideas, as it uses them itself, freely—nourished, and not bound by them.

MATTHEW ARNOLD, *Culture and Anarchy*

Vagueness and ambiguity. Most of the much-lampooned repetitiveness of legal language is the result of trying to make watertight statements. The danger of vagueness and ambiguity in legal documents is too obvious to need illustration. Perhaps it is only this life-and-liberty-saving importance that can make a writer hunt for ways of making perfectly clear whatever he has to say unless pride in his craft is enough to impel him to do so. The authors of these sentences are certainly slipshod in their work:

1. This seems to be just inconsistency in American philosophy. (Is "just" adjectival or adverbial? It makes a great deal of difference.)
2. This word designates any person who acts in a civil way. ("In a civil, that is, courteous, manner" or "in his capacity as a citizen or employee of the government"?)
3. The ordinary man must act as a check on any usurpation of the expert's powers. ("Usurpation of power by the expert" or "usurpation by someone else of power rightly the expert's"?)
4. He says that since all Americans have equal rights, no one goes out of his way to get out of that class, and that the people who were out slowly descended back due to their own lack of ambition. (This one needs a complete rewriting: "He says that, since all social classes in America have equal rights, almost no one goes out of his way to get out of the class into which he was born, and that those few who, for one reason or another, do move out return gradually because the advantages prove not to be worth the effort." It doesn't mean just that to you? No wonder.)
5. Humor is a very effective means for communicating discontent when used satirically, but when humorous analogies are applied to serious subjects, the humor becomes devoid of its purpose and indeed detracts from it. (Any reader patient enough to work over this sentence will finally discover that clearing up "its purpose" will do more than anything else to clear up the confusion in the sentence. "Its purpose" must be understood, apparently, to exclude satire. That makes the statement completely illogical, but at least it is no longer ambiguous.)

Inflation. The undisputed master of the inflated style is Dickens'
Mr. Micawber.

> The blossom is blighted, the leaf is withered, the God of day goes down
> upon the dreary scene, and—and in short you are ever floored. As I am!

It is funny in print; in life, it is often offensive and sometimes pathetic.
There is a marked tendency among good prose writers today to write
with as much simplicity as they can manage. (Mr. Churchill is a notable
exception.) But not all things can be said simply. And, more to the point,
not all people want to say things simply. It is no heinous offense to write
"Anyone who has a fair position in industry . . ." instead of "Anyone
who has a decent job in industry . . ." but the inflation, the slight pomposity, is there all the same. This is more noticeably stiff: "Higher education of excellent quality can be had at very lenient terms at state uni-
versities." Coupling a passive verb with "at very lenient terms" marks this
ineradicably for what it is—an attempt to make something simple sound
imposing. Like "Those who uphold the negative side of this question,"
it represents a kind of shrinking away from rude contact with things-as-
they-are.

It is a somewhat different psychological attitude that leads a writer
to load his text with phrases which send up their echo from a previous
century. He seems to know the rudeness of things-as-they-are but to
have turned to a golden past for words with which to enhance their dignity. He never "uses" but "avails himself of"; for him, people are "wont"
to do things. A third kind of inflation is that which seems to have no
cause other than the love of abstractions for their own sake; while it
may be indicative of a potentiality in the writer, it is certainly as annoying to the reader as any device one can name. One example should
be enough:

> The Editor claims that the two advantages of the proposal have since
> been rendered improbable, and, hence, the presence of the House Deans
> is *conducive to a feeling of surveillance.*

Euphemism. Euphemism is the use of a mild or vague or peri-
phrastic (roundabout) expression as a substitute for blunt precision or
disagreeable truth. Some euphemisms are simply matters of propriety.
(See H. L. Mencken's amusing remarks on "mortician" and on the invention of "ecdysiast" to meet the professional demands of a certain
Miss Sothern, *The American Language, Supplement One,* pp. 569 ff.
and 584 ff.) Probably most of the euphemisms which appear in students'
papers, however, rise from hypersensitivity, a vain fastidiousness almost
as repulsive as its counterpart, vulgarity. Hypersensitivity and vulgarity
are both bad in writing because they keep the writer from making honest contact with his material, that is, they make him *insensitive* to its

real character. The student who wrote "position" instead of "job" (see above, Inflation) has imputed to "job" certain unpleasant suggestions of meniality; he hopes to dignify by renaming, feeling that there is a kind of magic power in words which can alter the objects to which they are attached. The hope is illusory, and the act pretentious. A salary is not made bigger or better by being called an emolument, nor is a luncheon made more delicious by being called a collation.

Another kind of euphemism, a vicious kind, is that which attempts to put a fair face on foul matter. "Liquidation of undesirable elements" is murder, plain and simple. A "deliberate defection from known truth" is a lie, nothing more or less. Such terms, unless used mockingly, are attempts to hide the facts, not reveal them, to complicate rather than simplify communication.

Jargon. "Jargon" has two meanings. It is language peculiar to a trade or a profession, what we sometimes call "shoptalk." And it is the use of that language outside the trade or profession, as well as the use of overgeneral, empty words and combinations of such words. Jargon is offensive when its purpose is to create effect rather than convey meaning; like euphemism and inflated language, it is verbal pomposity, parade stuff portentously empty. Most of the sinning is done with a small number of words, each so broadened that it has lost all definiteness and power:

field	in this *field* of study
element	the traditional *element* in this situation
factor	and the third *factor* is
scale	on a national *scale*
degree	to a greater *degree* than
aspect	the basic *aspect* of this situation
level	less likely on this *level* of consideration
area	within this general *area* of thought

Consider next these all too typical sentences:

Disinterest will develop *on the part of* the rich.

Thought *centers on* slackness in public administration.

He thinks of national government *in terms of* community.

Problems that are general and uncomplicated *in nature* the people solve very well.

He has many trenchant views *with respect to* socialized medicine, and is considered quite an authority *in this regard.*

These sentences bear another unmistakable mark of jargon:

One of the *environmental factors* which affected him to the good was baseball.

It began its comments by immediately taking the students' opinions of deans for granted and then proceeded to belittle not only the *functional status* of the deans but to misinterpret their applications of the duties of their offices.

However, to form a rule or formula so as to *evaluate the causation* of this bane of humanity, wars, one would have to *evolve* a psychometer, so to speak, with which *the occurrences of certain attitudes and involved co-ordinating factors* could be gauged, compared, and *in the ultimate contrast* made self-evident in a *social science general rule.*

Calling attention to such expressions does not mean that they may never be used. It does mean that the writer should use them sparingly and that he should always test their appropriateness by considering the metaphor that is generally involved. Such a test would make him wary of using *crossroads* in this sentence, for instance:

The United States has come to a dangerous crossroads in its history; it must decide which path to take, for there is no middle road.

Or of using *factors* in this one:

"He frantically cast about" gives one the impression that, having found his position jeopardized, the President desperately sought to thwart the threatening factors.

Naturally, jargon will be most readily apparent to those who read and write a great deal. Students finding themselves charged with use of jargon not uncommonly protest their innocence and their inability to see how they have erred. This protest is entirely understandable, but it is also evidence of the subtle power jargon has over all of us. Even the most literate must make constant and conscious effort to avoid resorting to the convenient but vapid words we call "jargon." But if they are so convenient, why then, one may ask, should one avoid them so scrupulously? The best answer to that question is given by Justice Holmes in a letter to Harold Laski: "The minute a phrase becomes current it becomes an apology for not thinking to the end of the sentence." Jargon provides a way of not thinking and of not seeing. It is, therefore, an arch-enemy of a good style.

Triteness. An accomplice to jargon is triteness, the use of expressions so worn out that they produce no reaction in the average reader and only weariness in the person who is widely read. Moreover, like jargon, they close the eyes and numb the minds of those who use them. A person who writes as the author of the following passage did not only *sees* nothing and *thinks* nothing but *tells* nothing to his reader:

It was with a *feeling of awe* that I first entered Harvard Yard. A *mist came before my eyes* and I spoke *in hushed tones* to the man who had brought me with him, the *mentor* of my school football team. Before me the brick and stone buildings *reared their heads* proudly into *the wide blue yonder.* Across the *velvet sward* moved *bright youth and gray-headed age.* From beyond the walls came the *busy hum* of traffic and of the *daily round of life* on the Square. Here all was *as silent as the dead.* My *heart caught in my throat* and I said *in muted tones,* "So this is Harvard Yard!"

Happily, so disastrously bad a piece is rare. Yet, the trite term—or cliché, as it is often called—is always a temptation to the writer because it relieves him of the responsibility to probe his consciousness for a more precise expression of his thought. The temptation is increased for the student by the fact that the cliché may be new to him and therefore, from his point of view, not really trite at all, an unfortunate situation admirably described by Fowler in these words:

> The hackneyed phrases are counted by the hundred, & those registered below are a mere selection. Each of them comes to each of us at some moment in life with, for him, the freshness of novelty upon it; on that occasion it is a delight, & the wish to pass on that delight is amiable; but we forget that of an hundred persons for whom we attempt this good office, though there may be one to whom our phrase is new & bright, it is a stale offence to the ninety & nine.   *Modern English Usage*

The dilemma is resolvable for a writer only if he is willing to take correction and determined to make himself master of the words he uses.

⊄ *A Brief Glossary of Usage*

USAGE VARIES WIDELY according to situation. What is entirely acceptable in casual speech and writing may not be acceptable in formal prose.
The standard governing the judgments here is that of *language appropriate to serious written exposition.*

ability, capacity. *Ability* means *power to perform; capacity* means
power to receive, content, or *extent of room or space.*

aggravate, irritate. *Aggravate* means *increase; irritate* means *to excite
anger in, cause soreness:* His initial irritation was aggravated by the
second remark.

all right. The only acceptable spelling of this combination of words.

amount, number. *Amount* refers to unnumberable quantity; the amount
of reading; the number of pages.

and etc. *Etc.* is an abbreviation for *et cetera* which means *and others.*
The *and* in this expression is, therefore, redundant.

anxious, eager. *Anxious* means *worried; eager* means *keenly desirous.*

any place, every place, some place, no place. These are colloquialisms
when used adverbially. The correct forms are *anywhere, everywhere,
somewhere, nowhere.*

as to. *As to* is jargon in such expressions as: He knows nothing as to the
source of this statement. Use *about.*

beside, besides. *Beside* is a preposition meaning *near by* or *compared
with:* sitting beside me; looks cheap beside this one. *Besides* is a
preposition or an adverb meaning *in addition to* or *other than:* Besides running the store he acts as postmaster. (prepositional) Besides,
he is a boxer. (adverbial)

can but, cannot but, cannot help but. Write: I cannot help thinking that
he is superior.

common, mutual. *Common* means *shared equally; mutual* means *re-
ciprocal.*

comparatives. Comparative expressions should indicate all terms of the
comparison unless some are *clearly* implied by context: They are
more willing *than they once were* to do the work.

considerable. Use of this word to mean *much* is colloquial only, as in:
He spent considerable time on his project. Write: He spent several
hours (months, days) on his project *or* He spent much time on his
project.

contact.   *Contact* as a verb is colloquial; as a noun, it is overused and frequently jargonic.

continual, continuous.   *Continual* means *occurring in steady but not unbroken succession; continuous* means *without interruption.*

couple.   As a noun, *couple* means *two of a kind, a pair.* In the expression *He read a couple of pages and stopped,* meaning more or less indefinitely a small number of pages, *couple* is colloquial only. Write: two *or* a few *or* several.

data.   *Data* is the plural form of *datum;* it requires a plural form in the verb it governs.

different from, different than, different to.   The correct expression in American English is *different from:* His theory is different from any other I have heard. However, *different than* frequently introduces a clause, as an alternative to *different from what:* College life is different than (from what) I thought it would be. *Different to* is a vulgarism.

due to.   *Due* is an adjective. The expression is properly used with a preceding noun: His success is due to hard work. Do not begin sentences with this expression, as in: Due to unforeseen circumstances, the program has been canceled. Write: Because of unforeseen . . . . (It must be admitted that this expression is well on its way to becoming standard, and that is probably a good thing. It will serve at least to replace "owing to," which has been long advanced as a superior locution.)

end up.   The "up" is certainly unnecessary, even if emphatic: Everything will end as he predicted.

enthuse.   *Enthuse* is a vulgarism. Write: I am enthusiastic about . . . .

equally as good.   This expression is redundant. Write *either:* This edition is as good as the other *or* The two editions are equally good.

extra.   Used to mean *very* or *unusually,* this word is a colloquialism only.

firstly.   This is an obsolete form. Use *first* both as adjective and adverb. Not so, however, with other ordinals: *second* (adj.), *secondly* (adv.); *third, thirdly.*

imply, infer.   Implying is the action of the speaker or writer; inferring is the action of the hearer or reader: Do you imply that he is a fool, or am I making a false inference?

irregardless, disregardless.   Both words are vulgarisms. Write: *regardless.*

kind of, sort of.   These expressions are clearly singular and should be used with the singular forms of verbs, demonstrative adjectives, and following nouns: This kind of table has too little strength for our purposes. *Kind of* and *sort of* used to mean *somewhat* are colloquialisms.

lend, loan. *Lend* is a verb; *loan,* a noun. Only the fastidious regularly observe the distinction, however.

less, few. Like *amount* and *number,* these words are distinguishable as answers (respectively) to the questions *How much?* and *How many?*

liable, likely, apt. Formal written English makes useful distinctions between these words:

He is liable to arrest. (bound in law)

He is liable to fall. (unpleasant contingency)

He is likely to be elected. (probability without indication of unpleasantness)

He is an apt pupil. (able to learn readily)

His remark is an apt one. (suitable)

like, as. *Like* is either a preposition, requiring a noun or pronoun as object (He talks like a fanatic; he even looks like one), or an adjective meaning *similar* (.They are of like build). It should not be used in place of the conjunctive in a sentence like this: He speaks *as* I do.

most, almost. *Most* means *to a high degree; almost* means *nearly:* He spent most of the time praising what almost every critic has damned. *Most* also means *preponderant number:* Most of the critics were present.

most, majority. *Majority* means any number more than half; it implies a precise calculation. *Most* is a general word meaning *nearly all.*

outside of. Both colloquial uses of this term are objectionable in formal prose: Outside of a novel, he read nothing all summer (*Corrected:* He read nothing all summer but one novel); He went outside of the college for his information. (*Corrected:* He went outside the college for his information.)

over with. This expression is a colloquialism. Write *finished.*

per. *Per* is, in most instances, jargon for *a:* He earns nine dollars a day.

phenomena. *Phenomena* is the plural form of *phenomenon.* Like *data* it requires the plural form in the verb it governs.

plan on. Instead of the colloquial *plan on doing,* write *plan to do.*

proof, evidence. In careful usage, the distinction between these words is always observed. *Proof* is evidence sufficient to establish a fact; *evidence* is whatever is brought forward in the attempt to establish a fact.

rarely ever, seldom ever. The *ever* is redundant in these expressions: He rarely looks up from his reading when I come in.

reason is because. This erstwhile vulgarism can be avoided by the use of *that* in the place of *because,* but is now commonly heard even among educated people.

refer back. Another redundant expression: the prefix *re-* means *back.*

in regards to, as regards, regarding. All three expressions are overused, but only the first is incorrect. In place of it, write *in regard to*—but seldom!

said.   Used as an adjective (*said document*), this word is legal jargon. Like *party* (meaning *person*), it should be avoided.

-self.   The intensive suffix *-self* should be used to provide emphasis: He did it himself *but not* He gave it to John and myself.

split infinitive.   The split infinitive is objectionable because it separates the parts of a close verbal unit. In nearly all situations it can be and should be avoided: *Not* He decided to hastily skim through the last chapter *but* He decided to skim through the last chapter hastily *or* He decided to skim hastily through the last chapter.

too, very.   *Too* is superlative; *very* is intensive. Substituting the first for the second (He isn't feeling too well) produces emphasis at the expense of clarity: how well is too well or well enough?

try and.   This expression is a colloquialism for the more logical form *try to*. It is acceptable in England, not in the United States.

type.   *Type* is jargon in fully half of its current uses: that type of person, a Hollywood-type setting. Avoid it.

a while, awhile.   *Awhile* is an adverb meaning *for a short time:* He read awhile. *While*, in the colloquial expression *a while*, means *time:* It takes a while to get everything finished.

yet.   When *yet* is used adverbially, it takes the perfect tense in sentences like: He hasn't done it yet (*not* He didn't do it yet).

⊂ Mechanics

THIS BRIEF CHAPTER on mechanics is not intended to be a comprehensive reference but simply a convenient source of information about the technical matters which most frequently trouble college students.

CAPITALIZATION

1. *Names.* Capitalize proper nouns and the adjectives derived from them. Darwin, Darwinian theory; France, French policy; Republican party; Roman Catholic Church. When such adjectives come to be part of the name of an object in common use, capitalization generally disappears: china cups, india rubber, italic type, french fries, bermuda shorts, graham cracker.

2. *Honorifics.* Capitalize titles of honor which are followed by a proper noun: Rabbi Wise, President Hayes, Professor Wilson, Mr. Eliot. Capitalize titles of honor when they refer to a specific person: the President of the Board of Overseers, the Mayor of Boston. *But:* A corporation consists of a president, secretary, treasurer, board of directors . . . .

3. *Titles.* Capitalize the first word, the last word, and all other words except articles, one-syllable prepositions, and conjunctions in the titles of books, stories, poems, plays, essays, lectures, paintings, sculptures, motion pictures, and songs: *Twenty Thousand Leagues Under the Sea, Ode on a Grecian Urn, The Adoration of the Magi, Moonlight and Roses.* Within a sentence do not capitalize "the" if it is the first word in the title of a newspaper or magazine: the New York *Times,* the *American Scholar.*

4. *Courses of Study.* Capitalize as for (3) if the course of study has a formal title: Economic Theory, Drama since Ibsen. Do not capitalize such terms otherwise: Capitalism represents a change in economic theory from . . . . ; the development of the drama since Ibsen shows the influence . . . .

5. *Geographic Areas.* Capitalize words referring to geographic areas: the Far West, the Near East, the old South. When the reference is adjectival, the word is sometimes capitalized and sometimes not, depending on the tastes of the writer or the arbitrary practice of a publisher: a Western sandwich, a western sandwich; but if the reference is to an area of land or water whose boundaries are clearly fixed, capitalization will

occur: the Atlantic coast. Words indicating direction only are not capitalized: They will go west this summer. (*But:* They will visit the West this
summer.)

6. *The Deity.*   Capitalize nouns and pronouns referring to a deity:
Our God Who made heaven and earth sets His laws in the hearts of
men; Jehovah; Lord; Saviour; Allah; Zeus.

7. *Historical Matters.*   Capitalize the names of historical events,
personages, places, institutions, artifacts, memorials, and documents: the
French Revolution, the Commanding General, Faneuil Hall, the Shen-
andoah Valley, the Washington Monument, the Bill of Rights.

8. *Family Relationships.*   Capitalize words indicating family relationship when they are used in conjunction with proper names and when
they are used as a substitute for proper names: Uncle Tom; my surprise
at seeing Grandfather alone. Do not capitalize such words when they
are used generically or when they are modified by possessives: the three
sisters; my father, Mary's uncle (*but:* my Grandfather Perkins, Mary's
Uncle John).

9. *Quotations.*   Capitalize the first word of a quotation, if the quotation is itself a complete sentence, not if it is only part of a sentence: They
answered together, "We have done nothing wrong." (*But:* They swore
that they had done "nothing wrong.") If the quotation is interrupted,
capitalize wherever a new sentence begins: "They have done it again," he
observed, "and they deserve to win." "Don't put it there," he warned.
"The water may damage it."

Do not capitalize

10. *Seasons.*   fall, winter, spring, summer, autumn, springtime.

11. *Phrases or sentences following a colon.*   The long months had
restored his health: he was almost a new man. However, capitalization
may occur if the colon is followed by a rule, a proverb, a sentence cited
from a familiar text, or the like.

12. *Parentheses within sentences, even if they are complete sentences.*   He stepped further into the room (it was a library, he noted)
and cleared his throat noisily in hope of attracting attention. Again,
capitalization may occur if the parenthetical interruption is used for
providing examples which are complete sentences.

SPELLING

Spelling is a matter of convention based on linguistic development.
Without the convention, communication would be much more difficult
than it is. For that reason alone the convention deserves respect. While it
is true that some people have what appears to be a genuine inability to

spell even simple words correctly, the condition is so rare that no college student can use it as an excuse; if he has reason to think his disability is physical or psychological, he has an obligation to seek help from an oculist or a counselor.

The only "cure" for most bad spellers is the replacing of bad habits by good ones: each must discipline himself in proportion to his need. These procedures will help:

1. Always keep a dictionary within reach as you write; consult it, during revision of your text, whenever you are in doubt about the correct spelling of a word.

2. Check the spelling of words you seldom use.

3. If you habitually misspell some words, make a list of them and keep it where you can consult it readily.

4. Learn by heart the distinction between such pairs as these:

accept, except	peace, piece
affect, effect	precede, proceed
breath, breathe	presence, presents
capital, capitol	principal, principle
choose, chose	prophecy, prophesy
conscience, conscious	quiet, quite
costume, custom	rite, right
council, counsel	sense, since
decent, descent	sight, site
desert, dessert	stationary, stationery
foreword, forward	straight, strait
formally, formerly	their, there
hear, here	then, than
its, it's	threw, through
knew, new	to, too
know, no	vain, vein
later, latter	weak, week,
loose, lose	weather, whether
moral, morale	which, witch
of, off	who's, whose
past, passed	your, you're

5. If you are not certain about the spelling of words containing one of the following combinations, *always check by dictionary*. There are "rules" for each combination, but if you have not learned them by now, the likelihood is that you will master the combinations only by forcing yourself to check until they stick permanently in your mind.

a. *ie* and *ei* (*believe, receive, weigh*)
b. final consonants before a suffix (*refer, referring; travel, traveling*)

c. final vowels before a suffix (*arrange, arrangement; desire, desirable; change, changeable; judge, judgment*)
d. final *y* in plurals and verb forms (*lady, ladies; alley, alleys; stay, stayed; pay, paid*)
e. final *o* in plurals (*radio, radios; potato, potatoes*)
f. final *fe* in plurals (*wife, wives*); final *ff* in plurals (*sheriff, sheriffs*); but final *f* in plurals is variable (shelf, shelves; chief, chiefs)
g. plurals of compounds (*courts-martial, handfuls, menservants*)

6. Compound adjectives are hyphenated when they precede the noun unless the first part of the compound ends in *-ly* (*second-class citizen; poorly paid worker*).

7. Words at line end divide by syllable only (*pay-ing, be-gin-ning, un-pre-ten-tious*).

8. Possession is indicated for personal nouns (not for personal *pronouns*) by an apostrophe with or without an inflectional *s*.

a. Singular nouns not ending in *s* take *'s*.

Gibbon's *Decline and Fall*

b. One-syllable singular nouns ending in *s* take *'s*.

James's pragmatic philosophy

c. Multisyllable nouns ending in *s* take only an apostrophe.

Collins' *Ode to Evening*

d. Plural nouns ending in *s* take only an apostrophe.

the Goncourts' journals

e. Plural nouns not ending in *s* take *'s*.

Gentlemen's *Magazine*

Possession may also be indicated by prepositional phrases (the pragmatic philosophy of William James) and is preferably so indicated when the relationship is not so much one of possession in the sense of owning as that of whole-to-part (the streets of Paris, the paintings of the Romantic Movement, the speeches of the Senate).

PUNCTUATION

Unlike spelling, punctuation is less a matter of convention than of common sense. Properly used, it indicates relationships within sentences and between sentences so that the reader may proceed without uncertainty. Improperly used, it misleads the reader. A writer cannot afford to be slipshod in punctuating any more than in defining or in documenting opinion.

1. *The Period.*

   a. Declarative and imperative sentences end with a period:

> This one does.
> Make yours do so, too.

   b. Abbreviations require a period:

> Prof. G. L. Kittredge
> Vol. IV
> pp. 82-96

2. *The Comma.* Nine tenths of the errors in punctuation on students' papers are due to misuse of the comma. These are the principal situations in which errors occur.

   a. The use or omission of commas to set off appositive words and phrases depends on the relationship intended. If the appositive is an adjunct (Charles the Bald, Peter the Hermit), commas are omitted. If the appositive limits or restricts the word to which it stands in apposition, commas are likewise omitted:

> Europeans acclaimed the novelist James Fenimore Cooper as they once acclaimed Scott.

If the appositive is simply supplementary—if it adds information but does not limit or restrict, commas separate it from the word it supplements:

> The author of *Pathfinder,* James Fenimore Cooper, was a native of New York State.

Note that, if the appositive expression is to be set off by commas, it must be *completely* set off:

> The last part of *Dead Souls,* Gogol's greatest work, appears to be irrevocably lost. NOT: The last part of *Dead Souls,* Gogol's greatest work appears to be irrevocably lost.

   b. Restrictive clauses (those that materially qualify the referent) are *not* set off by commas:

> The chapters which remain show the powerful genius of that great novelist. (Restrictive)

> The remaining chapters, which have been translated into a dozen languages, show the powerful genius of that great novelist. (Nonrestrictive)

In the first example the phrase "which remain" limits the word "chapters." The subject of "show" is not merely "chapters" but "chapters which remain." In the second example the "which" clause adds information but does not limit "chapter" and does not govern "show."

c. Clauses joined by the conjunctions *and, but, or* ordinarily take a comma before the conjunction:

> He wrote the essay, and I read it as soon as he brought it to me.

A comma is always necessary when *for* is used as a conjunction:

> I read it at once, for the publisher was calling for copy.

d. Commas separate items in series:

> The titles of books, stories, plays, and moving-pictures should be underlined in manuscript.

> A wordy, abstruse, pretentious statement is seldom clear. *But:* A wordy, abstruse, pretentious introductory sentence may easily discourage a reader.

> (In this example the adjective "introductory" has a different relationship to "sentence" from that of the other adjectives; "introductory sentence" is a unit of the same kind as "moving-pictures" or "icebox," but does not have enough use to gain the hyphen of "moving-pictures" or the complete union of "icebox.")

e. Participial phrases are *completely* set off by commas

> Reading the report again, he discovered the important detail he had missed.

> He discovered, by reading the report again, that he had missed several important details.

> He spent the remainder of the day at home, reading the report once again.

—unless they are very short:

> He came home singing lustily.

f. Dependent clauses which explain or give a reason for the main clause are sometimes set off by commas:

> Ortega rejects this definition, for he believes "mass" is not a matter of number but of mental habit.

> BUT: He uses the term "mass-mind" whenever he refers to the mental habit of rejecting the unique or the original.

When dependent clauses *precede* the main statement, they are always set off by commas unless they are very short (note the punctuation of this rule):

Whenever Ortega refers to the mental habit of rejecting the unique or the original, he uses the term "mass mind."

g. Commas set off parenthetical expressions of various kinds:

Albert Einstein, the distinguished mathematician and physicist, was also an amateur musician. (appositive)

He said that, like other scientists, he found mathematics and music a congenial combination. (additive)

He insisted, moreover, that the two have fundamental similarities. (connective)

Both are, in their purest form, entirely abstract; both use an entirely symbolic, that is, nonrepresentational, idiom. (qualifying; explanatory)

h. Occasionally commas are needed where syntax does not require them simply to prevent misreading or to indicate a pause essential for correct reading:

In the open air drama takes on the dignity of its surroundings.

CORRECTED: In the open air, drama takes on the dignity of its surroundings.

What must be must be.

CORRECTED: What must be, must be.

i. Commas are used to separate numbers, dates, and addresses:

There were 19,170 more votes cast this year than last.

He was born on February 22, 1936, in Washington, D. C.

We are moving from Middletown, Connecticut, to Middletown, New York; our address there will be 29 Park Street, Middletown 14, New York.

j. Degrees and titles are separated from the names of their bearers by commas:

This report is the work of Samuel E. Jones, M. D., a friend of the late Consul General, M. Georges Faivre.

k. All forms of direct address are set off from the text proper:

And these, my friends, are answers to your questions.

If you want to come along, John, you are welcome to do so.

l. Commas set quoted words off from other parts of sentences that contain them unless the quoted words are interrogative or exclamatory.

"Virtue," she said, "is not the prerogative of bachelors."

"Isn't it?" he asked ironically.

"No, it isn't!" she retorted with vehemence. "You men are all alike," she went on. "You think you own the universe."

3. *The Semicolon.* The semicolon is a connection between independent clauses not joined by a conjunction:

History makes men wise; poetry makes them witty.

In such use, it suggests closer relationship and a more studied balance between units than is indicated by separate sentences. It may also separate a series of long, dependent clauses:

When a man has read deeply in history; when he has come to appreciate the subtle illumination of poetry; when he has mastered the knowledge of nature, animate and inanimate; when he has examined the moral and religious thought of all time: then, and only then, can it be said of him that he has a liberal education.

There is often confusion about the use of the semicolon with such conjunctive words as "however," "therefore," "nonetheless," "consequently." If such words introduce a clause, a semicolon precedes them; if they interrupt a clause, they are set off by commas:

He made up his mind without any investigation at all; therefore, his discovery of the truth taught him the folly of hasty judgment.

If he had investigated the matter, he would not have said what he did say. He blurted out his opinion, however, without making any inquiry at all.

4. *The Colon.* More often than not, the colon is confused with the semicolon. It has so definite a function in writing, however, that every student should learn its particular uses and practice them frequently.

a. The colon may introduce an enumeration:

Although he is known primarily as the author of the novel *Moby Dick*, Melville wrote sixteen books in all, demonstrating his skill in four different literary forms: the novel, the short story, the account of travel, and poetry.

b. The more important structural use of the colon is in expanding, explaining, or illustrating what precedes it:

War and Peace is the giant of Russian fiction: by sheer comprehensiveness it overshadows all other novels in the language. (explaining)

Like a giant, it gazes down on the panorama of Russian life: the debt-ridden extravagance of urban aristocrats, the poverty and obduracy of the peasants, the disorderly yet impassioned life of the military, the cynicism and anguish of the spiritually uprooted. (expanding)

And its gaze is not only wide but penetrating: it reveals the quiet nobility of Andrei as superbly as it displays the tumult and confusion of the battle of Novgorod. (illustrating)

c. If the enumeration or expansion or illustration is the grammatical object of a preposition or the grammatical object or complement of a verb, the colon does not occur:

The nations attending the conference are England, Denmark, France, West Germany, and the Netherlands.

The cake is made of a rich batter filled with candied cherries, ginger, citron, and nuts.

5. *The Dash; Parentheses.*   These two marks of punctuation are most frequently used to set off matter not grammatically related to its context. Of the two, the dash is the less formal.

Both men contributed—Beethoven the more powerfully of the two—to the enlargement of musical form.

Beethoven's third symphony (the *Eroica*) provoked a storm of protest.

The dash is also used—and too often so used—to produce emphasis:

To Beethoven, protest meant nothing, favor meant nothing; his life was focused entirely on one passion—music.

6. *Quotation Marks.*   Although the liberality with which quotation marks are used varies from writer to writer, general publishing practice has more or less established the conventions listed below.

a. Quotation marks are necessary for setting off phrases or passages not one's own (see the section entitled "Plagiarism"). They enclose *only* the quoted words:

Plutarch tells us that, although the Athenians continued to observe Solon's laws, they nonetheless "expected some change and were desirous of another government."

"Hence it was," Plutarch goes on, "that through the city . . . ."

Note that the commas fall *before* the quotation mark. That is true also of periods, even if a single quoted word occurs at the end of the sentence:

Plutarch is not specific about what the Athenians expected; he limits himself to the general word "change."

The placement of other marks of punctuation will depend on the sense of the passage:

How does Plutarch know that "all expected some change"?

When a quoted passage continues for more than one paragraph, quotation marks are set at the beginning of *each* paragraph but at the end of the *last* paragraph only. If the citation is longer than seven or eight lines, a more common practice is to indent the quoted passage, and to singlespace it in manuscript if the remainder of the text is double-spaced, omitting quotation marks entirely.

b. The terms of a formal definition and any other use of a word as though it were an object require quotation marks:

> In the title *Brave New World,* the word "brave" means something like "good" or "noble."

> His "Yessir" was immediate but a shade contemptuous.

c. Quotation marks may also indicate that a word is being used in a special sense, usually one which the author has established beforehand or feels will be readily understood by his reader:

> Seixas is genuinely an "amateur" tennis player, one who plays for love of the game, not for money.

d. Colloquial words and slang expressions, if used in a context which does not readily accommodate them, are often set off by quotation marks. The purpose of the usage seems to be largely protective, the author making sure by this means that the reader knows his choice of language to have been deliberate.

> Apparently teen-agers no longer "dig" Frank Sinatra as they once did.

> In our part of the country such "toney" people seldom have much to do with the hill dweller.

e. The use of quotation marks to set off passages of dialogue from description and explanation has a long tradition in English. The convention is simple enough to illustrate, but it is no longer so invariably observed, even in novels, as it once was:

> "You can do it, I think," he said, "but you will have to do it alone."

> BUT: He said that you could do it but that you would have to do it alone.

Contemporary writers often omit the quotation marks today, substituting a dash before the beginning of a speech or using no mark of punctuation at all:

> —You can do it, I think. But you will have to do it alone, he added.

> *Or:* He looked at her steadily. You can do it, he said, but you will have to do it alone.

Both of the foregoing examples get around the difficulty posed by the running together of "I think" and "he said" which is so neatly taken care of by quotation marks, but the fact that a difficulty arises may illustrate a sound reason for retaining the convention.

7. *Brackets.*   Brackets are commonly used as a means of indicating additions to a cited text which have been supplied by the citer of the text.

> The third of Haney's letters on the subject was more specific. It included full information about the location of the mine and an account of the operations so far completed. Then, in a sudden burst of candor, it concluded:

>> It is now only May [the letter is dated May 16] and already I have taken enough silver out of this hole to make me comfitable [*sic*] for the rest of my life.

(The bracketed *"sic"* is a device for indicating to the reader that the misspelling of "comfortable" occurred in the original text and is not a proofreader's or author's oversight.)

If a parenthetical expression occurs within another parenthetical expression, the internal one is set off by brackets.

8. *Suspension Points.*   In citing a text, a writer may wish to omit parts which are irrelevant to the purpose for which it is being cited. An omission is indicated by the simple device of inserting suspension points, or ellipses, at the proper place in the text:

> The fourth and final letter has undertones of tragedy, but it begins with characteristic cheerfulness:

>> Today I am going back to see Melia [Haney's only living sister] and I plan to take what I have got saved back with me. There is enough . . . for both of us, and some to spare . . . . It is a long trek, and I don't like to go it alone, but I must. Anyone who can stick it out here for ten months sure don't need to worry much about lasting through a little ten-day ride on horseback.

The first appearance of suspension points in the passage above uses only three since the omission occurs within a sentence. The second appearance uses three and a fourth to indicate the period at the end of the sentence from which the last part has been omitted.

In order to accommodate the text he cites to the sentence introducing it, a writer may break into the middle of a sentence or paragraph, or he may break off before the end. To indicate such interruptions he uses suspension points.

> In all the writing of these hardy adventurers there is something melancholy, a feeling—as one of them put it—of ". . . a hollowness inside that ore won't fill, a hole bigger'n a mine shaft and twicet as dark."

If a writer quotes a passage long enough to indent but still less (either at beginning or end) than the complete paragraph in the original, he indicates the omission of sentences in the same way that he indicates the omission of words from a sentence: by three suspension points before the quotation or four points after it.

⊂⊃ The Use of Sources

A DEFINITION OF PLAGIARISM

THE ACADEMIC COUNTERPART of the bank embezzler and of the manu-facturer who mislabels his product is the plagiarist, the student or scholar who leads his reader to believe that what he is reading is the original work of the writer when it is not. If it could be assumed that the distinc-tion between plagiarism and honest use of sources is perfectly clear in everyone's mind, there would be no need for the explanation which fol-lows; merely the warning with which this definition concludes would be enough. But it is apparent that sometimes men of good will draw the suspicion of guilt upon themselves (and, indeed, are guilty) simply be-cause they are not aware of the illegitimacy of certain kinds of "borrow-ing" and of the procedures for correct identification of materials other than those gained through independent research and reflection.

The spectrum is a wide one. At one end there is word-for-word copy-ing of another's writing without enclosing the copied passage in quota-tion marks and identifying it in a footnote, *both* of which are necessary. (This includes, of course, the copying of all or any part of another stu-dent's paper.) It hardly seems possible that anyone of college age or more could do that without clear intent to deceive. At the other end there is the almost casual slipping in of a particularly apt term which one has come across in reading and which so admirably expresses one's opinion that one is tempted to make it personal property. Between these poles there are degrees and degrees, but they may be roughly placed in two groups. Close to outright and blatant deceit—but more the result, per-haps, of laziness than of bad intent—is the patching together of random jottings made in the course of reading, generally without careful identifi-cation of their source, and then woven into the text, so that the result is a mosaic of other people's ideas and words, the writer's sole contribution being the cement to hold the pieces together. Indicative of more effort and, for that reason, somewhat closer to honesty, though still dishonest, is the paraphrase, an abbreviated (and often skillfully prepared) restate-ment of someone else's analysis or conclusion without acknowledgment that another person's text has been the basis for the recapitulation.

The examples given below should make clear the dishonest and the proper use of source material. If instances occur which these examples do not seem to cover, conscience will in all likelihood be prepared to supply advice.

THE SOURCE

The importance of the *Second Treatise of Government* printed in this volume is such that without it we should miss some of the familiar features of our own government. It is safe to assert that the much criticized branch known as the Supreme Court obtained its being as a result of Locke's insistence upon the separation of powers; and that the combination of many powers in the hands of the executive under the New Deal has still to encounter opposition because it is contrary to the principles enunciated therein, the effect of which is not spent, though the relationship may not be consciously traced. Again we see the crystallizing force of Locke's writing. It renders explicit and adapts to the British politics of his day the trend and aim of writers from Languet and Bodin through Hooker and Grotius, to say nothing of the distant ancients, Aristotle and the Stoic school of natural law. It sums up magistrally the arguments used through the ages to attack authority vested in a single individual, but it does so from the particular point of view engendered by the Revolution of 1688 and is in harmony with the British scene and mental climate of the growing bourgeoisie of that age. Montesquieu and Rousseau, the framers of our own Declaration of Independence, and the statesmen (or should we say merchants and speculators?) who drew up the Constitution have re-echoed its claims for human liberty, for the separation of powers, for the sanctity of private property. In the hands of these it has been the quarry of liberal doctrines; and that it has served the Socialist theory of property based on labor is final proof of its breadth of view.

> CHARLES L. SHERMAN, "Introduction" to John Locke, *Treatise of Civil Government* and *A Letter Concerning Toleration.*

1. WORD-FOR-WORD PLAGIARIZING

It is not hard to see the importance of the *Second Treatise of Government* to our own democracy. Without it we should miss some of the most familiar features of our own government. It is safe to assert that the much criticized branch known as the Supreme Court obtained its being as a result of Locke's insistence upon the separation of powers; and that the combination of many powers in the hands of the executive under the New Deal has still to encounter opposition because it is contrary to the principles enunciated therein, the effect of which is not spent, though the relationship may not be consciously traced. The framers of our own Declaration of Independence and the statesmen who drew up the Constitution have re-echoed its claims for human liberty, for the separation of powers, for the sanctity of private property. All these are marks of the influence of Locke's *Second Treatise* on our own way of life.

In this example, after composing half of a first sentence, the writer copies exactly what is in the original text, leaving out the center section of the paragraph and omitting the names of Montesquieu and Rousseau where he takes up the text again. The last sentence is also the writer's own.

If the writer had enclosed all the copied text in quotation marks and had identified the source in a footnote, he would not have been liable to the charge of plagiarism; a reader might justifiably have felt that the writer's personal contribution to the discussion was not very significant, however.

2. THE MOSAIC

> The crystallizing force of Locke's writing may be seen in the effect his *Second Treatise of Government* had in shaping some of the familiar features of our own government. That much criticized branch known as the Supreme Court and the combination of many powers in the hands of the executive under the New Deal are modern examples. But even the foundations of our state—the Declaration of Independence and the Constitution—have re-echoed its claims for human liberty, for the separation of powers, for the sanctity of private property. True, the influence of others is also marked in our Constitution—from the trend and aim of writers like Languet and Bodin, Hooker and Grotius, to say nothing of Aristotle and the Stoic school of natural law; but the fundamental influence is Locke's *Treatise,* the very quarry of liberal doctrines.

Note how the following phrases have been lifted out of the original text and moved into new patterns:

crystallizing force of Locke's writing

some of the familiar features of our own government

much criticized branch known as the Supreme Court

combination of many powers in the hands of the executive under the New Deal

have re-echoed its claims for human liberty . . . property

from the trend and aim . . . Grotius

to say nothing of Aristotle and . . . natural law

quarry of liberal doctrines

As in the first example, there is really no way of legitimizing such a procedure. To put every stolen phrase within quotation marks would produce an almost unreadable, and quite worthless, text.

3. THE PARAPHRASE

PARAPHRASE: Many fundamental aspects of our own government are
ORIGINAL: Many   familiar   features   of   our   own   government   are

apparent in the *Second Treatise of Government*. One can safely

apparent in the *Second Treatise of Government*. It is safe to

say that the oft-censured Supreme Court really owes its exist-

assert that the much criticized . . . Court obtained its being as

ence to the Lockeian demand that powers in government be kept

a result of Locke's insistence upon the separation of powers;

separate; equally one can say that the allocation of varied

and that the combination of many powers

and widespread authority to the President during the era of

in the hands of the executive under the

the New Deal has still to encounter opposition because it is

New Deal has still to encounter opposition because it is

contrary to the principles enunciated therein . . . . Once more it

contrary to the principles enunciated therein . . . . Again we see

is possible to note the way in which Locke's writing clarified

the crystallizing force of Locke's writing.

existing opinion.

The foregoing interlinear presentation shows clearly how the writer has simply traveled along with the original text, substituting approximately equivalent terms except where his understanding fails him, as it does with "crystallizing," or where the ambiguity of the original is too great a tax on his ingenuity for him to proceed, as it is with "to encounter opposition . . . consciously traced" in the original.

Such a procedure as the one shown in this example has its uses; it is valuable for the student's own understanding of the passage, for one thing; and it may be valuable for the reader as well. How, then, may it properly be used? The procedure is simple. The writer might begin the second sentence with: "As Sherman notes in the introduction to his edition of the *Treatise*, one can safely say . . ." and conclude the paraphrased passage with a footnote giving the additional identification necessary. Or he might indicate directly the exact nature of what he is doing, in this fashion: "To paraphrase Sherman's comment . . ." and conclude that also with a footnote indicator.

In point of fact, the source here used does not particularly lend itself to honest paraphrase, with the exception of that one sentence which the paraphraser above copied without change except for abridgment. The purpose of paraphrase should be to simplify or to throw a new and significant light on a text; it requires much skill if it is to be honestly used and should rarely be resorted to by the student except for the purpose, as was suggested above, of his personal enlightenment.

4. THE "APT" TERM

> The *Second Treatise of Government* is a veritable quarry of liberal doc-
> trines. In it the crystallizing force of Locke's writing is markedly apparent.
> The cause of human liberty, the principle of separation of powers, and the
> inviolability of private property—all three, major dogmas of American
> constitutionalism—owe their presence in our Constitution in large part
> to the remarkable *Treatise* which first appeared around 1685 and was
> destined to spark, within three years, a revolution in the land of its
> author's birth and, ninety years later, another revolution against that land.

Here the writer has not been able to resist the appropriation of two striking terms—"quarry of liberal doctrines" and "crystallizing force"; a perfectly proper use of the terms would have required only the addition of a
phrase: The *Second Treatise of Government* is, to use Sherman's suggestive expression, a "quarry of liberal doctrines." In it the "crystallizing
force"—the term again is Sherman's—of Locke's writing is markedly apparent. . . .

Other phrases in the text above—"the cause of human liberty," "the
principle of the separation of powers," "the inviolability of private property"—are clearly drawn directly from the original source but are so
much matters in the public domain, so to speak, that no one could
reasonably object to their reuse in this fashion.

Since one of the principal aims of a college education is the development of intellectual honesty, it is obvious that plagiarism is a particularly serious offense and the punishment for it is commensurately severe.
What a penalized student suffers can never really be known by anyone
but himself; what the student who plagiarizes and "gets away with it"
suffers is less public and probably less acute, but the corruptness of his
act, the disloyalty and baseness it entails, must inevitably leave an in-
eradicable mark on him as well as on the institution of which he is
privileged to be a member.

MAKING A BIBLIOGRAPHY; USING FOOTNOTES

Essays written for college courses generally require the use of
"sources": books, periodicals, and newspapers containing information
relevant to the topic of the essay to be written. The citation of such
sources occurs in one or both of two places: in footnotes; in a bibliography
appended to the essay.

Very simply, a bibliography lists the books, periodicals, and newspapers actually used in the preparation of the essay; a footnote indicates
very precisely the source of a quotation or specific statement occurring
in the text of the essay. For both, a more or less standardized system has
been developed so that readers anywhere can turn quickly from the footnote or the bibliographical listing to the proper source and be sure that

they have at hand the correct volume of the correct edition of the cited work. This section provides, in a form as abbreviated as clarity permits, the fundamental information you will need about these two tools of scholarly work.

BIBLIOGRAPHY

A bibliography lists the books, periodicals, and newspapers actually used in the preparation of an essay. (There are bibliographies, to be sure, which do more than that, but for present purposes the definition given above is accurate.) It is, therefore, a record for the reader of the kind and amount of research done in preparing the essay and, as such, it enables him not only to verify the documentation but also to make at a glance an estimate of the probable value of the paper. It is this latter function which occasionally leads the writer to make one of two errors in the compilation of a bibliography: (1) the listing of everything read during the period of research, whether or not it has any relevance to or value for the essay, a completeness which is both pretentious and wasteful of the reader's time and energy; (2) the listing of important or important-sounding volumes which have not been read at all or have only been "looked into," clearly a dishonest procedure.

The following examples illustrate the common kinds of bibliographical entry.

1. Lunt, W. E., *History of England* (New York: Harper, 1947).

The author's name is given as it appears on the title page of the book itself, but with surname first so that alphabetization of entries will be obvious.

The title is italicized. (This is the equivalent of underlining in typescript and manuscript.)

The place of publication, publisher, and date of publication are listed in that order and enclosed in parentheses. For books outside the copyright period, fifty-six years, it is customary not to give the name of the publisher ("Harper" above) unless it is desired to distinguish between editions of a book published by more than one house—as with many of the classics, for instance.

A colon is used to separate place from publisher, and a comma to separate publisher from date of publication or, if the publisher is not named, to separate place from date: e.g., New York, 1802; a period is used at the end.

2. Crosby, John, "Speechlessness at Great Length," New York *Herald Tribune,* CXI (July 23, 1951), 13.

The title here is set in quotation marks because it is only an article, a part of a larger work. Italicizing is reserved for the larger work (New

York *Herald Tribune*). The simple rule for capitalization of titles explains usage here and elsewhere: *capitalize all words in a title except articles and one-syllable prepositions and conjunctions, and always capitalize the first and last word.*

The volume number is given in Roman numerals to distinguish it from the numbers which follow. It is necessary for periodicals and news-papers because back numbers are bound by volumes for library storage.

The date of the issue and the page on which the article can be found provide all the additional information that is needed for quick access to the source.

3. "Haiti," *Encyclopædia Britannica,* 14th ed. (1936), XI, 81-83.

As is common in encyclopædias, the author of this article is not in-dicated. The entry therefore begins with the title of the article.

It is important that the edition be noted because the content of the article might be different in another edition and the location of it within the set would almost certainly be different.

4. *Œuvres de Turgot,* ed., Eugène Daire, 2 vols. (Paris, 1844).

The title appears exactly as on the title page (is not translated).

In this case the author's name is implicit in the title; the man who prepared the *Œuvres* (*Works*) for publication is listed after the abbrevia-tion "ed." ("edited by").

Note that the number of volumes has been stated. This is customary procedure if the work has more than one volume. Some bibliographers give the number of pages in one-volume works, but that is not necessary. Page numbers *are* given, however, in the second and third examples above because the source cited forms only part of a larger work whose other parts are not necessarily germane to the topic.

A final note: the items in a bibliography should be arranged alpha-betically, the first word in an item determining its alphabetical placement, unless the first word is an article (the, a, an); in that case, the following word is the basis for alphabetization.

FOOTNOTES

A footnote indicates very precisely the source of a quotation or specific statement occurring in the text of the essay. (It may also give in-cidental or supplementary information, of course.) There is some vari-ation in the form of footnotes, from one publishing house to another and even from one scholarly society to another. The instructions which follow, however, have the authority of most of the university presses in the United States and conform, as do those on bibliography, to the style sheet of the Modern Language Association. Only the most commonly used

terms are presented for study. These few simple generalizations deserve
prior attention and observance:

1. Number the footnotes consecutively throughout an essay.
2. Place the footnotes for each page at the bottom of that page; or, if you
   want to save yourself a great deal of space-calculating, assemble them
   all on a separate sheet at the end of the essay.
3. Make sure, in the final draft, that the numbers in the text correspond
   to the numbers attached to relevant footnotes.
4. Indicate the presence of a footnote by an Arabic numeral in the text.
   Ordinarily, this numeral should come at the end of a sentence. It should
   always be raised above the line of text:

   Jones vehemently denied the report.[6] When the . . .

5. Use footnotes sparingly. Their purpose is to inform the reader, not to
   impress him.

The series of footnotes which follows satisfies the most common situations. A full explanation follows the series.

[1] Theodor Wilhelm and Gerhard Graefe, *German Education Today* (Berlin:
Terramare, 1936), pp. 3-5.
[2] James Bryant Conant, "The Advancement of Learning in the United States in
the Post-War World," *Science,* XCIX (February 4, 1944), 91.
[3] Ibid., p. 92.
[4] *Jahrbuch des Reichsarbeitsdienstes,* 1937-38 (Berlin, 1937), S. 34.
[5] Conant, p. 94.

Explanation.   The first footnote is a reference to three pages in a
book published by Terramare in Berlin and written by two men. Their
names appear in the order in which they are found on the title page.
Note that they are not reversed so that the surname comes first as in
bibliographical entries; this is simply because there is no purpose in making the adjustment necessary for alphabetization when arrangement is by
order of occurrence in the text.

The second note refers to one page in an article which appeared in
volume ninety-nine of *Science* magazine. In such an instance it is not
necessary to name the publisher or place of publication if the magazine
is at all well known, but it is advisable to give the date of issue as well
as the volume number. Note that the page reference for a publication
does not use the abbreviation "p." (for "page") or "pp." (for "pages")
if the volume number is given. In the first example (where there is no
volume number indicated because the work is published in a single
volume) the abbreviation *is* used.

The third note is a reference to a different page of the same work as
that referred to in (2). "Ibid." is an abbreviation for the Latin word

ibidem meaning "in the same place" and always points back to the immediately preceding work.

The fourth note refers to a yearbook, a compilation of statistics (in this case, concerning state work projects). Such a volume is the work of a host of men, and there is no point in indicating either editor or author for any particular section. The abbreviation "S." stands for "page" in German.

The fifth note is also a reference to the article by Mr. Conant. This time, however, "Ibid." could not be used since another reference intervenes. Therefore, the author's name and the page number alone are given.

These additional footnote abbreviations occur frequently in scholarly texts:

cf.	*compare*	loc. cit.	*in the place cited;* (different
ch.	*chapter*		from op. cit. because it
et al.	*and others*		refers to the same *passage,*
ff.	*following*		not simply to the same
l.	*line*		work, as previously cited)
ll.	*lines*	passim	*throughout the work, here*
v.	*see*		*and there*
viz.	*namely*		

Just as honesty requires quotation marks around any statement copied directly from a written source, it requires a footnote to indicate the place from which information has been gathered or from which paraphrased reconstructions are woven into the text.

A fine bibliography and careful footnoting, no matter how ably prepared, will not make up for deficiency in reasoning, style, and substance of the essay proper, but they do enhance the value of good scholarly writing because they act as auxiliary agents in the process of communication.

Analyses of Three Essays

IT IS OFTEN HELPFUL to have at hand, as a means of confirming one's command over generalizations recently encountered, some examples to show the relevance of those generalizations to the actual processes from which they arise. The three essays which follow were written by college freshmen. Each is reprinted exactly as its writer presented it to his instructor. In a column parallel to the student's text, comments and questions occur at appropriate places, and at the end a fuller and more general analysis of the essay appears. The essays appear in order of quality, the first being the best.

I

A CRITICAL ANALYSIS OF
"AMERICAN NOTIONS OF ARISTOCRACY"

The title is entirely descriptive.

Thomas C. Grattan, in his interpretation of American life, has criticized the tendency of a large minority of Americans to seek an aristocratic social organization. From his experiences with American society, he makes the following observations:

The writer defines his topic in the opening sentence. Why does he not indicate his attitude toward Grattan's statement at this point?

Americans misunderstand the words "aristocracy" and "gentlemanly." To them, the words mean something quite different from what they mean to Englishmen. Newspaper articles, with their constant use of the words "high life" or "fashionable," illustrate clearly both Americans' yearning for aristocracy and, at the same time, the depth of their misunderstanding of what aristocracy and gentlemanliness really are. The fact is, Americans simply cannot measure up to the English conception of an aristocrat. Their manners are too diversified and therefore they have no social precedents so necessary to the aristocratic form

He begins a new paragraph to set off the summary which follows from the introduction of the topic. This accounts for the unusual brevity of the opening paragraph. He manages this paraphrase throughout both without openly injecting his own presence and without using mechanical aids ("Then he says . . . ," "He further notes . . . ," and so on).

Which assertions are statements of fact? Which are supporting statements? In what order do they come? Do any of the sentences give a subtle indication of the writer's opinion of the material he is summarizing?

187

of society. American society is not at all equipped for aristocratic social distinctions. No important family has been established; no titles are given, nor is merit or dishonor passed on to the children of worthy or disreputable parents. Large landed possessions with dependant tenants either cannot be found in some parts of the U. S. or in other sections are owned by unrefined possessors.

Finally an ignorance of the arts exists among the wealthy, for nowhere can one find a patron of artistic endeavor. America, then, lacks everything necessary for an aristocracy, and Americans should realize that the term has no application to themselves. The error that many make on both sides of the Atlantic is that American and English societies and institutions are comparable. Actually they are not, and if the leading classes of Americans realized this, they would not try to emulate European characteristics, which they are utterly incapable of attaining. What these Americans should do is to originate their own plan of social organization, one which would be consistent with their institutions. An aristocracy can only grow in a congenial surrounding. It is incompatible with a republic.

Thus Grattan sees many Americans yearning for a social system which is completely alien to their own institutions. To examine his analysis of the problem we may divide it into three parts: the terminology Grattan uses; his objective in writing the essay; and the conclusion he reaches.

One cannot but feel, after reading Grattan's essay, that many important words have been used, but only vaguely defined. For instance, "aristocracy" is rather a broad term. We may assume that the author restricts it only to the British notion of the word;

a variant spelling
The closing sentence is awkward though understandable. How can its emphasis be made stronger?

The beginning of another paragraph here is a mistake for two reasons. What are they?

Notice how deftly the writer makes apparent the shift from analysis to conclusion in his paraphrase.

The slight change in tone here is meant to reproduce for the reader the tone of Grattan's advice. What is that tone? How does the writer convey it?

Here the summary concludes, with two sharp sentences which themselves summarize the summary.
What is the function of "Thus"? Can you suggest a more effective expression for that function?

The writer uses the editorial "we" as a mechanical aid. He might have written: "An analysis of his statements requires inquiry into the terminology he uses. . . ."

The markedly ambiguous words in Grattan's statement (see paragraph one) are identified, and each is dealt with separately. They are used both to illustrate what, according to the yet even in this sense we cannot get a complete idea of what the author means until we have finished the whole essay. What is an aristocrat? First we learn that it takes three generations to make one; then, that it is something that doesn't use public washrooms, but washes its feet every day, and finally, that it patronizes the arts. Even if we accept this notion of the aristocrat, we must then inquire into the author's charge that a "large minority" of the American people wish to be one. Obviously "a large minority" could mean almost any number. It is a term that needs restriction and receives little. We do learn that a "large minority" does not include the "great mass of the people," but does contain the leading social classes, political leaders, and intellectuals. This is still far from being specific, and often one wonders just whom Grattan is criticizing.

If one accepts the terminology of the essay, however, he may then consider the supposed objective of the author: to show how American notions of aristocracy are inconsistent with the kind of aristocracy many Americans are trying to imitate. It would seem most important and necessary that as a first step in reaching this objective, the author should prove that a large minority of Americans really do wish to copy the English social organization. This Grattan completely fails to do. Since he has evidently gained this impression during his stay in the United States, there should be some evidence which has led him to this belief. Yet the only evidence he produces in support of the charge consists of some newspaper articles. The statement that Americans desire to imitate European aristocracy is not a truism, as Grattan suggests. Rather it is a controversial question

writer, is the ambiguity of the entire essay and to show the weakness of the topic sentence in particular. How does the writer make this an opportunity for another indirect indication of his opinion of Grattan's analysis?

Once adopted, the editorial "we" is maintained.

Notice how the concession is made here simply by the use of the emphatic auxiliary "do."

Consider the shift from "we" to "one" ("one first appeared at the beginning of the previous paragraph). If intentional, what is its effect supposed to be?

This passage shows clearly that the writer has put questions to the text and that he knows what tests to apply to statements of fact and opinion.

Compare the tone of this paragraph with that of the preceding paragraph. What is the change and why is it made?

The connectives that tie these sentences together are all admirably unobtrusive.

which needs adequate support. News-paper articles are not adequate sup-port, for they do not give a true and complete picture of American society.

Most of the essay, then, is devoted not to proving that a large minority of Americans desire aristocracy, but that their notions of aristocracy do not coincide with English social dis-tinctions. The author shows this very well—so well that it would seem that Americans are just about as far from English aristocracy as it is possible to get. Even President Buchanan, a po-litical leader who should be trying to imitate this aristocracy, is evidently trying *not* to imitate it. The news-paper article about the President cer-tainly shows that Americans are ig-norant of English manners; yet it also praises this lack of aristocratic bear-ing, and thus to some extent contra-dicts Grattan's assumption that there is a tendency for Americans to desire social distinction.

Finally, the conclusion the author reaches may be criticized. One can agree with him that Americans should not try to imitate British aristocracy, but not that they should try to origi-nate their own social organization. A society is not something that can be planned on paper. Rather, it evolves from varied forces acting upon a group of people. The American social organization has evolved, as has the English aristocracy, not from a pre-arranged plan, but by a historical process.

Grattan's essay has shown that Americans are not aristocratic in the English sense of the word. It has not shown that a large minority of Ameri-cans desire that kind of social organi-zation. If this latter assumption cannot be supported, there is really no point in writing the essay. The article then

Here the writer disallows Grattan's principal claim and points out the real focus of Grattan's comments.

The reference to President Buchanan assumes (correctly in the case of this paper) that the reader of the analysis has also read Grattan's essay. If that assumption were unwarranted, how might the reference be made ade-quate in this context?

The writer turns Grattan's own "evi-dence" against him.

Grattan's "conclusion" is embedded in the writer's rejection of a part of it—a good way of doing two things at once.

The disagreement requires support, so the writer begins with a premise.

The writer goes no further with his argument than a statement of premise and an illustration. Why?

"That kind" has no explicit anteced-ent; "the English form" would be bet-ter.

appears to be not so much a constructive criticism of American society as an excuse for the author to ridicule what could be called American lack of refinement. Perhaps Mr. Grattan has failed to grasp the more important aspects of American life. At least he has focused his attentions on what appear to be rather petty considerations.

A summary should make clear the main judgments arrived at

and also reinforce the tone of the writer's analysis. This summary does both things neatly and emphatically.

The faults of this "critical analysis" are few, and its virtues are many. The scheme of organization is more explicit than necessary but never annoying to the reader. Its arrangement—thesis, paraphrase, analysis, final commentary—provides an admirable, though restrained, crescendo. This climactic order is made more apparent by the gradual introductions of the writer's opinion: first, with the suggestion of irony, then with a humorous oversimplification, and after that with increasingly direct objection.

The language is unaffected, the syntax generally sound, and rhetorical effect always subordinated to meaning. The writing is not brilliant but it *is* competent, and the analysis itself is astute.

The composite of qualities—clarity, sound organization, conciseness, penetration—makes this essay a thoroughly commendable piece of work; and a certain amount of subtlety and a consistent dignity in expression add appreciably to its literary quality.

II

CRÈVECŒUR'S OPTIMISM
UNWARRANTED TODAY

Crèvecœur based his optimism on conditions and attitudes which have changed markedly in the one hundred and eighty years since the writing of "What Is an American?" These conditions and attitudes have, in my opinion, changed sufficiently to render the optimism expressed in his article unwarranted.

The title sounds like a newspaper headline. Adding a verb will make it more appropriate to the text.

Both the topic of this essay and the writer's contention about it are made explicit in the opening paragraph. That is all to the good. But the first sentence needs altering, and "in my opinion" is superfluous in the second.

Crèvecœur represented the American people of his day as a pioneering group, composed mainly of agrarians and frontiersmen. To the fortitude of these men Crèvecœur looked for the vigor which would strengthen America. Do we find this same vigor to-

The writer proposes a first point

and presents his counterpoint in the form of a rhetorical question. Would the counterpoint have been as con-

day? Can we today boast of energetic tillers of the soil and enthusiastic pioneers to expand our borders? I think not. Conditions under which a farmer's subsistence was obtained only as the result of diligent labor have been replaced by parity prices, guaranteed incomes, government purchasing, and government subsidy. The frontiersmen and pioneers exist no longer. Alaska, for example, has been for some time open to development and exploration, unhindered by hostile tribes or the danger of starvation. Yet Alaska remains virtually unsettled. I doubt if Crèvecœur would have found encouragement in such a spectacle.

A second source of hope for Crèvecœur was the loose relationship between the government and the governed. The passage of the income tax amendment and the degree of taxation present in our day would distress Crèvecœur. Federal laws, enforced on a nation-wide basis, have destroyed frontier lawlessness. In so doing, the federal laws have put a halt to the siphoning of the "offcasts" of American civilization from the cities to the frontier. Crèvecœur would attribute the existence of the vagrants seen in our midst daily largely to a lack of interest in the development of such areas as Alaska. Crèvecœur would probably see this lack of interest as having been created by the increase in individual security and partly by the extension and broadening of federal law. Whatever the reason, the fact remains that the automatic purging of American society has stopped. Crèvecœur would hardly be optimistic upon seeing the halt of this, one of the main guarantees of America's continued strength.

The "bad blood" of the America of Crèvecœur's day was constantly being drawn from the main arteries of

vincing as a flat assertion? More convincing?

This sentence is clear but would be more striking if it were put into the active voice: "In 1770, a farmer's living depended entirely on his diligence; in 1950, it depends . . . ." Is "replaced by" accurate—no "diligent labor" now required?

Use of example to support contention.

Taken seriously, this is a historical error. No one can know what Crèvecœur would think were he living today—he might be a Socialist!
The writer signals his next step rather obviously by "second" and, with more subtlety ("source of hope"), reminds his reader of the main topic of the essay.

"Degree of" is jargon.

There is annoying redundancy in this sentence. The writer does not follow up this suggestion but switches back to the one in the preceding paragraph. Why?

What does "whatever the reason" (a good enough phrase in itself) suggest about the writer's argument on this point?

"Automatic purging" is concise and vivid.

Two things are wrong with the first half of this sentence; the second half is nicely emphatic.

American life by the frontier; it was being replaced by European transfusions of all types. Today the latter have been ended almost as completely as the former. Immigration restrictions, added to barriers of distrust and suspicions, have cut the lifeline which served to invigorate our nation one hundred and eighty years ago. Any traces of foreign ancestry are, by contrast, today frowned upon. Such cries as "You foreigner!" and "It's un-American!" would seem very strange to Crèvecœur. Yet he would meet them if he journeyed to America today. Unless he were a high diplomatic envoy, Crèvecœur would now find himself investigated and searched before being admitted. If he decided to settle here, he would soon find that society, rather than seeking his ideas as a contribution to the growth of America, now would demand that he become "Americanized." Crèvecœur would, undoubtedly, have difficulty in hiding his disillusionment.

His letdown would become complete when he beheld the change which had taken place in the classless America of his day. Behind the financial barons of 1952, he might readily see the ghosts of the manor lords. Although the former situation would be seen as a great improvement over the latter, the lines separating employer from employed—the "upper-uppers" from the "lower-lowers"—have returned as one of the trademarks of current life.

Crèvecœur summarizes his article with a hopeful tribute to America's past and future. He sees in the admixture of races and the vigor of the people real reason for optimism. Were Crèvecœur to claim such optimism now, his reasons would have to be greatly altered. The reasons given by Crèvecœur one hundred and eighty

The transition between these paragraphs is what we have called, in this handbook, "organic." The writer could have improved it by making the first clause subordinate to the second.

The "transfusions" metaphor is an arresting one. Does "of all types" damage or improve it?

"Lifeline" continues the metaphor.

"Today" is misplaced.

Compare this section of the paragraph with the preceding section. Dependence on "would" has markedly reduced the immediacy of the account.

This transition is effective because it uses the dramatic development as a way of marking another step and, at the same time, of announcing the completion of the "argument."

"The former situation" is ambiguous.

"Contemporary" would be more precise than "current" in this phrase.

This conclusion mentions two of three matters treated in the text and repeats (overrepeats, indeed) the writer's thesis. It is flat, however, flat and unprofitable.

years ago have become outdated. Their current application would hardly give rise to optimism.

Examination of the marginal comments, necessarily incomplete though they be, will show that this essay does not have the firm control of language and of ideas which characterized the previous essay. The faults are not rudimentary or gross but they are faults nonetheless. Still, the line of development is clear and steady here, and the organization is compact and efficiently managed. The writer has represented Crèvecœur's position accurately and has found *specific* conditions in contemporary society to use as evidence of change.

The most serious charge to be brought against the essay is the one, marginally noted, of historical error. If the use of a revivified Crèvecœur is only mechanical—a time-machine device for enlivening the comparison —the worst that can be said is that it is trite. If, however (and this frequently seems to be the case), the writer wants us to take his use of Crèvecœur solemnly—our forefathers disapproving the decay of American society—he has committed a bad historical mistake. This is simply the projection of his own views, which may be right enough, into a person who will give those views added weight even though they are not his. Because it takes some imagination to make an error of this sort, making it *once* is not reprehensible. To repeat it would be.

This essay is neither so sound nor so firmly expressed as the previous essay, but it has a respectable content and a generally clear, if not subtle, presentation.

III

"THOMAS COLLEY GRATTAN'S ARTICLE, 'AMERICAN NOTIONS OF ARISTOCRACY,' IS NOT HONESTLY CRITICAL AND DOES NOT HAVE THE SINCERITY OF THE BRYCE ARTICLE."

The writer adopts the quotation set for analysis as his title.

It is evident throughout the work that Mr. Grattan is sneering at American customs and at the mannerisms of the people. Certainly it is true that American notions of what a gentleman is differ from European notions. But it is not true that Americans imply that the people described as gentlemen in America would be considered gentlemen in Europe or vice versa. The word is spelled the same but carries a meaning as different as the accents in America are different

"His article" would be a clearer reference than "the work."

Error: historical personages are not referred to as "Mr." Simply "Grattan."

The opening sentence is forceful. The two that follow balance each other effectively.

The outworn Latin phrase is more convenient than felicitous.

from the accents in England. The same principle applies to the word "aristocracy." The English and the American words are not the same; therefore it is senseless to compare American concepts of aristocracy with European concepts of aristocracy.

The next sentence apparently states the "principle" alluded to here.

The author seemed shocked by the manners of Americans, they seemed to him very vulgar and unrefined. In his illustration concerning President Buchanan it is evident that he feels English customs and mannerisms to be definitely superior to their American counterpart. In his allusion to the Englishman mentioned in the article he states that he would only have imitated his host for the purpose of becoming more popular and implies that such action would ordinarily be unthinkable by such a person. It is true that English society was more refined at the time Mr. Grattan wrote his article. But I wonder how refined the people of any European country were when their country was as undeveloped and unsettled as was America at that time? The people, it is true, did not pay much attention to music and art. The main reason was not a lack of refinement but a lack of time. They were too busy developing and in too unsettled a state to have leisure time to devote to the arts. The youth of the country and the tempo of its development, rather than the lack of European custom tended to make Americans less refined than Europeans. However, this is not the only aspect of the situation. The refinement of Americans in general as compared to Europeans in general is definitely in favor of American society even at the time when Mr. Grattan wrote. Education, confined to certain classes in Europe, is universal in America. Even in Buchanan's time the poorest American had a broader outlook on

Compare this sentence with the opening one. Can you tell what is to be the principal preoccupation of this essay?
Change of tense without reason.

A comma is the least *helpful mark of punctuation here. Is the redundancy expressive or annoying?*
Why not "he finds" for "he feels . . . to be"?

Error: "mannerisms" for "manners."

The writer does not give his reader enough information to make this comment understandable. It is awkwardly expressed, besides.

Idiom: "unthinkable to"
"More" than what?

Is this a question? Would a flat assertion be more or less expressive? How do you account for the form the writer has chosen? What is its effect?

What "people"?

This part of the essay accounts for the lack of refinement conceded above. What is its tone?

Incomplete punctuation
This sentence signals a shift in direction. Unfortunately, it is woefully trite.

Study this assertion, ignoring for the moment the inaccuracy of "is." What is its relationship to the passage preceding "However"? What is its relationship to the final sentence of the first paragraph?

life than did the typical European peasant.

Mr. Grattan's final point—that there will never be an aristocracy comparable to the European aristocracy in the United States because the conditions for its growth are poor—is unquestionably true. Certainly one of the goals of the republic was to abolish such a system.

The final paragraph, though not entirely effective as a summary, is well contrived (the unexpected willingness to agree followed by the turning of tables) and admirably terse.

This essay is markedly inferior to the preceding ones in content, procedure, and expression. The argument suffers from underdevelopment and contradiction; the order is, so far as the reader can tell, haphazard; and the expression is principally notable for a lack of concreteness and vividness.

Still it is apparent that the writer has some ear for language (in both the first and final paragraphs, for instance) and that his mind is not supinely receptive. There are several technical errors but not so many that the reader is distracted.

Index

☞ Index